An Inclusive Blueprint

BEING TOLERANT
— IS FOR —
COWARDS

LEADERSHIP THINKING
TO DISRUPT THE STATUS QUO
WITH PURPOSE

CRAIG B. CLAYTON, SR.

A GLOBAL TRANSFORMATIONAL STRATEGIC THOUGHT LEADER

© Equitable Workplace Institute Publishing

Copyright Page

Being Tolerant Is For Cowards © Copyright 2021 – Equitable Workplace Institute / Craig B. Clayton, Sr.

All rights reserved. No part of this publication may be reproduced, distributed or transmitted in any form or by any means, including photocopying, recording, or other electronic or mechanical methods, without the prior written permission of the publisher, except in the case of brief quotations embodied in critical reviews and certain other noncommercial uses permitted by copyright law.

Although the author and publisher have made every effort to ensure that the information in this book was correct at press time, the author and publisher do not assume and hereby disclaim any liability to any party for any loss, damage, or disruption caused by errors or omissions, whether such errors or omissions result from negligence, accident, or any other cause.

Adherence to all applicable laws and regulations, including international, federal, state and local governing professional licensing, business practices, advertising, and all other aspects of doing business in the US, Canada or any other jurisdiction is the sole responsibility of the reader and consumer.

Neither the author nor the publisher assumes any responsibility or liability whatsoever on behalf of the consumer or reader of this material. Any perceived slight of any individual or organization is purely unintentional.

The resources in this book are provided for informational purposes only and should not be used to replace the specialized training and professional judgment of a health care or mental health care professional.

Neither the author nor the publisher can be held responsible for the use of the information provided within this book. Please always consult a trained professional before making any decision regarding treatment of yourself or others.

For more information, email info@beingtolerantisforcowards.com

Dedication

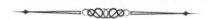

LETTER TO MY SONS & BEAUTIFUL BRIDE

After watching the verdict in the George Floyd murder trial, it gives me hope. Not false hope, but genuine optimism that my children and grandchildren will have a better opportunity to be treated with dignity and respect. This book captures some of the life changing and character shaping experiences that have enabled me to awaken every day with a sense of purpose. I dedicate it to my sons and of course my beautiful bride.

TO MY SONS: There was a movie I saw as a young man that changed my life. It was called "Roots," and it was about the story of one black man who was able to trace his family heritage back to a specific part of Africa and found his roots. During slavery, a pervasive mentality caused people to treat us as less than human to be bought and sold like property. When I held you, shortly after birth, I also repeated the line from the movie:

'Behold The Only Thing Greater Than Yourself!'

Know that you are beneath NO ONE but God! I was not exaggerating when I said the movie Roots had an impact on me. Years later, I would be instructing a class for a client in Arizona. One of the students in my class had a last name that sounded like it might have an ethnic origin outside of the USA. During the week-long workshop, I found out he was from Senegal. I also found that he and his wife had invested their retirement into building a home and school for street children in Senegal. Their goal was to give these children a skill and help them become self-sustaining. He told me these street children were relegated to begging at intersections, barefoot, walking in broken glass and animal feces, trying to scrounge up enough money for their overseers to then feed them.

Ten days later, I was on a flight with him back to Senegal. Before leaving, I was able to find a source for a unique solution to provide children in developing countries with shoes. It is called the 'shoe-that-grows'. It expands and fits a child for up to five years! We took duffle bags full. Getting them through customs was a tremendous risk, as they could easily have been assumed to be a business venture and the items confiscated. We were able to make a difference in the lives of these children.

The day before I flew to Senegal, I received my DNA test results, which confirmed family stories that our heritage was from West Africa. I soon discovered that my family heritage was likely linked to slave traders that would have forced men, women, children, and infants onto slave ships from Goree Island.

This island was a slave trading post is located just off the coast of Senegal and served as a significant West Africa Slave trading hub. Visiting that island was linked to the connection that I felt as a young man to the TV Series Roots. After being sold, the slaves from Goree Island had to walk a wooden plank from the door of the island prison to the deck of a waiting slave ship.

DOOR OF NO RETURN

The door you pass through from the island prison to the waiting slave ships to be chained to the deck; has been called the 'Door of No Return' for years. Hundreds of thousands of slaves were forces to leave their homes through this door. If they got sick or died during the transit, they were thrown overboard and fed to the sharks. The 'lucky' ones were able to make it to America, be sold into slavery, and beaten. I brought flowers with me as I took the Ferry ride to the island. I tossed them in the water from the 'Door of No Return'. For me, it was closure for my family.

We Returned…..

I was there to represent those in our family who thought they would never return. To my sons and grandchildren…. I can say, hold your head up high. I also thank those fellow Africans I met during my visits, who heard me speak, realized I was an American and then said, at least once a day: *"Welcome Home Brother, Welcome Home!"*

Goré Island, Dakar, Senegal

From…The Door Of No Return
To…The Path From Which I've Come!

From Goré and Back
Once Chained… Now Free!

JOSHUA, MY BABY BOY, WHERE DO I START. You are now a father of two beautiful boys (Josiah & Caleb) and husband of a god-fearing Christian mother and wife, Taylor. I am so grateful that God allowed me to try to get fatherhood right. I know I failed you in many ways, but it was never because of a lack of effort. One memory I will share with the angel Gabriel, Auntie, and the family already gone home; is when you preached one of your first messages at a church in Lansing, Michigan, as a 14-year-old boy. The church took up a love offering and presented the basket to you. There were hundreds of dollars in the basket.

I remember YOU going over and telling the Pastor you couldn't accept the money because God has already taken care of you. You then handed the basket back to him. Once, he explained that you HAD to accept it because these folks gave the money to you, knowing that they were blessing a man of God and that God would, in turn, bless them. The Pastor said you couldn't say no because it would stop their blessings. Without missing a beat, you asked if anyone in the audience needed prayer and had them come to the altar. After praying for them, you wondered if anyone there was praying because they had lost their job.

A young man with his wife slowly raised his hand. You took the basket of money and gave it to him, telling him, "My father has taken care of all my needs. Take this money and be blessed." The young man tried to refuse, but you told him HE couldn't because it would stop YOUR blessings. This comment came from a 14-year-old with no coaching or instruction other than following your heart for those in need.

I am so PROUD to call you, my son. I know that God has great things in store for your life. I pray that he spares me long enough to see those things. I am so pleased in the young man, husband, and father that you have become.

JASON, MY MIDDLE SON. You have often told me that you are the son that is most like me from a personality perspective! I carry the biggest regrets about how much I was missing from your life after your mother, and I divorced. My living in California and you in Florida with your Mom; became an excuse. The miles became months, became years. You have given me a great understanding of the term 'grace'. It would have been easy for you to have walked past me at your high-school graduation when we reconnected. You extended grace to me then and now.

Watching you become a father of two boys (Jaise-Paul and Jackson) and one princess (Allison) has shown me that you focus on being the best father you can. Don't be so hard on yourself, son. You had to learn how to be a man, father, brother, and friend with no man around the house to model. That is because your mother and I were not adult enough to work out our issues. I have always admired your willingness to serve. I am grateful for the foundation you received at FAMU. Dr. Sybil Mobley and the business school gave you a great foundation in academics and accountability. Your participation and success in the ROTC Program and subsequent service in the U.S. Army also added to the man you have now become. As of this publication, you are a Major, and I am confident that Lt. Colonel is in your future.

Your heart for people is evidenced by your interactions and compassion for others. Son, with the kind of heart you have, there will be times when people will take advantage of that. Don't let it crush your spirit.

There will always put people in your life to re-affirm your goal and destiny. Continue to make smart choices and always be cautious of people or opportunities that seem too good to be true. I am not saying don't trust, but trust has to be earned; it is a privilege and not a right.

When you find yourself in a situation that you are unsure of… remember you can ALWAYS find a way out! Occasionally, you may have to swallow your pride to take the way out. If the house is on fire, you won't hesitate to climb out a window, in a new suit or your birthday suit, right! Don't let pride cost you your reputation or your life.

My First Born Son - Craig:

I doubt you will ever read this. I have tried to reach out over the years to no avail. Therefore, I decided to honor your request to stay out of your life. When you were born, I was 19 years old. I knew very little about being a man and even less about being a father. The one thing I knew was I had to go to work. I worked two and three jobs even while in the military. That also meant I wasn't around as much as I should have been.

Son, I am sorry that you have felt for years that your life is better off without me in it. I will always love you, and I know that I did the best I could, even with all the mistakes of omission not commission in your life.

TO MY BEAUTIFUL BRIDE

Jennifer... "My Boo" - I know how you hate that term of endearment. But you are my 'Boo-T-Ful Bride' that God loaned me until death do us part. I have been so blessed to have you as my partner in life. I have made so many mistakes in the 35+ years we have been together, yet you stood by me anyways.

I traveled the world on business trips, and you were always supportive of whatever was needed to keep the household together.

- ❖ *I see you, and I thank you.*

   You managed a career spanning almost 40 years with AT&T, and still provide love and attention for our children....

- ❖ *I see you, and I thank you.*

   You have managed to uplift so many with your beautiful smile and the light that shines in your eyes.

- ❖ *I see you, and I thank you.*

   When I read the attributes of a Proverbs 31 Woman – I realize that God has allowed me a chance, despite my frailties, failures, and fallings, to understand that a virtuous woman is more precious than rubies.

   I have been blessed with rubies in abundance.

- ❖ *I see you, and I thank you.*

   I love you to life. I know that there is something special in store for each of you, don't let the plans of others prevent you from reaching your dreams.

NEVER DREAM SMALL….

- Why waste sleep?

ALWAYS DREAM BIGGER THAN YOUR REACH

- Just because you can't see it doesn't mean it's not around the corner waiting!

<u>REMEMBER</u>

- 6 most important words: I admit I made a mistake.
- 5 most important words: I am proud of you!
- 4 most important words: What is your opinion?
- 3 most important words: If you please.
- 2 most important words: Thank you.
- 1 most important word: You or We…not "I"

Know that you are loved.

Always remember that…

Authors Note

For Over twenty years Craig has been a global consultant and an expert on Transformational Leadership, Organizational Effectiveness, and Inclusive Human Capital Strategies. For twenty years, he also served as the Director and Diversity Strategist with the University of Houston's International Institute for Diversity & Cross-Cultural Management located in the C.T. Bauer College of Business.

Craig B. Clayton, Sr., is the founder of the Equitable Workplace Institute and is responsible for creating, developing, training, and implementing strategic approaches to creating equitable workplaces.

His approach includes integrating inclusive strategies to develop, hire, retain, recruit, promote, on-board, create inclusive succession plans, conduct talent assessments and reviews, inclusive performance management practices, and more.

He developed the 'Diversity Profit Equation' linking inclusive human capital models to the top line (revenue growth), the bottom line (cost reduction) and the pipe line (recruiting, retention and talent management) in quantifiable measurable ways.

He has established diversity councils, created business resource groups, developed supplier diversity programs, integrated learning and development into talent management processes, and created accountability models.

He specializes in providing organizations with executive strategies and business practices that create measurable processes that improve employee performance, productivity and profitability through creating culturally competent leaders, managers and organizations.

Creating equitable workplaces has tangible business impacts; after all margin enhancement is everyone's responsibility!

PARTIAL CLIENT LIST: Representative clients Craig has worked with include but are not limited to University of Pittsburg Medical Center, Kaiser Permanente, Deloitte, Johnson Controls, Hewlett-Packard, Wal-Mart, Bank of America, Turner Broadcasting, Motiva, Grainger, Exxon Mobil, MD Anderson Cancer Center, Shell, Texas Instruments, Astra-Zeneca, Abbott Labs, AT&T, BP, and many more. (Not An Endorsement)

MEDIA EXPERIENCE: He has been interviewed on radio and television including PBS, ABC, CNN, CBS, NBC and Fox Affiliates. He also filmed a half-hour special on PBS focusing on *"Corporate Bullying – The New Sexual Harassment in the Workplace."*

Contents

Introduction

The Socio-Political History Of Tolerance

Y ou have already checked your social media, looked at your phone, watched TV or listened to the radio to check today's news. It happened again; there was something on the news involving race, gender, ethnicity, religion, education, or politics. People are choosing sides. If you are one of the few women in the organization, you may be hesitant about the upcoming coffee room discussions. If you are a white male, someone who is often referred to as privileged, you are concerned about saying the wrong thing. You want to show empathy without being seen as patronizing, so you say nothing. If you are one of the few people of color in the organization, you know the question is coming; "What do (Black People, Latinos, Asians) think about this issue?" It is as though you were voted as the spokesperson for an entire group of people. If you were, you might have missed that meeting. If this hasn't happened to you or someone you know in your organization, consider yourself lucky. Your turn to answer that question may be coming tomorrow.

People are whispering on the elevator. You are a leader in the organization. People are going to be standing at your door, asking what the company's position is. Your biggest fear, they are going to want to know what YOU think. If you say something that people consider to be insensitive, will it impact your career? If you don't take a stand, will they wonder if you are a leader? If you try to walk the middle ground, how is that leading?

Not many individuals can change a country or society. But you can change your house, your family, your team at work, your business unit, your company.

You can be that disruptive thinker that is willing to speak truth to power regardless of the consequences. There is an all too commonly held belief in the workplace, that if a comment isn't specifically directed at you, then you stay quiet, put your head down, and do your job. If the goal is to avoid finding yourself in toxic workplace cultures, the opposite is true. When you want to change organizational culture, you need courageous people. Most great leaders desire to have people who are willing to be disruptive thinkers, as well as sources of creative friction and abrasion.

My Aunt Suzie did domestic work all her life. She spent hours a day on her knees, scrubbing floors, toilets, cooking for other people, and preparing their meals. Aunt Suzie had a third-grade education but was one of the wisest women I ever knew.

She would always challenge me to speak my truth. She said, speaking truth to power was like being an "agitator." She thought Montgomery Wards, a once-thriving department and mail order store, was the ultimate end-all of stores. For some reason, she called it 'Monkey Wards.' Aunt Suzie once said to me, *"If I took my hard-earned money, scraped together by ironing other people's clothes, taking care of their children, and went to Monkey Wards and bought an expensive washing machine, then go to Winn Dixie* (a popular grocery store in that part of the south) *and buy me some expensive soap powder, darling, if I put my dirty clothes, in my expensive washing machine, with that fancy soap powder, but there ain't no agitator in the machine, at the end of the cycle, all I have is wet, soapy dirty clothes!"* She then closed by saying, "Be an agitator baby. Remember, in a washing machine, the agitator is what puts in the friction, and the friction gets the dirt out!"

Aunt Suzie's – Apron Wisdom
"Friction gets the dirt out!
Be An agitator baby!"

2

CALL TO ACTION: Today, we need more people willing to be 'agitators' in society, in organizations, in the workplace. Are you ready to provide the creative abrasion that gets the dirt and toxins out of the organizational culture? We need more people that realize being tolerant is for cowards. This book is a blueprint for instilling courage! *It provides leadership thinking to disrupt the status quo, with purpose!*

Organizations today need disruptive thinkers, sources of creative abrasions (agitators), people who are willing to dissent, and people who are eager to find their voice when someone is being treated disrespectfully. Someone who will say, *"I heard what was said! I saw something that made me uncomfortable! I will not tolerate it."*

How Would You Answer These Questions?

- When topics like bullying at work, harassment in the workplace, the latest offensive tweet, a breaking news story occurs or a racially insensitive comment dominates the headlines, what are you going to say?
- Are you concerned about being seen as weak?
- Are you worried that you are going to be seen as stirring the pot?
- Every organization has some ugly children. Are you willing to call the baby ugly?
- Can you put a pebble in the shoe of those you influence?
- Are you willing to risk your career by saying and doing what's right?
- Do you have the courage to really lead?
- What will your friends and peers say if you do?
- What will your children say if you don't?
- Are you willing to be the source of 'creative abrasion' in your organization?
- Will you speak truth to power?
- How will you make a decision that has such a significant impact on the anxiety you feel, the frustration and overwhelming angst?

- Are you ready to make a stand that can possibly impact your life, your livelihood and even your future? After all… **Being Tolerant Is For Cowards!**

These questions are not easy to answer in the least confrontational times in our sociopolitical history. In today's hypersensitive social and political times, these questions are even more difficult to confront. Social media provides opportunities to have your personal and professional character assailed in ways that are hard to understand or imagine. The vitriol that can come raining down when you speak truth can create serious challenges. The potential ramifications can impact your professional life, character, and in some cases even your personal safety as well as the safety of those in your family.

I feel your pain. I have been in your shoes. I have had to make choices such as these. Do I stay quiet and protect my paycheck, or do I speak up for what is right, even if there are personal costs and pain associated with the decision? As a leader, I sat in a meeting where the discussion turned to practices that I knew were wrong, racially insensitive at the least, possibly even illegal. The impact of the organizations' plan was going to negatively impact people who had NO voice in that room except mine.

I could choose between being accepting, indulging, even tolerating. After all, that was the easy way. It was also cowardly! It was clear that if I chose to speak up and say what was right, it would come with a significant price. On one previous occasion, I had decided to keep quiet because of fears about how people would respond, the potential for a confrontation, and it even meant my safety could be at risk if I spoke up.

I remained silent. I have regretted that decision every day of my life since then. It taught me that the price of tolerance (silence) could sometimes be your pride, self-esteem, and even your dignity.

This time, I chose to make a stand. It cost me my job. It created personal uncertainty about my ability to make a living to support my family.

However, it led to the most rewarding career I could have ever imagined. It has allowed me to connect what I do with who I am. It opened the door to my living my best life and fulfilling my destiny. I have not worked in the last 25 years as a result of that decision. My avocation (equity) has become my vocation.

There Is Truth To The Saying:

"If You Enjoy What You Do You Never Work A Day In Your Life!"

If you apply the tools identified in this book, you will gain insights to help you become more courageous when you are confronted with situations that require tough choices. These situations can arise with your peers, family members, clients, customers and even your boss.

Interacting in tough situations in ways that are respectful and inclusive is a learned behavior. In some organizations, as well as aspects of our society, there has been acceptance, not just tolerance, of cultures of disrespect. The willingness to tolerate incivility has been rooted in the achievement of what has been perceived as more significant goals.

For example, as long as the corporate financial goals are met, there can be a willingness to look the other way. Various political parties have been willing to accept and tolerate comments and behaviors that would have been deplored, as long as they can win an election, regain or maintain a majority. Individuals have allowed someone to target them and turned that into victimization because of an unwillingness to make or take a stand.

If your organization develops wide-ranging strategies and inclusive competencies among their managers, leaders, and talent professionals, then the efficiencies that come from engaged employees becoming enabled will result in respectful, equitable and profitable places to work for all stakeholders.

If you develop the skills to take your power back, then no situation where you have been targeted will become a scenario where you will be victimized. You cannot stop someone from putting you in their crosshairs because of some perceived difference that they don't respect. What each of us can do is prevent that targeting from becoming victimization.

Martin Luther King once said to the sanitation workers in Memphis, Tenn. during the civil rights movement in America, "Whenever men and women **straighten** their backs up, they are going somewhere, because a man can't ride **your back** unless it is bent."

You may be wondering, "Who is this guy that he can help me, my team, or my organization to accomplish these tasks identified in this book?"

Well, to begin with, my professional qualifications include working for over 20 years as the Director and Diversity Strategist of the International Institute for Diversity & Cross-Cultural Management at the University of Houston's C.T. Bauer College of Business.

In that role, I conducted quantitative and qualitative research for dozens of organizations to determine the impact of creating inclusive and respectful workplace cultures, management practices, inclusive talent strategies, and other aspects of organizational effectiveness.

I have developed methodologies and processes that quantify the impact of having an inclusive mindset on the top-line (revenue growth), bottom-line (cost-reductions), and pipeline (recruiting, retention, and human capital practices).

Simultaneously, I have consulted for and worked with over 200 of the Fortune 500 companies in various capacities. I have traveled professionally to over 15 countries, including Brazil, Mexico, The Philippines, Indonesia, Hong Kong, Jamaica, China, Singapore, Senegal, Kenya, Ethiopia, South Africa, and more.

I am also the Founder and Executive Director of the Equitable Workplace Institute (EWP – Institute). This institute offers dozens of instructor-led courses to increase and improve organizational culture. I have worked with for-profit, not-for-profit, government, military, law enforcement, intelligence agencies, and educational organizations.

I have assisted organizations with the creation of 'Respectful Workplace Policies' and the development of behavioral standards, inclusive talent management policies, and created the Intercultural Agility Model, which allows organizations to develop the skills needed to have inclusive talent, leadership, and management professionals. Through all of this, I have become a global leader on the topic of inclusion, respect, and workplace equity.

All Of That Describes What I Do. It Also Tells You Who I Am.

My journey has been an ongoing process of life-long learning for me. It comes from a place of empathy. Alfred Adler said, "*empathy is when you listen with the ears of another, see with the eyes of another, and feel with the heart of another.*"

I have assisted and worked in organizations where individuals' dignity and self-esteem were being attacked every day. I have personally experienced workplace bullying. I have seen the real impact of what happens when organizations are not inclusive and respectful.

My journey started as a result of my personal experiences with disrespect and people choosing to be tolerant when they witnessed these behaviors. I have spent over two decades helping to create ways for individuals, leaders, and organizations to be more inclusive while building self-esteem.

This book was written as a culmination of over twenty years on this journey. The ideas come from research, from my experiences, and from the many conversations I have had with people on these topics. I do not profess to have all the answers, but where I don't, I have always used critical analysis and research in my approach to finding the way forward. The research is then translated into success toolkits to help institutions maneuver from organizations of tolerance to organizations of inclusion and respect.

The world is changing in measurable ways. I will show you as a reader that not only is it possible to change organizational culture, but it can also improve performance, productivity, and profitability to the benefit of all stakeholders. I can help provide readers with optimism about the consistent changes impacting their lives and workplaces around the world. I understand how change and challenges can be difficult for societies, organizations, and individuals. Internal and external environments can have an impact on competitiveness, feelings of teamwork, and the overall sense of belonging.

These forces will continue to create angst and concern for thought leaders and practitioners. I recognize that the sources of competitive advantage for most societies, organizations, industries, and teams is usually rooted in some aspect of their ever-changing people strategies. These stressors will only increase in the next five to ten years. I have facilitated sessions with key stakeholders and can appreciate the impact of what will happen if teams, divisions, and organizations do not get it right.

I know that many organizations and key stakeholders assume that issues involving inclusive behaviors, respect, dignity, and civility are considered soft skills and are deemed to be hard to quantify and predict. I understand this frustration and you are not alone. I appreciate the difficulty in developing a process-based approach and then creating ways to hold people accountable for making the team, institutional, organizational and societal changes that are required to move from best practices to being best in class.

There are many aspects of the human diaspora that present additional complications such as the differences in generational perspectives and practices as well as difficulties associated with race and gender topics. Additional challenges include the growth in the importance of global and cultural implications on hiring, recruiting, management, community, societal, and leadership practices. I realize this can seem like a daunting and sometimes overwhelming task; yet key stakeholders are expecting you to inclusively understand, manage and drive these efforts.

After All... If The Competition Manages Inclusivity Better Than
You Do...They Win; It's That Simple!

Driving solutions to these challenges and more has been my life's work. I want to give you some insights about ways to identify a path forward. This book will address the topic of moving from revulsion, avoidance, and tolerance to value and respect on several levels.

- **Section One**: THE SOCIO-POLITICAL HISTORY OF TOLERANCE – In this section of the book, the foundation for the issue of tolerance will be outlined. The current events in the news that have put this topic at top of mind awareness with issues dealing with race, gender, ethnicity, religion, education, politics, as well as other divisive concerns.

  Additionally, you will be provided societal connections to the topics of tolerance as well as some statistical insights about the prevalence of derailing behaviors, the link to the global socio-political climate, and whose responsibility it is that disrespect is escalating. Lastly this section will conclude with the links between incivility, power, and privilege.

- **Section Two**: THE PERSONAL JOURNEY - In this section, this book will explore the personal journey that you have just embarked on. By choosing to move from tolerance to respect, equity, and inclusion, you have chosen to take a personal journey that will require you to stretch your cultural comfort zone. You will need to think about many things you take for granted, including the need to adjust your own unconscious biases. The second section of this book will also address issues associated with the personal filter through which we see the world and our immediate surroundings and personal skillset. Included will be topics such as:
    - Understanding is tolerance.
    - Why it is important to move beyond tolerance.

- What are the implications on teams?
- Understanding:

The range of respect and forms of blind spots.

This section will also explore why we think the way we do and provide a framework to use that will help us understand how to move from tolerance to inclusion. Having an inclusive mindset is critical to the ability to treat people with dignity and respect. We will illustrate, define, and provide insights about why and how to develop an inclusive mindset.

- **Section Three: THE TEAM JOURNEY** - The third section of this book will focus on how to move from being an organization of diverse groups to an organization of inclusive teams, by demonstrating the negative impact of stopping at the point of tolerance within teams.
It will explore the importance of developing inclusive teams and moving away from merely forming diverse groups. This section also looks at how teams work when there is an inclusive mindset and how the most successful managers treat people with dignity and respect. The link between inclusive leaders and inclusive teams is also analyzed to provide tools to develop courage among your team members.

- **Section Four: THE LEADERSHIP JOURNEY** - The focus of the fourth section of this book is on leadership, more specifically, inclusive leadership with purpose. This section will look at how effective servant leadership is enhanced when it's based on two things - inclusion and purpose. This section includes a look at what it means to lead inclusively and how this requires courage to move beyond the status quo. It will analyze different management theories and how these can be beneficial for innovation and creativity. It will then look at what leading with purpose means and how this can be achieved.

The tools to lead inclusively will incorporate information on how to lead with emotional intelligence, social intelligence, and empathy to boost productivity and increase your organizations' long-term sustainability. Leadership that creates empowerment, enabling, and engaging inclusively, is also addressed. These tools are sketched out to provide a holistic approach to leadership that can transform your organizations' ability to develop effective leadership at all levels.

- **Section Five**: **THE ORGANIZATIONAL JOURNEY** - This part of the book provides insights about the application of all these tools (Individual, Team, & Leadership) to build better organizations that have moved beyond tolerance.

   Using intercultural agility tools, leaders can develop an organizational culture of respect that increases engagement, raises the levels of discretionary effort, and drives productivity. Inclusive leaders can enable their employees and transform their corporate culture based on creating an environment of respect and inclusion.

   Through being intentionally inclusive and embracing creative abrasion, successful organizations can be built that will outlast their competitors. With purposive decision making, quantified with a culture of metrics and analytics, organizations can develop quantifiable strategies to become goal-focused at every level.

I want to provide you with insights to help you on a personal level, as a team, a leader, and an organization. I have years of experience helping organizations accomplish these goals and I am certain that I can help you and your organization too.

Are you ready to stretch your personal cultural comfort zone? Are you up to the task of looking in the mirror and facing the need for change? Are you ready to begin to move your group towards becoming an inclusive respectful team? Are you willing to move past tolerating differences to respecting and valuing them? Is it time for you and your leadership team to become more inclusive, more aligned with their purpose? Is your organization ready to build and leverage the 'people to profit' chain? If so, let's get started by moving beyond tolerance towards acceptance of differences and respecting them!

"Tolerance of intolerance is cowardice." –Ayaan Hirsi Ali

Chapter 1

The Socio-Political History of Tolerance

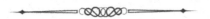

This book is not about the history of racism, xenophobia, or misogyny, and it does not attempt to solve the historically rooted systemic issues facing the United States and other parts of the world. The topics covered in this book are closely linked to disrespect, prejudice, unconscious bias, discrimination, and racism. The idea of tolerance is one that is rooted in the differences we have always had. By simply tolerating each other, we are being cowards and not facing this problem head-on.

Tolerance is not just a social justice issue; it has a significant impact on the bottom line of every organization. If you want your organization to have a competitive advantage, then you are going to have to face and move beyond the topic of being tolerant when dysfunctional behaviors manifest in your organization. You are going to have to figure out how to understand and leverage differences to your benefit and grow your organization through developing an inclusive mindset in your workforce, workplace, and marketplace strategies.

This book will address how to move organizations from being tolerant to becoming inclusive. As we know from history, this is not an easy problem to solve, but it is a problem that all organizations will have to face at some point. The first aspect of this journey will be the personal one. Let's start with taking a look at the history of tolerance.

Incivility Has Reached Epidemic Levels

Workplaces are becoming increasingly more diverse. This phenomenon is happening on a global basis. For example, in the United States, according to the U.S. Department of Labor, in 2018, over 75% of people entering the workforce in the USA are either women, immigrants, or people of color.[1]

Disrespectful behaviors are also increasing to almost epidemic levels. This disrespect is also happening on a global basis. A recently conducted longitudinal survey was conducted by the Equitable Workplace Institute, measuring the prevalence of derailing behaviors in the workplaces of the USA, over a fifteen-year window. The original study measured the prevalence of workplace bullying, acts of disrespect (incivility), micro-inequities, and micro-aggressions.

In 2004, seventy (70%) percent of employees stated that they had witnessed or experienced these behaviors in the last twelve months. In 2018, that number had risen to 86% of employees. [1] Many of these incidents of disrespect were perceived to be connected to aspects of difference related to either race, gender, generations, and sexual orientation.

The Global Political Climate of Incivility

In 2018 and 2019, there was a global wave of immigrant-bashing that is occurring at alarming rates. Protectionism, isolationism, xenophobia, and misogyny are rampant in every corner of the globe. The media showed children floating on shores in Europe, floating in the river between the USA and Mexico border region, and screaming crowds accosting families looking for a better life.

The alt-right was on the rise across the globe, and news coverage seems to be filled with hate speech. Elected and authoritarian government officials were consistently spewing hatred, discriminatory comments, and outright racism. Many of their followers were emboldened to do the same in their communities

---

[1] Equitable Workplace Institute 2004 & 2018. www.ewpinstitute.org

and in the workplace.

In Great Britain, one of the key forces that drove their voting to withdraw from the EU was due to an overriding concern about being disenfranchised and potentially displaced by an increasing flow of immigrants.[2] Germany saw internal upheaval linked to the policies that allowed increasing numbers of Syrians to enter their country.[3] France had an increase in the popularity of political parties that espouse the philosophies of isolationism, primarily directed towards immigrants and refugees.[4]

In the USA, a current populist movement of the right had philosophies that drew support from the alt-right in increasing numbers. As societies around the world continue to drift further and further to the right, there has been an increasing number of centrists who were not comfortable with how far things went, yet they did not feel compelled to speak their truth in public settings. This silence had the effect of being seen as tolerance. To many average citizens, if political leaders speak in racially offensive, xenophobic terms with no consequences, then why can't they? To be clear, this book is not about political ideology on the left or the right. The main focus and emphasis are linked to the topic of respect, courage, and purpose.

How many people in your organization suffer from too much respect at work?

Everyone is entitled to be treated with respect. This starts in our homes, our communities, our workplaces, our society in general. Respect starts with civility. When incivility is the norm, respect goes by the wayside.

The focus of this book is to emphasize the importance of having an

---

[2] https://www.theguardian.com/politics/2019/nov/11/labour-promises-managed-migration-eu-brexit
[3] https://www.irishtimes.com/news/world/middle-east/syrian-refugees-unwanted-in-germany-afraid-to-go-home-1.3978624
[4] https://www.nytimes.com/2019/11/06/world/europe/france-macron-immigration.html

inclusive mindset in all aspects of how an organization manages its most important asset, its people.

Respectful workplaces have become the anomaly and not the standard anymore. Common courtesy is not so common anymore. The ability to have a civil conversation seems to be negatively impacted by the level of incivility that is at epidemic proportions.

In a recent workshop on the topic of having an inclusive mindset and being respectful in the workplace in the south, I had a line-level supervisor in the organizations' operational department, who forcefully spoke up about halfway through an all-day session and said:

> *"I'm really sick of hearing about all this respect crap. I really*
> *don't care if someone doesn't like what I have to say. This is*
> *America, and I have the right to say anything I want. This*
> *organization has forgotten what the first amendment stands for.*
> *In fact, if I choose to walk out of this session today and use the*
> *N-word five or six times when I am talking with a coworker, it's*
> *a private conversation. If someone walks up and hears that*
> *discussion and gets offended, that's their problem! They should*
> *stay out of my conversation."*

His boss was in the room as were numerous other first-level line supervisors. Several of his bosses' peers were also in the room. None of them found their voice. They all just looked at me. Then one of his peers spoke up and endorsed his little diatribe and said, *"That's right, this is America, and we can say whatever we want, right?"* Three or four more of the guys in the room started speaking, saying: *"That's right! Yeah man, we're Americans and we have rights too?"*

Everyone in the room looked at me to see how I was going to respond. I couldn't believe in 2020 that this was something he was comfortable enough to say, but I also knew I had to address it head-on right away.

I told him, *"You know what, you are right. This is America. You have the right to say anything you want. The first amendment absolutely gives you the right to speak your mind."*

In fact, I told him: *"You can falsely yell fire in a crowded movie theater, but as Supreme Court Justice, Oliver Wendell Holmes stated, your free speech comes with consequences."* I went on to tell him that he also has the right to tell racist jokes and make racist comments at work, just as he said, however, with grown up choices, come grown up consequences!

I advised him that after exercising his free speech rights the company also had rights of their own. This included the right to introduce him to an invention that works both ways; it's called a 'doorknob'. Just like he used the doorknob to enter the workplace, if he chose to exercise his free speech in the way he expressed, I was confident that the company would demonstrate to him a unique aspect of that same doorknob. This time it would be used to let him out, just like he used it to get him in.

> *"A Bad Attitude Is Like A Flat Tire. You Can't Go Anywhere*
> *Until You Change It!!"*

To my surprise the company chose to ignore his outburst and did nothing about it. This is at a publicly traded company. In fact, shortly after this session, I was chastised for the way I spoke to their employee. I terminated my engagement with them shortly after their response.

Who Is Responsible For The Rise In Disrespect?

Many aspects of the disrespect and incivility that has become widespread is not just laid at the feet of the recent political turmoil that is occurring. We, as a society, have been trending this way for the last twenty years. When parents treat their children in a way that demonstrates entitlement, then there is an air of superiority that accompanies that mentality.

The feeling of entitlement is not a race or class issue. The psychological definition of entitlement is "an unrealistic, unmerited, or inappropriate expectation of favorable living conditions and favorable treatment at the hands of others." The ultimate expectation that comes from this mindset of entitlement is the feeling that you **deserve** preferences and resources that others do not. A healthy dose of entitlement can lead to confidence and self-assurance. An unhealthy, almost obsessive dose can lead to narcissism. At the core of most alt-right philosophies is an excessive amount of narcissistic, admiration of oneself, one's race, or one's perceived level of significance in the world's order.

Aunt Suzie's – Apron Wisdom
"Entitlement is Like Being Born on Third
base. Thinking You Hit a Triple!!"

An entire generation of this self-absorbed entitled mentality has been nurtured by the overabundance of helicopter parents who reared their children, thinking they are more important than the teacher, the school's rules, the law, or society in general. After all, these children were told THEY were the most important thing in the world.

As I said, this is not intended to be a political diatribe on my part, yet these contributing factors are hard to ignore. The fallacy associated with the errant mentality of entitlement exists in all aspects of our society, on both sides of the political spectrum, in all socio-economic layers of humanity. The expectation of entitlement exists in different ways but is still dysfunctional in all of its manifestations. It is often associated with privilege as well as parents who overindulge their children and create the egocentric, self-centered, entitled, narcissistic adults who feel they can disrespect anyone for any reason. After all, they are so self-absorbed, they are entitled to insult whomever they choose.

The Link Between Entitlement And Privilege

These two terms are different sides of the same coin. There is a subtle but distinct difference between the two words. Privilege is something that most see as having won the ovarian lottery. They were born into circumstances that provide advantages that you did nothing to deserve. Your luck allowed you to be in the front of the line.

Entitled is something one often sees themselves to be because they are better than others, for no reason. It is usually something that is taught. People who feel entitled take their privilege for granted and believe it is their birthright.

Many in the current political upheaval have taken the word entitlement and assigned the characteristics of getting something for nothing, a handout. Ironically, many of those same people don't see their fortune, having been born into most forms of privilege, is getting something for nothing as well.

"Unlike confidence, which requires absolute belief in your abilities, courage only requires one thing: that you act. To be courageous is to do things you're afraid to do."

—Written by Ashford University Staff

The Privilege Conundrum and Tolerance

When the topic of privilege arises, it causes many people to recoil. Some even now refer to the use of the term privilege as a sociological weapon meant to demean or disparage those who have some forms of privilege. Some see it as an assault by the PC-Police (politically correct). When you take race out of the equation, the existence of privilege is easier for most to accept. Privilege is simply being given the benefit of the doubt!

DEFINING PRIVILEGE: Privilege is a right, immunity, or benefit enjoyed only by one category of people beyond the advantages of others. The advantage is completely out of your control. Let's face it; we all benefit from some of privilege.

Privilege Is Simply Being Given The Benefit Of The Doubt!

Accepting the fact that you have privilege can be a challenge depending on which form of privilege it is. The most insidious aspect of privilege, whatever type you may have, is when you begin to think that the benefits you derive from your privilege are things that you actually deserve because you are somehow better, smarter, or more deserving than others are - entitled. Everyone has privilege of some sort that they did not earn even if you do not like the form of privilege that you have.

The most important thing that can be learned from understanding how privilege manifests is to recognize that others may not have our form of privilege. This often means they must run their race by starting from a different starting line or across different terrain that we have to run on our race.

Privilege Is Being Born on Third Base Thinking You Hit a Triple!

TYPES OF PRIVILEGE

Among the types of privilege that exist, of which there are many, let's take a look at a few examples:

- Socio-Economic Privilege
- Gender Privilege
- Religious Privilege

SOCIO-ECONOMIC PRIVILEGE: This form of privilege is not indicative of someone being super-rich. Even the phrase super-rich is a relative term. I have traveled to five African nations and seen incredible wealth in parts of Pretoria, Johannesburg, and Cape Town. I have also seen the extreme poverty brought about by living across the ridge in the townships. This type of privilege is a combination of education, income, and occupation.

> EXAMPLE: If you were born in a suburb with middle-class, working parents, you might not have the socio-economic privilege of someone born in the Hamptons outside of New York City, or someone in Belaire outside of Los Angeles, or in Highland Park outside of Chicago. But you have a significant amount of socio-economic privilege over someone born in many inner-city neighborhoods or certain developing countries.
>
> All of these are privileges that you did nothing to achieve or deserve. Your access to education and upward mobility is easier. Your likelihood of obtaining a better job is higher; your access to healthcare is greater. All of these are benefits of privilege that are not based on you deserving these things. It is based on your having hit, as was said earlier, the ovarian lottery.

GENDER PRIVILEGE: In most societies, this form of privilege is given to men. There are many ways this privilege manifests. Women recognize these forms instantly. Many men deny they have privileges and often don't acknowledge them even when pointed out. In patriarchal societies, these privileges are more pronounced.

> EXAMPLE: Men are most often those with power in societies. This power includes political, educational, social, economic, and even moral authority. These privileges are unearned, though many men won't

acknowledge this. In my opinion, if any man doesn't recognize the existence of male privilege, he is in denial.

RELIGIOUS PRIVILEGE: The manifestation of this type of privilege depends significantly on where you live. In many parts of the United States, this is manifested as Christian Privilege. Holidays associated with Christianity will be realized much more frequently than those related to other religions.

There is a higher likelihood that politicians will be aligned with your faith and, as a result, will pass laws linked to your faith practices. In other countries, there will be significantly different religions, holiday celebrations, types of food, and laws that are aligned with their dominant faith beliefs.

All of these types of privilege, as well as some not mentioned, are real and often easier to acknowledge and accept until they impact you. When people look into the privilege window, it quickly can become a mirror. *There usually is significantly less ownership of the existence and impact of the mirror than there is the window.*

It's easier to look through the window, than it is to look in the mirror. – C.B. Clayton, Sr.

The form of privilege that causes the most animosity in discussions is white privilege. The association of the topic of tolerance and white privilege must be confronted. Privilege of any sort disadvantages someone. For example:

- Socio-economic privilege disadvantages those who were not born into wealth nor have access to education.
- Gender privilege, normally afforded to men, disadvantages women regardless of the society that it manifests in.
- Religious privilege disadvantages those not from the dominant religion

22

in a given country or society.

White privilege is no different. It disadvantages all those who are not white. The mere discussion of this privilege is met with the most pushback and angst. Yet we tolerate the differences it affords those who have it, and many times see it as an entitlement, instead of something one has based on societal and sociological happenstance.

WHITE PRIVILEGE: This type of privilege is the one that causes the most rancor in discussions. This form of privilege is most often prevalent in the United States and other European countries. This is best understood if you take all other attributes of difference and create an even playing field, and then examine the impact.

> **EXAMPLE**: In the USA or a European country, take two individuals of the same gender, socio-economic background, educational achievements, parental environment, geographic location, physical attributes, language, community, support systems, as well as any other attribute of difference with one exception. One is Caucasian, and the other is not. Here are some ways that privilege exists according to Peggy McIntosh's, White Privilege: Unpacking the Invisible Knapsack article:[5]
> - Can you go shopping, pretty well assured they will not be followed or harassed?
> - Can you go grocery shopping and find foods that fit with cultural traditions?
> - Can you get upset without your anger being attributed to your race?
> - Can you do well in challenging situations without being called a

---

[5] https://nationalseedproject.org/Key-SEED-Texts/white-privilege-unpacking-the-invisible-knapsack

credit to your race?

- Are you never asked to speak for all the people of your racial group?
- Can you criticize a politician without being told to go back where you came from?
- Can you get pulled over by the police without fearing for your life?
- Can you easily buy greeting cards, dolls, and toys, featuring people of your race?

The only reason these distinctions and many others are so prevalent is that it is easier to be tolerant. It takes courage to speak up. It takes courage to be willing to call out these forms of privilege whenever they appear, whether they are based on race, gender, religion, education, or any other attribute of difference.

As mentioned, privilege also leads to an arrogant and self-important mindset that makes it easy to be disrespectful. Individuals reared with an entitlement attitude see no need to respect someone they see as subservient or beneath them. For every parent who has reared their child to think they are unique, that is not the problem. The real challenge is also teaching your child that everyone else is just as talented and deserving of respect as they are.

Many people today are disrespectful, with no feeling of remorse because they have been taught by parents that they deserve special treatment, and others are less significant than they are.

An Example In The USA Confederate Flags

For the last several years, the news has been full of examples illustrating that we are still struggling as individuals, communities, and as a nation to accept and deal with the tremendous pain and emotional injury connected to the history of racism, xenophobia, and intolerance in our country.

For example, one illustration that the fabric of our society seems to be bursting at the seams involves the reverence for symbols of the confederacy in the USA. One of the critical issues driving the Civil War in the USA was the topic of slavery.

The south (the confederacy) wanted to maintain the institution of slavery. The ability to keep enslaved labor that provided the plantation owners with wealth and social status was of paramount importance. Despite having lost the war to the Union Army of the north, many southern states, decades after the civil war ended, erected monuments to the losing generals - generals who led an effort to revolution, an internal war, against the United States. Most of these statues were not erected during or immediately after the war ended. The majority of them were put in place during the Jim Crow South as a way to pay homage to the 'good ole days' when African-Americans were enslaved. It was a subtle way to imply the entitlement, privilege, and superiority many white southerners felt they possessed.[6]

There have been national-level discussions in the USA about removing these confederate statues. In 2017, the nation witnessed far-right nationalist groups murder someone protesting against their hate-filled rhetoric in Charlottesville, Virginia.[7] The moral threads of our communities seem to be unravelling at an alarming pace. As a nation founded on principles of faith and fairness, it looks as though civility and civil discourse have devolved into an expectation of what each individual wants, instead of the greater common good.

For example, when looking at the removal of the confederate statues, an announcer on TV provides an illustration that might make some think twice. The circumstances are not identical, but the concepts have enough parallels.

Imagine a Jewish family whose grandmother survived the holocaust, was now living in the United States. They walk to the local elementary school to enrol their 7-year-old

---

[6] https://www.history.com/news/how-the-u-s-got-so-many-confederate-monuments
[7] https://en.wikipedia.org/wiki/Charlottesville_car_attack

granddaughter. *The school is named Hermann Goering Elementary, and it is located next to "The Third Reich Park", complete with a statue of Adolph Hitler.*

Hanging on the wall of the school, next to the American Flag, is another flag with a swastika on it. In the science class, there are posters of a man named Josef Mengele.

It is hard to imagine a scenario like this unfolding in the United States. And yet, in every state in the United States, there is an African American family whose grandmother knows the story of her grandmother surviving slavery. Many have a family member that was one of the 5,000 people who were lynched in the USA, who have to face a similar dilemma.

They must enrol their children into schools named after people involved in slavery and proponents of the kind of racial hatred and divisiveness that still tears the USA apart. These families must face the confederate flag, an enduring symbol embraced by those of like-minded alt-right philosophies, daily. The rationale expressed is pride in their heritage. Why is the former unacceptable, yet the later deemed acceptable in America?

The Link to Social Media

It appears that topics, such as these are becoming more frequent. Differences in the workplace, schools, and social organizations are becoming more prevalent. So is the rise in tensions about the significance of certain identities and insignificance of others. Are we more divided, or do we have more outlets and vehicles to discuss these differences, so it seems to be more prevalent?

It has been said that the rise in police violence against minorities has not significantly increased in the last ten years. Some say what has increased is the ability for people to capture these incidents on their phones, which has made it seem much more prevalent.

It has gone beyond which version of events you want to believe. Way too often, you can watch incidents unfold, and still, people see things in opposed perspectives.

The rise of social media has led to an increase in how much news we consume, which news do we want to watch, and how much information we share. Often this process reaffirms what we want to hear because we listen to and watch what will reaffirm our pre-existing outlook.

This has led to an increase in the number of challenging and confronting conversations we have about topics that require us to choose a side. Sometimes it seems that escaping these conversations is impossible. They are happening with friends, with family, with strangers, online, and of course, in our schools.

They are also taking place in the workplace with coworkers seeing issues based on the cultural, generational, and social filters that are each impacted by attributes of difference.

These conversations are also happening in parking lots, cafeterias, and on the phone. People are talking in elevators. During coffee breaks, people will bring up the latest news from their smartphone, and they will ask you where you stand on specific issues.

They will ask coworkers what they think of the latest news on an issue associated with immigrants, women, minorities, or the LGBTQIA community. They are looking to leaders and management for insight about what the organization's position is, and everyone will take a stand. As a leader or someone of influence, finding your voice has to be rooted in equitable, fair, and respectful insights. Sometimes these answers are contrary to the prevailing thoughts and attitudes that permeate the popular press. In the workplace, you as a leader are not afforded the anonymity that comes along with hiding behind a social media post or a tweet.

It is for this reason that this book is being written. It is a blueprint to instill courage, move beyond being tolerant, and provide leadership thinking to disrupt the status quo with purpose.

Something to Think About: Questions For You

To begin this journey, I would like you to ask yourself some questions. Whether you are a leader in an organization or not, you cannot run away from these questions. They are an inevitable part of our changing workplaces:

- When you are asked to take a stand on difficult issues, what are you going to say?
- Will you be concerned about appearing weak or insensitive?
- Are you worried that you are going to stir up issues and problems unnecessarily?
- What if others disagree with your values?
- What if your coworkers all have different opinions from yours?
- What if your coworkers and leaders hold discriminatory views?
- Will you do what is right, even if it may risk your career?
- In a situation where your coworkers push offensive opinions like workplace bullying, racism, or ostracization, will you speak up?
- Are you willing to be the source of creative abrasion in your organization?
- Would you be willing to take a stand when it could impact your lifestyle, livelihood, and future?

Answering some of these questions is hard. It isn't easy to rock the boat, especially if you are the only person who stands up for what is right. After all, we all have jobs, families, and obligations that could be on the line if we choose to speak the truth to power. It can be a difficult thing to be tolerant of someone or something that you know is wrong. It should be more difficult to **not** be tolerant of indifference and exclusion.

As I said before, I feel your pain. I have been in your shoes. More than once, I have had to make a choice of whether or not to speak out or stay quiet. In one case, I made a decision that I will regret all my life. I was a coward and chose not to speak up. I was tolerant of someone else's disrespectful and racist comments. Sometimes being tolerant is the easy way out, I understand that. However, that doesn't make it right.

Aunt Suzie's – Apron Wisdom

"Truth Doesn't Need Help. All It Needs Is Light."

Being tolerant, whether it is in your workplace, at home, or in your community, is the easy thing to do, and subsequently, it is something we all have done. It's easy to tolerate the status quo. Who wants to rock the boat? It takes courage to decide to move from tolerance to respect and inclusion.

Don't Make A Character Choice That You Will Regret….I Did.

(Jasper Texas 1999)

Keeping It Real

Choices That Become Defining Moments

I was conducting a series of workshops throughout a week-long training engagement after the murder of James Byrd in Jasper, Texas. James Byrd had been dragged to death behind a pickup truck, and two people from Jasper accused of the murder. They were being tried separately. One of the trials was going on while I would be in town conducting training sessions on workplace respect.

As I prepared to leave for my week in Jasper, my wife made me promise I would not get into a debate with people in town about the merits of the trial. She was afraid for my safety in this small Texas town with a history of race problems.

I told her I would try not to get into a debate or dispute with anyone. She made me promise that I would do more than try. She asked me to promise her that I would honour her request. I promised.

There were no hotels in Jasper, only motels. I was conducting training for a store where one of the people arrested for this heinous crime formerly worked. Employees in the store were taking sides claiming that this former co-worker, who was on trial for murder and a hate crime, was not a bad guy.

I was doing one training session in the morning and a second workshop in the late afternoon, in a meeting room at the motel. After my morning session, I would return the key to the front desk, at their request.

They advised me they had other things happening, and this was the only meeting room they had. On the afternoon of the first day, I went to the front desk to get the key to the training room for the late afternoon session.

One of the employees in the morning session thought the person arrested for the crime, was getting a bum deal. I later found he was related to one of the motel employees and shared his thoughts with his relative at the front desk. He told her that he thought the class about respect was a waste of time. When I went to the front desk to get the key for the training room, the employee put the key on the counter and placed her hand on top of the key.

She said, *"So you're the guy here doing this training about the Byrd case, huh?"* Her hand was still covering the key on the counter. I responded: *"Yes, ma'am. Can I have the key, please?"*

She said: *"I don't understand why people are coming to our town and making such a big deal out of this!"* I heard my wife's words…bit my tongue and said, *"Yes, ma'am; may I please have the key for the training room?"*

She wasn't getting the response out of me she hoped for, and not saying anything was tearing me apart. However, I honoured my wife's request and bit a hole in my tongue. This employee of the motel then stepped WAY over the line and said: *"Well, this isn't that big of a deal; it's not like they dragged him that far!!"*

For context, these two men were accused and ultimately convicted of chaining James Byrd behind a pickup truck, and dragging him down a dirt road, for three miles until they decapitated him.

With her hand, still on the key, she stared at me, as I was seething inside. She was waiting to see how I was going to respond. I was thinking about my promise to my wife and could still hear her words. I thought to myself, *"Lord, you gotta give me some words. I don't know what to say next!"* I responded, *"Well ma'am, that's an opinion; a pretty unique one, but still an opinion. I still need that key, please."*

She pushed the key on the floor, slammed the door behind her, and walked into the motel office. I slowly picked up the key, walked into the meeting room, closed the door behind me, put my back against the door, slid to the floor, and I sat there, and cried. I wasn't crying because of anything she said. I was shedding a tear because of what I DIDN'T say. I erred to the side of safety, bit my tongue, kept my promise, and felt completely ashamed and devastated that I had been SUCH A COWARD!

I'm telling you; I know that being tolerant is for cowards. I have been one. But I promised it would never happen again.

Be more concerned with your character than your reputation,
because your character is what you really are, while your
reputation is merely what others think you are.

What Is The Purpose Of This Book?

This book will identify the choices leaders and organizations need to make to move from tolerance to respect and inclusion as individuals, as teams, and as leaders. If you bought this book and are now reading it, then I hope that this means you have started your journey of moving beyond tolerance towards an inclusive mindset.

This book is for leaders who want to move beyond tolerance but do not know where to start. The book will show you what types of leadership thinking you need to disrupt the status quo with purpose. The last part of that sentence is probably the most important part, **with purpose**. Becoming inclusive for the sake of being politically correct is not the purpose of this book.

This book will focus on how to make your organization **more productive** by developing an inclusive organizational culture. It will show you how you can instill courage among your leaders, executives, and team members. The process of developing an inclusive mindset and leadership thinking that allows you to challenge the status quo is a process. Once you have done this, you can develop an inclusive organization that has moved beyond tolerance.

The tools described are researched, practiced, and proven to be a best-in-class approach to developing individual and organizational inclusion and respect. These tools are not merely about checking boxes; they are about creating a change in attitude and mindset. It is about creating an organizational culture based on inclusion and respect. The ultimate business goals for most organizations are to either increase revenue (top line), reduce their bottom line (expenses), or effectively leverage your pipeline (recruiting, retention & talent management) or some combination of all three.

After All, Margin Enhancement Is Everyone's Business!

Getting Started: An Inclusive Mindset

As organizations are becoming more diverse, including different ethnic backgrounds, generations, thinking styles, leadership styles, and more, it is increasingly more important that all aspects of the human capital life cycle (recruiting, retention, sourcing, onboarding, leadership, learning and development) have an inclusive mindset.

In particular, demographically speaking, the USA and the world are seeing a significant shift in minority populations. From data collected in the last U.S. census, it is estimated that by 2042, more than 50% of the population of the U.S. will be a member of what has historically been considered a minority group.[8]

---

[8] Toossi, 2012.

From this data, it is apparent that becoming diverse is really not a challenge. Most of that 'visible diversity' is clustered at the entry-level of the organizational hierarchy. The real issue is creating equitable workplace cultures where people have access to all aspects of talent management systems and processes on an equitable basis.

If this is achieved through a transformation in your leadership thinking, then the productivity benefits will be felt in your organization for decades to come. Moving beyond tolerance will make your organizational culture more inviting and accepting for all stakeholders.

"Tolerance becomes a crime when applied to evil."

—Thomas Mann, The Magic Mountain

Inclusiveness In The Workplace

An inclusive workplace is a working environment that values individual and group differences within its workforce. It enables an organization to embrace the different backgrounds and perspectives of employees, which in turn increases their talent, innovation, creativity, and contributions.[9]

We have all relied on our instincts to make decisions. Unfortunately, you cannot rely on your instincts alone when making talent-related decisions involving such organizational critical tasks as attracting, selecting, recruiting, engaging, managing, leading, developing, or retaining talent. An inclusive mindset is becoming increasingly more critical as the workforce is becoming more global, multicultural, multi-generational, and multi-lingual.

Inherent in the decision-making process is an opportunity for our instincts

---

[9] https://www.linkedin.com/in/siyanasokolova

33

to be impacted by cognitive bias, as many I/O Psychologists will state.

There are dozens of cognitive biases that manifest at a subconscious level. They can impact our perceptions of measurable and even predictable ways. An ***inclusive mindset*** involves becoming aware of the most prevalent forms of cognitive bias and developing steps and processes to identify and mitigate them before they create opportunities to impact our decision-making processes in non-productive ways.

MINDSET

Definition: The term mindset defines a person's way of thinking about their abilities and capabilities. It is a collection of thoughts and beliefs that shape your outlook on your competency and proficiency. It primarily involves the ***inward*** look we each make to assess ourselves.[10]

INCLUSIVE MINDSET

Definition: Having an *inclusive mindset* is the outlook or framework one uses when looking ***externally*** at others. It is significantly impacted by the way our cognitive biases have been developed. Regardless of where or when you were reared, we all have generalizations, stereotypes, and stigmas that have become ingrained, even at a subconscious level, in our way of seeing and interacting with others.

Proactively developing an inclusive mindset is a business requirement, especially for managers, supervisors, leaders, HR, and talent professionals. Having an inclusive mindset is directly associated with your outlook and perspective. Being inclusive is a mindset issue because you have to **choose** to be accepting of the inevitable differences that exist in organizations.

The work in 'mindset' has been aligned with the research of Dr. Carol Dweck, Professor of Psychology at Columbia University. Her work in the area of motivational psychology is widely recognized as seminal in the field of

---

[10] https://en.wikipedia.org/w/index.php?title=Carol_Dweck&oldid=920026765

motivation. She divides people into two categories or approaches people take when assessing their own abilities. She categorizes people's self-tape or self-view as either being driven by a 'fixed or growth' mindset. This self-tape drives people to see their basic qualities as either static or fluid.

> **Fixed Mindset:** A static or fixed mindset is when someone sees their qualities as etched in stone. Your personality, intelligence, personality, moral character, are what they are and there is no changing them. This is linked to the colloquial statement that you: *'can't teach an old dog new tricks'*. The view that *'this is the hand I have been dealt'* is seen as an end state that one can do nothing about.

> **Growth Mindset:** Those with a growth mindset see the cards they have been dealt as a starting point and not the destination. Every failure is an opportunity to improve, learn, and get better. This mindset believes that everyone can change and grow. [11]

This doesn't mean, according to Dr. Dweck, that everyone with a growth mind can become Einstein or Beethoven; instead what she is saying is that it is impossible to know what someone's true potential is and that with hard work, insights, development, and coaching, people can always go further than they might initially think, or than what others have told them they should think!

Real Life Examples: There are so many examples of people achieving more than they were told they were capable of achieving!
- Walt Disney was fired from the Kansas City Star in 1919 because his editor said he "lacked imagination and had no good ideas."
- Michael Bloomberg was let go when he was working as a partner at

---

[11] https://en.wikipedia.org/w/index.php?title=Carol_Dweck&oldid=920026765

Salomon Brothers, an investment bank. He is now a multi-billionaire.

- Oprah Winfrey was an evening news reporter and apparently got fired because she couldn't sever her emotions from her stories!

- Elvis Presley was told by the concert hall manager, after a performance at Nashville's Grand Ole Opry, that he was better off returning to Memphis and driving trucks (his former career).

There are dozens of more examples of people being told their abilities and skills were fixed, but their mindset was not limited by other people's perceptions. Their internal 'growth mindset' drove them to see failure as a learning opportunity. Developing an inclusive mindset is much more than a feel-good social issue or a sensible employment practice.

It is a critical approach to protecting and enhancing profitability and to leveraging workplace and workforce differences for competitive advantage. Like any critical approach, the first stage in addressing this will be to understand and acknowledge the problem. We know that our society and therefore our workforce is changing. In some organizations, there are as many as five generations in the workforce.

We know that organizations that embrace differences are more successful than others[12]. We also know that organizations that are brave enough to become inclusive organizations are even more successful than those that are just merely tolerant of differences.

But there is now more to this problem than meets the eye. Twenty years ago, becoming diverse would be considered a goal. As society has changed, so has this goal.

Now, having a diverse workforce is not an accomplishment; it's an inevitability. Many organizations cite the increased level of diversity that exists within their organization as though they have made great strides to achieve those

---

[12] Tulshyan, Ruchika, 2015.

increases. The numbers are quoted on their websites and in their corporate documents with a tremendous sense of pride.

It is common to read that Silicon Valley companies even compete against each other to see which organization can have the best "diversity percentile." However, **becoming diverse, just like being tolerant, it is no longer the goal.**

If becoming diverse is not the goal, then what is? How do organizations find out what goals are suitable for their organization? How can you link these goals surrounding the changing workforces with your organization's wider goals for success? How important is addressing this problem?

"To be truly successful, companies need to have a corporate mission that is bigger than making a profit." - Marc Benioff, Salesforce

---

Growth Mindset And Inclusive Mindset

In today's increasingly diverse workplace, workforce, and marketplace, having a growth or fixed mindset is more than a personal issue. It is key to how you view yourself, your team, your workplace, and your organization. Missing in the work of Dr. Carol Dweck is the topic of the EXTERNAL look that we take.

How do we view others? How inclusive is our mindset?

When looking at others, do you view people from an INCLUSIVE or EXCLUSIVE mindset? Do you look beyond your personal biases and stereotypes that can cause you to have a jaded view of someone's abilities and even their capabilities? Are you even aware of the spots you may have on your lens? The hardest look for most of us to make is the look in the mirror. There are a couple of ways to get some clarity about where you may be on the Personal

Bias Continuum. The continuum ranges from explicitly (consciously) biased to being unconsciously inclusive.

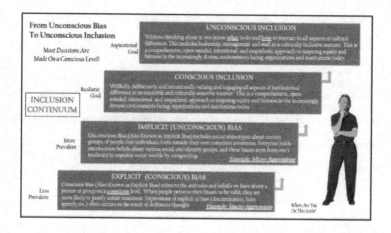

An Inclusive Mindset Starts By Understanding Your Biases

Part of understanding how to develop an inclusive mindset is understanding where your existing biases are on certain attributes of difference. We each have a **worldview** that has been programmed into our subconscious over our lifetime in overt as well as covert ways. This is referred to as implicit bias or implicit social cognition. It drives our attitudes, biases, and prejudices in subtle ways that are not at top-of-mind awareness for most of us. If the goal is to develop an inclusive mindset, one of the first steps is to determine what are the blind spots we already have.

Each of us has been programmed by our families, the area where we were reared, our religion, friends, and more. This impacts our outlook on all aspects of how we view, interact, judge, and make decisions. Our own cultural lens has a direct bearing on our worldview, stereotypes and misconceptions. Inclusive leaders have a thirst for wanting to learn more about cultural differences without judging those differences. Inclusive leaders are capable of changing their interactions based on non-verbal as well as verbal feedback.

Being An Inclusive Leader Doesn't Mean Changing Identity; Just Being Able to Adapt as Needed

Moving from unconscious incompetence (You don't know what you don't know) to unconscious competence (you perform without thinking about performing) is a progressive journey that starts with awareness, followed by training, and then practice! A key step recommended to gain a better understanding of where you are on this journey involves taking an implicit aptitude test. The most robust way to accomplish this baseline understanding is through 'Project Implicit'.

This project in an international collaboration by researchers at Harvard, Yale and dozens of other academic institutions, and non-profit organizations who are interested in implicit social cognition. This focuses on thoughts and feelings that are normally outside of our conscious control or awareness. Included are our blind spots relative to race, religion, age, disabilities, sexuality, weight, gender in specific careers, skin tone, and more. Harvard University hosts the online assessment.

Some critics have assailed the assessment as unreliable. Its use should be seen through the prism of providing insights to drive reflection and awareness and not as an academic psychometric test consisting of numerical reasoning, verbal reasoning, diagrammatic reasoning, and situational judgement.

There are now several different Implicit Aptitude tests including the above-mentioned social attitudes assessment, as well as a mental health assessment, that helps identify associations about self-esteem, anxiety, alcohol, eating disorders, and more. For more information click here: https://implicit.harvard.edu/implicit/

Being aware of your own cognitive biases can help reduce them occurring at an unconscious level. A key enabler of having the ability to be inclusive in your interactions with people from different backgrounds, thought processes, cultures, and social backgrounds is also connected to various types of intelligence.

Intellectual capability (IQ) has never been questioned when looking at the skills of those tasked with managing and leading in the workplace. Progressive organizations are becoming increasingly aware of the importance of leaders having other forms of intelligence as well. Emotional intelligence (EQ), social intelligence (SQ, and cultural intelligence (CQ) have a significant impact on the ability to have an inclusive mindset and approach.

Inclusive Mindset & Emotional Intelligence

Definition: Emotional Intelligence (EQ) refers to the capability of a person to understand, manage, and control his or her emotions. It also includes having the ability to recognize, manage, and influence the emotions of others as well. In other words, a person with high EQ has an impact internally and externally.

Key to the ability to effectively demonstrate a high EQ, is the ability to have an Inclusive Mindset. Emotional intelligence provides you with the understanding of your own emotions and the ability to influence others. With workplaces becoming increasingly more global, multi-generational, and diverse, emotional intelligence is becoming ever more significant in the ability to have an inclusive mindset.

There can be up to five different generations in the workplace, as well as different cultures, thinking styles, and more. Having a high EQ may mean you have increased potential to influence others; however, it doesn't mean you will have a **desire** or the cultural and social intelligence to positively impact those around you. It also doesn't mean you will be **accepting** of those differences.

Having the intelligence (IQ) to understand those differences must be partnered with a willingness to have a mindset that is open to and accepting of the differences that you intellectually and emotionally understand. For example, when looking at generational differences:

INTELLIGENCE QUOTIENT (IQ): Having the intellectual capacity to understand that each generation has a set of values and precepts that impact how they approach work, their coworkers and their commitment to the organization, doesn't mean you **value and respect** those differences.

EMOTIONAL INTELLIGENCE (EQ): Having the **ability** to understand the importance of different backgrounds, thinking styles, cultural, and generational dissimilarities doesn't mean that there is a willingness to be inclusive.

Emotional intelligence refers to the ability to identify and manage one's own emotions, as well as the emotions of others. Empathy is typically associated with EQ, because it relates to an individual connecting their personal experiences with those of others.

Emotional intelligence is generally said to include at least three skills:

1. Emotional awareness, or the ability to identify and name one's own emotions;

2. The ability to harness those emotions and apply them to tasks like thinking and problem solving;

3. And the ability to manage emotions, which includes both regulating one's own emotions when necessary and helping others to do the same.[13]

SOCIAL INTELLIGENCE (SQ): This refers to having the ability to get along well with others, as well as the ability to get others to get along well with you. One of the key skills in this type of intelligence is communications. Social Intelligence develops from experience with people and learning from success and failures in social settings. It is more commonly referred to as tact, common

---

[13] https://www.psychologytoday.com/us/basics/emotional-intelligence

sense, or street smarts. [14] Daniel Goleman, in his book, Beyond IQ, Beyond Emotional Intelligence, identifies two types of behaviors that are typical, based on your level of social intelligence. He describes toxic versus nourishing behaviors. Take a look:

TOXIC BEHAVIORS

- Ignoring Coworkers
- Inappropriate Jokes
- Monopolizing the Conversation
- Talking Over People / Interrupting
- Gossiping / Violating Confidences
- Insisting on Getting Your Way
- Ridiculing / Putting People Down

NOURISHING BEHAVIORS

- Acknowledging Coworkers
- Using Humor Constructively
- Inviting Others to Share Thoughts
- Hearing People Out
- Keep Confidences
- Compromising, Cooperating
- Affirming Others; Empathizing

---

[14] [1] The Man Problem: destructive masculinity in Western culture, Palgrave Macmillan, New York.

The goal is to have leaders and others that exhibit more nourishing behaviors than toxic. Your level of social intelligence has a bearing on your approach to having an inclusive mindset, being respectful, and the ability to move beyond tolerance to respect.

Ultimately, every single decision you make for your organization comes down to one thing; does it make the organization more effective? Effective organizations have a purpose, are more productive, and more productive organizations are more profitable.

Profitability at all costs can be a dangerous path to choose, and ultimately, organizations must ensure that they have an organizational culture that best matches the values of the entire workforce.

Focusing on profit places competition above cooperation and places productivity over values. This can work for the short term but will soon create an organization that is based only on the needs of stakeholders. This ignores your main customer – your workforce. Focusing on profit alone also ignores long term sustainability. This is the primary goal of any business, and that is an accurate measure of the success of an organization. That can only be achieved by focusing on values that are based on creating a productive workplace.

"Inclusion and fairness in the workplace . . . is not simply the right thing to do; it's the smart thing to do."

- Alexis Herman

In any situation, making organizational change is hard. It is not easy to try to change how workforces do things. Changing corporate culture is just as difficult. This will be discussed at length in section five and throughout this book. The aim of the tools provided in every section of this book is to provide you with a way to overcome this challenge.

What You Will Learn In This Book

Let me start by telling you what you will not learn from this book. You will not learn how to reverse systemic racism, and you will not learn how to stop societal racism and prejudice. I wish I had the answers to these substantial systemic problems, and I wish I had ways to convince our leaders to act to reduce the damage that they are doing to our society. Perhaps these will become part of another book focusing on society and the ways in which we can treat each other more civilly.

For this book, my focus is on something a lot more concrete, more succinct, and a lot more tangible. This book is focused on how we move from being diverse to becoming inclusive in our organizations and what types of leaders can create this type of change.

The focus was intentional. The aim in writing this book was to share my research and experience of what I have learned about working in Inclusion Management, and to use this to provide success toolkits. If these are taken on and used in your organization, they will not only improve inclusive competencies, but they will improve your organizations impact on the world in a positive way. This can help you to define long term strategies that allow your organization to grow in more effective and efficient ways.

"We find comfort among those who agree with us - growth among those who don't." -Frank Clark

---

What you take from this book is subjective. It depends on many different factors about who you are as a reader. Hopefully, at a minimum, all readers will take away the following key points:

- **This book is not about social justice; this is about business.** One of the critical things that you will take away is that becoming an inclusive organization is not just the right thing to do, but it is the smart business thing to do.

- **This book is not about merely checking the box for compliance.** This book will also show you that the concept of inclusion is not just something you need to do because you have been told to do. If you want your organization to grow and respond to the changing workforce, workplace, and marketplace, adapting to have an inclusive mindset and leadership style is something you must do.

- **Being inclusive will stretch your cultural comfort zone.** Changing organizational cultures requires effort, and it requires rethinking ideas that you may see as irrefutable. Your cultural comfort zone will be challenged, and this is a good thing. It will help you to learn flexibility and innovation and to use these skills to grow your organization.

- **Being inclusive means treating others how they want to be treated. (The Platinum rule)** We always hear that we should treat others how we want to be treated, but this is not entirely correct. To really create inclusive and effective organizations, we need to understand how others want to be treated and develop ways in which this can be achieved.

- **Respecting and valuing differences and being inclusive is hard work.** Just as changing organizational culture takes effort, so does respect and valuing differences on an individual level. This requires taking a good look at your value systems and adjusting them to drive change. The impact on a personal level is higher outputs professionally and personally.

- **Moving towards being an inclusive organization requires courage.**
  Bringing about change in any lasting way, in any organization, is about disrupting the status quo. There will always be people who are against this as they want things to remain the same. To develop change and to stay committed to it requires courage in the face of this difficulty. Leaders will need the courage to implement the toolkits in this book to create more effective leadership thinking in their organizations.

- **Being inclusive gets more out of less.** The workforce is growing, and as it does, we need to get more out of the workforce in order to achieve organizational growth. Being inclusive allows organizations to achieve this without diverting extensive costs towards this exercise.

- **Becoming inclusive help you move from a group to a team.** It is well documented that teams are more productive than groups. Equally, it is well documented that forming workplace teams is easier said than done.[15] Workplace groups are easily formed; they are the natural effect of what happens when more than two people work together. Teams must be created and supported; they must be cultivated and nurtured. Developing inclusive competencies helps to achieve this.

- **Becoming inclusive requires inclusive leadership.** Traditionally, measures to improve acceptance of differences and develop an inclusion mindset has been the responsibility of the Office of Diversity. This can be detrimental to the success of both of these initiatives as for organizational change to be successful and long-lasting, it must be

---

[15] Agrawal, Jagdish Prasad, 2017.

owned by senior management and driven by those with talent management responsibilities. Inclusive cultures require leadership thinking that is prepared to disrupt the status quo with purpose, and this starts in the C-Suite.

- **Leading inclusion change processes requires leading with purpose.** We all know leaders who just seem to drift along from quarterly report to quarterly report providing just enough growth to be seen as successful. They do the best they can to just get through the day and get through the next quarterly reports. They end up losing their energy, their enthusiasm, and any vision they once had. This becomes reflected in the organization as employees and co-workers become less motivated to excel, less motivated to be innovative, and less motivated to inspire others around them. Leaders with purpose, on the other hand, have specific, expressed strategic reasons for existing in their role. They have a vision for what they want the organization to look like, and that vision is their primary goal; subsequently, it becomes the organizational goal. Rather than just focusing on shareholder wealth creation, leaders with purpose have a powerful effect on long term strategies and so long-term success of any organization.

This is not an exclusive list. There are many more topics covered in the chapters that follow. Hopefully, there will be more that you will learn from this book. It will be covering a wide variety of topics in bite-sized sections and should provide enough for you to be able to develop a success toolkit for yourself and your organization to bring about positive, inclusive change in your workplace.

> *"No one can whistle a symphony. It takes a whole orchestra to play it."--HE Luccock*

Before being able to address the implications of not moving beyond tolerance as a leader, team or organization, we must first take a closer look at these issues through an individual filter.

Are You Ready? Assimilation or Acculturation?

In the last section, I mentioned that what you learn in this book is subjective. A large part of this is whether or not you are ready to change the way you have been thinking about tolerance and inclusion.

In a sense, this book is asking you to question your confidence in how you have been viewing these topics. Why should you do this? Why should you take on such a large change? Why shouldn't you leave this to others to pursue?

The answer to these questions is quite simple. The business environment of today is filled with challenges around culture, skills, and demographics. Organizations have two choices.

- The First Choice: Ignore these and carry on with the status quo of operating "tolerant" organizations, managers, and leaders that focus on assimilation.

- The Second Choice: Take on the challenge, explore your organizations challenges, and find long lasting continuous solutions that focus on acculturation.

Many organizations are still stuck in the past with archaic cultural norms and expectations that are preventing them from reaching their institutional and organizational destiny. As the global demographics are changing it means the talent pool is also becoming increasing more diverse in all attributes of difference.

For years there has been an expectation of assimilation that has been ingrained in organizations. Part of the on-boarding process for many organizations has always included helping new employees understand the way things are done after they become a part of a company. The purpose for these coaches, sponsors and mentors is to continue their legacy of inculcation and adaptation that often eliminates the uniqueness that was inherent in selecting that new employee in the first place!

IBM was one of the biggest proponents of having an assimilate or leave mentality. For years the expectation of assimilation went beyond their hiring based on a specific academic, personality, and mentality that fit the IBM mold.

They even made sure there was an expectation of how you dressed and the specific colors and styles that were considered acceptable versus those that were seen as outliers. Blue suits, white shirts, red ties were the uniform of the day.

Many organizations are still limiting their access to some of the brightest minds, thus negatively impacting their growth, performance, and productivity. During the interview process, many candidates are eliminated from consideration because of a couple of code words that are often used and rarely challenged.

When someone on your interview team or a hiring manager eliminates a candidate based on saying they are 'not the right fit' or that they are not 'comfortable' with the candidate, an inclusive mindset should always ask why? What is it about the candidate that you are uncomfortable with? Why do you feel they are not the right fit? The acid test for such decisions should be the following:

ACID TEST: Is The Decision Based On Business Requirements
Or Personal Preference, Convenience Or Tradition?

If the decision is not based on business requirements, then the decision should not be made for reasons of convenience, tradition, or personal preference. There has long been a focus on homogeneity in the hiring and promotion processes of organizations. Homogeneous organizations consist of people who remind us of us. If everyone on a team thinks the same way, when one person misses something, everyone misses it.

I have a friend whose son has 14 years as an officer in the Army. When I had this discussion about homogeneity with his son while he was home on leave, he mentioned that in the Army, the process of homogeneity was routine. People were promoted based on how well they fit in with the command squad. In his unit, they had an incident where lives were lost. They examined the processes they followed in retrospect. They realized that one of the key factors in being promoted in his unit was based on people who the commanding officer felt reminded him of himself at a younger age. After all, that couldn't be a bad thing; he had risen to the rank of Colonel. As part of the lessons learned processes, they have a tremendous understanding of the value of different styles, approaches, and mindsets. In their case, if everyone thinks the same, people can lose their life.

When I started on my first job, I came home after work, and Aunt Suzie asked me that evening how it went. I told her they had some stringent expectations in the hiring process, and I was surprised I was accepted. My surprise was not in the fact that I didn't meet the requirements. I was confident that I exceeded them, or I wouldn't have been hired.

I told her that everyone dressed the same, talked the same, acted the same, and even seemed to think the same! She asked me how many people were on this job. I told her there were about six people in my department. In her usual wisdom she said;

Aunt Suzie's – Apron Wisdom
"Baby, if there are six of you there and y'all think
the same, talk the same, approach problems the
same, then five of you don't need a job, do you??"

EXAMPLE: Garden Salad or Gumbo?

An illustration of the difference between assimilation and acculturation is with two types of food items. When Aunt Suzie made stew or gumbo, by the second day, the ingredients in the pot would all taste the same. When eating a spoonful of stew, the carrots would taste like the potatoes, and the potatoes would taste like the celery because they all took on the flavor of the gravy.

When she made gumbo, it would be the same. The chicken would taste like the shrimp which would taste like the sausage, because they all took on the flavor of the roux. This is an example of assimilation.

When you make a garden salad, the lettuce, bell peppers, red onions, and radishes all maintained their individual flavor. While they combine to make the salad, each of the ingredients still retains its distinct taste and flavor. This is an example of acculturation. The ingredients all blend together to make the salad, but each still maintains its own uniqueness.

There is a benefit to having an expectation of assimilation when it comes to organizational policies and practices. In order to be equitable in the application of rules, workplace expectations, safety, and more, there is a business reason for there to be some degree of assimilation.

Many organizations still have policies that were designed for the homogenous workplaces that predominated before women and people of color grew in numbers and acceptance in the workplace. There have been significant increases in news accounts of employees being fired and bringing lawsuits for things like their hair styles. Several states, including New York and California, have had to pass laws prohibiting an employer for terminating someone because of an Afrocentric hairstyle.

- A prominent Wall Street law firm even had an employee, who was an intern, told that, she needed to 'straighten out her hair' in order to fit in.
- An employee at a nationwide department store told an African-American woman her braids were not appropriate for their store.

- A high school wrestling athlete was made to cut his dreadlocks by a referee before being allowed to compete.

The expectation of assimilation is still very prevalent in many organizational cultures. If the way you style your hair, the color of your shirt, suit, or tie is that closely linked to the organizational culture, imagine how many ways it impacts creativity and innovation in an organization.

One study, conducted by the Equitable Workplace Institute in conjunction with the University of Houston, found that respondents who had NOT submitted new ideas at work explained their reasons as follows:

- 44% Said: I Tried in the past but kept getting no response.
- 38% Said: My input doesn't seem to be wanted
- 14% Said: No one has ever asked me for my ideas!

If organizational cultures are not inclusive and willing to acculturate, these ideas will never be received and the benefits of them will be lost.

Reasons To Become Inclusive As An Organization

Making the choice to become inclusive as an organization has little to do with social justice or legislative instruction. Making this decision will determine your organizations performance and long-term success. There are four main reasons for this success, which will be discussed throughout the book:

1. Workers who feel included in an organization are more satisfied in their work and more willing to "wear the company t-shirt." Neurologists have shown that we have evolved to be more collaborative, innovative, and productive when we are working as part of a team. In fact, they have demonstrated that when we are working in inclusive teams, we naturally produce healthy energy and create positive hormones that increases our productivity. This creates satisfied workers and the more satisfied your

workers are, the longer they stay in organizations. Satisfied workers are also more likely to help to recruit competent workers to your organization. With inclusivity, productivity goes up, while talent management costs go down.

2. Our organizations do not exist outside of our communities; the makeup of our organizations is a reflection of our communities and therefore they are a reflection of our customers. By being inclusive organizations can get a better understanding of their customers and also of how to reach more of those customers. Inclusive teams are more likely to be able to understand the behaviors of our communities at large and so will be better able to tap into those behaviors.

3. Embracing inclusion creates innovation. If your strategic thinking comes from the same people with homogenous thinking, then innovation is harder to achieve. By including the values of everyone in your organization, creativity and innovation are valued and promoted above static ideas.

4. Inclusive organizations become employers of choice; people naturally want to work in places where they feel valued and can participate fully. This strengthens an organization's ability to hire and retain the best. Organizations that are inclusive will become more competitive in securing talent especially when the skill is in high demand.

So back to the question. Why should you move from being tolerant to having an inclusive mindset? Very simply, organizations that don't build cultures that are truly inclusive, will be left behind. They will not perform as well as those companies that are inclusive.

Moving towards inclusivity is essential but it is also a change that fills many with apprehension. This is a natural reaction. Moving towards inclusivity requires a specific change in not just organizational culture, but also in the way that employees think.

Moving from tolerance to an inclusive mindset is what Daniel Kahneman in his 2011 book called moving from "thinking fast" to "thinking slow"[16]. Kahneman, a psychologist who looks at our irrational behavior, divides our thinking into two different "systems", system 1 and system 2.

System 1 thinking is thinking fast; it is based on intuition, metaphors, and associations. Picture yourself at a stop light. The light turns red, so you pull up to stop. The person in the car next to you starts waving at you. They wind down their window and say something to you. Your window is shut; you have to decide if you wind down your window and talk to the stranger.

In that split second, subconsciously, you use your system 1 thinking to decide what to do. You use your previous experiences and habits to judge the other person in the car; you associate them with behavior you have seen before, and you use metaphors to quickly describe that moment in reality.

System 2 thinking on the other hand is thinking slow; it is more analytical and more deliberate. When we activate system 2 thinking we deliberately control our thinking. It requires effort, and we use evidence and logic to justify decisions made from this thought. As a consequence, system 2 thinking is slow and is more rational.

Picture yourself back in the car. You have arrived at your destination and you are driving around the parking lot looking for somewhere to park your car. After driving around for a while, you finally find one narrow spot, but it is in the corner of the parking lot and all the spaces around it are full. In reversing into that narrow parking spot, you are activating system 2 thinking. In this case, your intuition takes a back seat. Instead, you need to think carefully about your actions, you need to be deliberate with what to do, and carefully control your actions. While you are parking, if someone asked you to multiply 37 with 11, you would struggle to concentrate on this additional task. Your mind is occupied on one task and has slowed down to think about how to execute it. If you used

---

16 Kahneman, 2011.

system 1 thinking and tried to park your car in a quick way without thinking about the action, it is likely you would say goodbye to your side mirrors.

When we think about being tolerant, we often use system 1 thinking to deal with the challenges. We use habits and quick judgements. When we move onto thinking about being inclusive, we are more likely to use system 2 thinking; we are more deliberate, more thoughtful, and analyze problems in a more collaborative and detailed way.

The analogy is not perfect and there have been some critiques of Kahneman's theory, but it serves as a good basis for discussing inclusion. To achieve successful inclusive competencies in your organization, the thinking process behind it needs to move away from system 1 thinking and follow the patterns of system 2 thinking.

Many leaders will be apprehensive about introducing change that requires their employees and coworkers to:

1. Put in a lot of effort over a continued period of time.
2. Stretch their cultural comfort zones.

This apprehension is normal, but it should not be debilitating. Apprehension is an amazing opportunity; it provides you with a chance to assess where you are, take stock, and try to understand what is making you feel nervous about a particular action. Sections of this book will provide the tools to do just this. We will look at how organizations can take stock and figure out what inclusive competencies they have already.

This is a great step in addressing apprehension as often when taking stock, organizations realize that they have more inclusive competencies than they thought. One way to address apprehension is to keep reading this book!

"I must follow the people. Am I not their leader?"

— *Benjamin Disraeli*

This book acts a guidebook from a coach on what steps to take next. The book will help you to learn and develop in the areas of tolerance, dignity, respect and inclusion with a key focus on teams and leading with purpose. This book will act as a coaching tool to help you improve your performance and help you to move from tolerance to developing an inclusive mindset. The skills you will gain from the book will help you to start building a success toolkit that you can then use for workforce, workplace and marketplace strategies in your organization. Ultimately the question to ask is not just "are you ready?" Instead, it asks "what are you waiting for?"

Chapter 2

The Personal Journey

"Stretching Your Cultural Comfort Zone"

SECTION INTRODUCTION: *The Way I See It*

The workplace is changing in many ways. There are many different cultures in most organizations. While at the University of Houston for the last twenty years, I found that the students spoke over 160 languages. In many organizations, there are as many as five generations in the workplace. Stretching your cultural comfort zone is no longer an option. It is a required competency that means learning new skills as well as appreciating unique approaches and solutions.

CELL PHONE CHALLENGE

Most people feel they are making efforts to expand their cultural surroundings by going to ethnic restaurants or attending celebrations and community festivals. These are all great ways to begin the journey of exploring other cultural differences and approaches.

Please take a quick 'cell phone' challenge on the topic of stretching your comfort zones. Start with the letter "A" in your contacts on your phone. How far would you have to go into the letters of the alphabet before getting to the third person of a different ethnic background that you have had at your home for dinner?

Having someone at your home for dinner is completely different than having a meal in a restaurant. In a restaurant, it's easier to stay focused on 'safe' conversations. When someone is at your home, the discussions are much more personal. Much more open. Much more revealing. Much more human. It is easier to see through some of the generalizations we make about each other that often become stereotypes. Stereotypes, biases, and blindspots are taught. People are not innately racist, bigoted, misogynistic, nor xenophobic. It has never ceased to amaze me how people poison the minds of their own children and families.

RACISM IS TAUGHT!

I want to share two examples of circumstances that illustrate what I mean. The first illustration is from my college days in East Tennessee. The second illustration happened in 2019.

MILLIGAN COLLEGE: I attended college my freshman year in east Tennessee. First-year students were not allowed to have cars on campus. Athletes were required to be on campus a week early. There were less than 1,000 total students, including commuters.

The first evening on campus, there was nothing to do. Some of the tennis team members were hitting volleys on the court located in the center of campus. I grew up in Florida and was accustomed to wearing what we called 'flip-flops' most of the time.

I had a seat in the grass by the tennis courts watch them practice hitting balls. I noticed a fellow student was sitting in the grass near me. She seemed to be staring at the ground near my feet. I looked on the ground to see if something was crawling around, I should be aware of. I saw nothing, yet she starred even harder.

At one point, she realized I was aware of her stare, and she broke her gaze away and started crying. I asked her if she was OK, and her tear then turned to sobs. She finally gained her composure enough to tell me how stunned she was.

I asked her what was so stunning, and she said, with tears in her eyes, "You

Have Toes!" I looked at her incredulously and said, "Huh?!?" Her following statement stunned me. She said her father told her that black people didn't have toes. We have claws that had not developed into toes from an evolution standpoint yet.

I asked her what else she had been told? She then said, through her tears, her father also told her black people had a piece of tail at the base of their spine. This appendage was part of our tails that had not completely evolved.

LITTLE ROCK AIRPORT: The second instance of how racism is taught occurred in 2019 while working on a project across Arkansas. I had just flown in and was walking through the baggage claim area heading to the rental car area. At six feet four and 275 pounds, I usually wear my cowboy hat and boots most of the time. As I walked past passengers, families, and businesspeople waiting on their luggage, I notice a little boy that appeared to be no more than five years old. He was sitting on his father's shoulders. I saw him staring at me as I approached. Without a concern, he loudly says to his father, while pointing at me:

"Look, Daddy, A Ni@%*r with a cowboy hat on!"

Everyone turned; some looked incredulously at the little boy and his dad; others seemed unphased. Some seemed almost shocked. I slowed my stride, never changed my expression, looked at the father to see what his response would be. Without missing a beat, he said: ***"Yeah, son, I see him."***

FREEDOM OF SPEECH IS NOT FREEDOM OF CONSEQUENCES

While there are teachable moments and people who have a hunger to learn, not everyone is concerned with treating people with dignity and respect. Racism, xenophobia, and misogyny are all taught behaviors. I have learned to go where I am celebrated and appreciated and not where I am simply tolerated.

Workplaces, workforces, and marketplaces are changing in many ways.

These changes are impacting entire organizations, divisions, operational units, teams, as well as individuals. All institutional change actually has to be seen through the impact on individuals. As the topic of culture takes on many meanings, it requires that each person must take stock of how they view the issues involving corporate culture, occupational culture, global culture and more.

Once we take stock of where we are on these issues it can require that we establish goals associated with our present state as well as determining our desired state.

- For example, in many operational settings, men have dominated the workforce and the leadership structure. Women are becoming increasingly more prevalent in these settings.

- In the global capitals of most countries as well as the larger metropolitan cites of the world the level of ethnic and religious diversity is creating environments that are significantly different than they were twenty years ago.

- With improved access to healthcare and the need to maintain a level of income that supports the lifestyle many have grown accustomed to, people are not only living longer but working at a much older age than in the past. In many organizations today, there are up to five generations in the workforce.

- As societies become more accepting of gay, lesbian, transgender, and transsexual employees, people are finding that their personal or religious perceptions are not aligned with the organization or societal acceptance of these differences.

The first step in creating organizations where moving beyond tolerance is expected is the need for many individuals to take stock of where they are personally on this journey and determine in what areas might they need to stretch their cultural comfort zones.

Whenever organizations undertake change initiatives, they are usually based on operational goals that are ultimately plans for a more successful organization. Best in class organizations realize that the goal setting must go beyond the operational targets and performance related expectation.

Included are many goals specific to human capital related opportunities and potential challenges. Workplace respect, acceptance, equitable treatment, eliminating bias, creating opportunities for people to acculturate, and not just be expected to assimilate, are important in today's changing societies.

Goals, whether operational or human capital specific, are basically targets we want to reach; ideals we set for how far we want to go in the process of improvement. So, in this way, with each goal you set yourself as a team or individual, the key question you will need to ask yourself is how far you are willing to stretch yourself.

Thomas Oppong argued that "many people are so comfortable they're miserable and that comfort can lead to self-absorption, boredom, and discontent. Breaking a habit, trying something new, taking a risk, making new connections, or putting yourself in a totally new situation won't be easy, but it's worth it. It's exhausting but rewarding."[17]

Dr. Elizabeth Lombardo, Psychologist and author of "Better Than Perfect", says people who regularly seek out fresh experiences tend to be more creative and emotionally resilient than those who remain stuck in a routine. "Breaking your own mold can only make you stronger and more confident to reach higher levels in your professional and personal life."[18]

To achieve any goal, we have to stretch ourselves to some degree. When we are talking about making changes involving culture, we have to realize that this will begin as a personal journey that involves moving out of our comfort zones.

---

[17] Oppong, Thomas, 2017.
[18] Ibid, Oppong.

"A leader takes people where they want to go. A great leader takes people where they don't necessarily want to go, but ought to be."

— *Rosalynn Carter*

When looking at apprehension and how it can be seen as an opportunity to be used to bring about positive innovative change, we must remember that when stretching outside of our comfort zone this can first of all be seen as a positive way to boost confidence among our teams and ourselves. If we set goals that are easy to achieve, we do not get much sense of achievement from it. If our goals are ambitious, yet realistic, when we complete them, we get a big sense of achievement.

Mark Murphy discusses this in his book "Hard Goals."[19] In this book he dismisses our traditional acceptance of searching for SMART goals. He argues correctly that if we really want to succeed, or be innovative, or bring about real change, we need to set hard goals - goals that we think would be really difficult to achieve.

Think about a goal you have set yourself recently. It was probably specific, it was probably measurable, and it may have been time bound. But was it realistic and achievable? Or was it probably a bit crazy? No one sets a goal to try to run part of a marathon. They aim to run the marathon and it is hard and at the start it is often extremely unrealistic. Ask anyone who has quit smoking if they think that the goal of quitting smoking was an easy goal to set for themselves. And we all know that losing weight is definitely not an easy goal; just ask my personal trainer about that!

When setting targets for moving from being tolerant to inclusive, the goals need to be hard. They need to involve your whole organization stretching their

---

[19] Mark Murphy, 2010.

cultural comfort zone. However, the first step is you clearing your lens and reaching beyond your personal discomforts. It will be difficult, but this is a good thing. Setting hard goals in this scenario will help everyone involved and give them a sense of being part of a big achievement. By setting hard goals, you are also telling your coworkers, your teams, and yourself that you are capable of achieving big things. By setting hard goals, you are telling everyone involved that they have the skill and aptitude to achieve this. You are giving them a reason to perform at their best ability and you are giving them a reason to be committed to the change project.

You Can't Expect To Get To A Recital Without Having Gone Through The Rehearsal

By setting hard personal goals for ourselves, we can be rewarded by growing and developing both professionally and personally. This is especially true for leaders. By setting hard professional goals, leaders are rewarding coworkers and employees by pushing them to develop. In environments that are constantly changing, asking people to stretch their cultural comfort zones is a hard goal, yet is one of the best ways for organizations to develop key talent, leaders, and teams.

As we discussed in Section 1, it involves Kahneman's system 2 thinking. It asks people involved to use our analytical thinking to produce results that are more creative, innovative, and longer lasting. By using this type of thinking we are working harder, and it involves more effort.

Setting goals that are difficult and require more effort, involves being willing to embark on a personal journey of stretching our cultural comfort zones. It also stresses the importance of the change even when it seems out of reach. Imagine you work in an organization and the CEO decides to introduce some inclusion related competencies to the organization. The CEO decides to do this by sending out a memo that asks everyone to be more inclusive by being more respectful of others.

No one is asked to change to do anything specifically to change their behavior, nor are they asked to stretch their comfort cultural zones. There is nothing said or done to ensure that people have the tools to become more inclusive. The existing KPA's, KPI's, and OKR's are not modified, changed, or altered to emphasize how people will be held accountable for becoming more inclusive.

While this is an extreme example, by not setting any goals that would be considered a hard goal and not having actions that take people out of their comfort zone, the CEO has implicitly told everyone in the organization that this goal is not that important. Stretching our cultural comfort zones **through establish hard, but not impossible goals,** is fundamental to being able to maximize the positive benefits available from moving from a mindset of tolerance and mediocrity to an inclusive and equitable culture.

"If your actions inspire others to dream more, learn more, do more and become more, you are a leader." – John Quincy Adams

---

In this section of the book, the idea of setting hard goals will be elaborated upon. We will introduce the idea of tolerance and discuss why tolerance is an "easy goal" and why it is not a good place to be for other reasons. The sections will also look at the Range of Respect Continuum, which looks at the range of behavioral options we have when dealing with the changes occurring in organizations and the importance of cross-cultural competencies. The section will also look at why having an inclusive mindset takes effort and why it is individually and institutionally valuable.

One of the main reasons why having an inclusive mindset is a somewhat difficult task, involves the need to stretch our cultural comfort zones. We are built with cognitive biases that make it hard for us to recognize the perceptions of difference and our neurological responses to our blind spots. In this section, we will discuss this in relation to how we can look in the mirror and address these as critical parts of a personal journey we all need to take to become more inclusive. We will also look at different forms of cognitive bias and examine how we can control these to be able to move beyond tolerance.

This section ends with a discussion on why this is important. Moving beyond tolerance takes courage and involves understanding the importance of treating others **how they want to be treated.** It also includes expanding our comfort zones so that we can support inclusive environments and speak out against the damage done by simply being tolerant. If we don't speak out against tolerance, we are part of the problem. This is the personal journey that we must all take to build better organizations that reflect positive values.

Ultimately however, organizations that do not move towards inclusion now, are going to be left behind. Change is happening no matter what you do. How your organization reacts to this will fundamentally determine your organization's long-term success.

What Is Tolerance?

If you ask ten people to define tolerance, you will get eleven different answers. Tolerance is a complicated word. It has many meanings and means different things to many people. When most people hear the term tolerance, they think about it as a positive way to interact with people. To simply tolerate someone in the workplace who is different than you is seen as a good thing. For this book, the core concept of tolerance is defined as 'putting up with' or 'enduring' the existence of something that we don't agree with or someone we don't like or want to be around. Some definitions refer to tolerance as allowing something or someone to exist or to practice something that we do not like or agree with, yet we don't hinder it, obstruct it, or interfere with it. From this definition, it is clear that it is passive.

Tolerance in the workplace asks us to passively react to the differences between genders, religions, sexual orientations, cultures, or ethnicities. The idea of tolerance has a long history and was discussed by philosophers in ancient Greece. Equal Employment Opportunity laws put in place in the 60s and the 70s, brought back this ancient ideology to the forefront of organizations. Workforce dynamics changed with the civil rights movement of the 60s, the women's liberation movements, and the word became more frequently used. In the early 2000s, as demographics shifted again, tolerance emerged once again.

With the changes occurring in workplaces today, including ethnic, gender, and multicultural differences, the likelihood of interacting in the workforce, workplace, or marketplace across multiple attributes of difference is inevitable. Customers and clients are becoming increasingly more diverse, and so equally, the likelihood of interacting with someone whose aspect of difference makes you feel uncomfortable is inevitable. It may be the accent they speak with, the way they dress, or it may be based on their generation or because of multicultural differences. It may be the fact that the majority of your peers are men, and the organization has hired the first woman in a particular role.

Any of these situations could create an environment where your responses, thoughts, or interactions, even on a subconscious basis, imply or indicate that instead of accepting or respecting these differences, you are uncomfortable with them and so you tolerate them.

When people attempt to become tolerant of someone's differences, the person to whom those feelings are directed at can feel that they are not viewed or treated like their peers. Workplaces are becoming less tolerant of behaviors that make others feel uncomfortable and interfere with the ability of people to accomplish their tasks. Many organizations have adopted a zero-tolerance policy for disrespectful or demeaning behaviors. Some of these derailing behaviors don't rise to the level of violating the law, but people still feel violated. Some organizations are instituting Respectful Workplace Policies (RWP's) to make sure employees understand what is and is not acceptable in their specific organizational culture. (More on RWP's in the Organizational section of the book.)

In the workplace, we are often told that tolerance is about having open minds with others around us. Tolerance is seen, at best, as **treating others the way we want to be treated,** even though they may have different opinions, beliefs, and values. We are told that we need to recognize other people's beliefs, values, and differences and **tolerate** them. To be tolerant, we must be accepting; we need to embrace the differences of others and refrain from expressing negativity about these differences. For most people, tolerance is seen as a **good thing** and as the basis for ethics statements in organizations.

How many times have you been told in your workplace that the principle of tolerance will create a better organizational culture and a better society, one that improves productivity and morale? Organizations are so enamored by the term that they often brag about how tolerant their organization has become without questioning what being tolerant actually means.

What Things Do You Tolerate?

While tolerance is a starting place for creating a respectful, inclusive environment, it often is seen as the destination. We believe that using a tolerant approach and mentality alone can create problems instead of solving them. Tolerance is not a process; we think that if we achieve it, it is the endgame. As a passive approach to an inclusive mindset, it reduces our ability to create long-lasting solutions to problems that inevitably result from our differences, and it prevents us from benefiting from creating a genuinely inclusive and respectful environment and culture.

If we want to stretch our cultural comfort zones and create understanding and inclusion, we need to be brave and move beyond tolerance.

"Vision without action is a daydream. Action with without vision is a nightmare." - Japanese Proverb

The problem is that we have all been cowards at some point or another. I have shared a few examples of my cowardice in hopes that it may make you think about how you would act in the future, or maybe how you have already acted in the past. When we use tolerance outside of the workplace, it can also come with negative connotations.

In every aspect of our lives, there are things that we tolerate; things we accept and allow to happen, even though they may disagree with our values or cause us harm. We let them happen. Why? So that we don't "rock the boat" or disturb the "status quo." In this way, we are all cowards to some extent. A great way to find out the true meaning behind tolerance is to look at your own life and examine what kinds of things you tolerate.

Aunt Suzie's – Apron Wisdom
"Hang in there, sweetie; Remember
Kites Don't Fly Without Resistance!!

We all use tolerance as a conflict resolution tool and as a way to deal with differences, but is it the best tool to use? If you run a google search for things that people usually tolerate, the first eight pages are articles telling you somethings that you should **not** tolerate! There are articles on what not to tolerate in a relationship, what not to tolerate from your coworkers, what not to tolerate from your family, from your friends, there are articles on every type of tolerance you can avoid. So, what things do we tolerate?

Personal Tolerance

On a personal level, we all tolerate things from time to time. We tolerate poor behaviors in our loved ones and tolerate actions that we don't like from those that live in our communities. There are many other things that we tolerate in our personal lives:

- **We tolerate unhealthy lifestyles**. We get stuck into a routine of life that does not include looking after our mind, body, and soul. Without looking after these, we cannot live a full life. We end up tolerating the fact that we don't exercise regularly or eat too many fast-food meals.

- **Letting money dictate our life.** It is impossible to ignore the fact that living in society today requires money. We all need money to live. Often, we let money dictate our lives, and we begin to tolerate this. Money should help you to live a full life; it is not the most important part of our lives.

- **Unhappiness.** This is a big one. It has become very common for people to accept and tolerate living a miserable life. It becomes something that is considered normal or acceptable. We settle for less than 100%, and this leads to us living unfulfilled lives.

- **Poor life skills in others.** This is often the underlying cause of many things we tolerate. Poor timekeeping, poor communication, poor listening skills, aggression, and selfishness are some of the most common things we tolerate in our personal lives. We all have seen this behavior in others **and in ourselves**. We tolerate many of them every day and do not try to improve these life skills.

- **Dishonesty.** Turning on the news today, you probably saw dishonesty from politicians or TV news personalities. Dishonesty creates false realities that do not live with integrity. We allow dishonesty to creep into our personal lives, and we tolerate it coming from our friends and families too. Just as it can appear in our workplace and on our TVs, we have come to tolerate it as part of our personal lives. It is something we see, and although we shake our heads, we still tolerate it. Our society has become more and more dishonest, and so the tolerance for this has become higher and higher

- **Lack of integrity in our lives.** Sometimes we can end up living a life that is not in line with our values, and we begin to tolerate this. How does it happen? Sometimes it sneaks up on us, and sometimes it is something that is caused by additional stress. Regardless, when we live a life that tolerates values we don't believe in, we can feel guilty, our energy is drained, and we can lose our self-esteem.

Work Tolerance

The essence of this book is on tolerance in the workplace and how to move from tolerance to inclusion. So, what do I mean by tolerance in the workplace? There are many forms of this behavior; many are linked to how we deal with differences in the workplace. These are some of the work-related ways we let tolerance impact our lives:

- **Working at a job you hate.** Many of us have been in this situation. You have to settle for a job that you do not enjoy or a job that does not make you happy or fulfill you. We have all been there. We tolerate it. Why? The paycheck keeps us there. In many circumstances, we tolerate jobs we don't like, and we use them as a way to climb the ladder. That job you did while studying at college, flipping burgers to save money to start your own business, or working in a junior position so that you can climb up the company ladder. We all do these jobs, and we tolerate them, hoping for a change to a better job. We all have to remember that we will spend much of our lives in the workplace and getting stuck in a job that you hate means that you will live a life that you hate.

- **Long commutes to work.** This may seem like a trivial thing, but commuting is a stressful and down heartening experience. If you spend an hour commuting to work, that adds up to 2 hours a day, and 10 hours a week. Over a lifetime that would add up to 20,000 hours spent travelling to and from work. That is nearly 70 months or 6 years of your life spent just getting to and from work. We tolerate this as we think we need to do this to make sure we get a good job. Imagine what you could do with that time if you chose to not tolerate this long commute.

- **Negativity.** This is common in organizations with little or no teamwork. The lack of cohesion brings people down, and so coworkers become negative. This can become constant, and it is something that others in the organization will begin to tolerate, not realizing it will give them a negative mood as well.

- **Harassment.** This is one of the most tolerated things in the workplace. Harassment is a legal term encompassing being treated negatively because of a specific attribute of your identity, such as your age, race, gender, ethnicity, nationality, ability, or religion. It often seems like every day the news has another breaking story of someone who was abused or harassed in the workplace. This is illegal behavior, but it is difficult to prove. Sometimes reporting abuse and harassment can have such negative effects on one's career that many people do not report it. It is tolerated in organizations all around the world and allowed to flourish. It can be in the form of sexual or racial harassment or discrimination against someone's physical disability. Sections further on in the book will include more detail on the definitions of these and what can be done to avoid this type of behavior.

- **Workplace Bullying.** This is similar to workplace abuse and harassment but differs slightly. This negative behavior is not specifically because of your identity. In the USA, as this book is being published, there are no laws covering bullying in the workplace. The closest thing to eliminating bullying is in the State of California. They have a state statute that requires organizations to conduct annual training for their employees to eliminate abusive behaviours in the workplace. These abusive behaviours would be defined as workplace bullying in most organizations. Unfortunately, as of 2020, this type of negative behaviour is still tolerated in most workplaces. Studies, by the Workplace Bullying Institute, have found that bullying happens four times more than illegal harassment. It is found everywhere, and recent studies have shown that in 75% of workplaces there is bullying.[20] The effects of bullying in the workplace are enormous. Work productivity is lowered, and employees can experience extremely negative mental health problems as a result of this tolerated harmful behavior. Later in this book, we will discuss the implications, costs, responsibilities, and ways to mitigate bullying in the workplace.

- **Low productivity.** Being part of a high functioning team in any workplace is known to boost our self-esteem and our confidence in our ability to do our jobs. If our organizations are not high functioning for whatever reason, we can quickly become despondent and even tolerant of this level of productivity. Often this is beyond our control; we may have a boss who is incompetent, for example, and so we tolerate the low productivity. It is often difficult to change this and so, we tolerate it as part of the negative aspects of the job. This can be very problematic as it has obvious negative repercussions for an organization's success, and

---

[20] Comaford, Christine, 2016.

it destroys office morale.

- **Losing self-respect and lowering integrity.** You may have seen this or tolerate this yourself. This can happen in certain situations when you are asked to act or behave in a way that feels wrong to you. Say for example, you believe in working with every team player and building up their skills, but your boss wants you to be stern and use aggression to push your team. In these situations, we tolerate this behavior to stay at the job and get that paycheck. We start to hear ourselves saying, "I don't like who I have become" and realize we are tolerating values that we should not and that we have lost our self-respect by doing so.

- **Ignoring your health.** We all have to work hard at our jobs and put in extra hours. Sometimes we can be pushed to work too much, and this can then damage our health. We can become depleted, depressed, exhausted, and over-stretched because we tolerate working too much, pushing ourselves, taking work home, staying at work too late, tolerating negative behavior, tolerating high levels of stress, and ultimately, not managing our work-life balance. The irony is that by sacrificing our health to try to work successfully, we prevent ourselves from working successfully. I know of many people I have worked with who have become burnt out and have lost their jobs or have left their jobs because they over-worked themselves and did not balance their lives. Unfortunately, they had become tolerant of letting their work-life become unhealthy.

- **Ignoring our life purpose.** There is someone in every office who is tolerant of this, The mail person who is a passionate artist; the accountant who is passionate about playing the drums the coworker who writes fiction books. We all have passions and things that give us meaning and finding that in our work can be extremely rewarding.

If we don't find this at work, we can experience something similar to burn out – BORE OUT.

If we are not passionate about our work and what we do, we become disinterested, we don't push ourselves, and we become bored at work. **We bore out.** Just like burn out, it leads to low productivity and low job satisfaction. We tolerate it for the, yes, you guessed it, that paycheck.

All of these examples are based on tolerances I have seen in places I have worked, and within organizations I have consulted for. There are many more, and you might have seen them in organizations where you have worked. We tolerate so much in life as a way to deal with conflict resolution and as a way to minimize chaos in our lives. We seek out comfort, routine, and the stability that comes from a regular paycheck, and this leads to us tolerating things that we should not necessarily be accepting.

"The greatest danger for most of us is not that our aim is too high and we miss it, but that it is too low and we reach it." - Michelangelo

---

If you look at personal tolerance and workplace tolerances in your own life, you could probably be able to come up with many similar examples as the ones listed.

Reflective Questions

- What areas of your life do you just tolerate the way things are going?
- When you acknowledge this, how does it make you feel?
- Does it bring you joy or wellbeing to be tolerating these things?
- Do you think it helps you to lead a fulfilled life?
- How does it impact your relationships with the people around you?
- Do you think it is possible to change this?
- What can you do differently to change this behavior?

For workplace tolerances, the next sections will talk about their impact and also what steps can be made to move beyond tolerance. We will look at how you can pay attention to the things you tolerate and let them go, to live positive lives and create positive workplaces. We need to make this change as we are the sum of what we tolerate.

Why is it Important to Move Beyond Tolerance?

In the summer of 2017, The Under Armour CEO and member of the President Trump's Manufacturing Council, Kevin Plank wrote on Twitter:

> *"I love our country and our company and will continue to focus my efforts on inspiring every person that they can do anything through the power of sport which promotes unity, diversity and inclusion."*[21]

---

[21] Plank, Kevin, 2017

Stocks of Under Armour had been falling for nearly a year but it was racist remarks made by President Trump that caused Mr. Plank to release this statement. Regardless of how you view the intent of the remarks made by President Trump.

> *Part of being inclusive is knowing that you don't just own the*
> *intent of your comments and actions, you also own the impact!*

Along with the comment made by the President & CEO of Under Armour, he also left the President's Manufacturing Council. Since then, Mr. Plank has been critical of the President and has supported sports people who protest against systemic racism. While there is no doubt that he was motivated by social justice, but he was also motivated by the bottom line. The lack of inclusion that was demonstrated by the President was affecting the bottom line of Under Armour. Had Mr. Plank remained on the Council, the impact on Under Amour's stock price is unimaginable. Consumers would have moved away from the associations with the comments coming from the President, and so the negative impact on Under Amour's stock would have been severe.

As society moves beyond tolerance and towards demanding inclusive organizations, companies will have no choice but to follow their consumer base. Moving beyond tolerance is more than this. It is about building organizations that get the most out of their employees. Moving beyond tolerance is a way to focus on this. It is a focus on things that have a direct effect on bottom line.

Inclusion boosts the quality of decision making and encourages creativity, diligence and hard work. These qualities are vital for innovation. As our societies become more diverse, building inclusive cultures means your employees are prepared to thrive in a diverse world. Your teams become smarter, the more inclusive they are and this in turns allows you to attract better workers who then become smarter and so on. This helps to boost the image of your organization, which also boosts profits.

Derailing behaviors, discussed in detail in a subsequent section of this book, create organizations that are at the opposite scale of inclusive organizations. They reduce profit by reducing the values above that create and generate the innovation necessary for profit. The next section will focus on how and why inclusion can help you to achieve organizational success.

Workplace Implications of Tolerance

When I logged onto my social media accounts today, I saw that a civil rights activist I follow, had reported an "Alt Right" account for some extremely abusive content. The report included a screen shot of the abuse from the "Alt Right", which read as follows: "Why should we tolerate political correctness?" As I am writing a book on tolerance, this piqued my interest. I opened the post and examined what they said. I won't repeat the precise wording, for obvious reasons. Ultimately, this post was a good example of what happens when we merely tolerate things.

The author had no understanding, curiosity, or awareness of the differences they were describing. They have merely acknowledged their existence and had done no more than that. It was no surprise that the opinions they had on the differences were based on a very low level of information about those specific differences. Had the author attempted to move from tolerance to a position of acceptance, and had they been encouraged to do so by a wider understanding of the damages of merely tolerating things, the author may have understood the issue much better.

"Men build too many walls and not enough bridges."

- Joseph Fort Newton

We cannot expect simply tolerating differences to bring about an understanding and acceptance of the changes we are facing. Nor can we expect tolerance to provide the benefits that inclusion can provide. Tolerating, as we discussed in the last section, is more passive. If we tolerate a problem, we are passively avoiding the conflict rather than acting on it to bring about positive change. Having permissive attitudes towards differences is an important skill and one that we need to use on a daily basis in our workplace and personal lives.

Imagine trying to negotiate your life without being tolerant about **all the differences** in race, religion, nationality, practices, and opinions around you. At some point, in order to function as a person, you need to tolerate these differences. However, **this is not the desired end state** in our personal lives or at our workplaces. If you did not make any attempts to accept these differences, to understand them, and to include them in some way, you would struggle to function in a harmonious and productive way in today's society.

This is truer of the workplace where there are clear and measured negative consequences for merely passively acknowledging diversity. For organizations, tolerance especially is not a good place to be. More specifically, tolerance produces:

- An organizational culture that does not actively address, embrace, leverage or accept differences.

- Goals that are not hard to achieve; it is easy to tolerate something, much harder to act to understand, appreciate, or value it.

- An organizational façade: a tolerant organization might look like they are inclusive but there is little understanding among coworkers.

There was a recent commercial in Denmark that illustrated what happens when we focus on tolerance. In the advertisement, called "All That We Share", a group of Danish people are gathered in a room. They stand in a row at the back of the room. The organizers tell the group that they will read out some

78

statements. If the statements are true, the people in the group need to move to an area in the room and stand there until the statements read out are not true. The group participating is a very diverse group, representing a wide variety of people in Denmark.

The organizer begins to read out statements such as "I was a class clown at school" or "I feel lonely." As the group members regrouped with the statements, they all learned that they had more in common than they thought. Most of the participants were shocked by the exercise. Why? Because they found out that they had something in common with most people in the room. "It's easy to put people in boxes. There's us, and there's them." That is the introduction to the video. It challenges the assumption that we live in an "us" vs "them" world. It also demonstrates what happens when we merely tolerate people around us. If you tolerate the person from another background, you do not accept them or understand them and you will never find out that they, like you, were once a class clown. Tolerance ignores that we have more in common than our differences and it blocks attempts to find out about these commonalities.

In organizations, if we fail to understand this and fail to move beyond tolerance, we can ostracize and isolate coworkers and employees. The easiest way to explain this is to look at how tolerance affects us in our personal lives. Say for example, you move to a new neighborhood and decide to join the local church, the first Sunday you can, you and your family go to the church. When you enter, you see many of your neighbors and you also see that the entire congregation is a different race than your family. As an African American that wants to be in a church that is welcoming, not necessarily all of the same race as yourself, you walk in and you enjoy the church service. After all, it is a part of your consciousness that one of Dr. Martin Luther King's quotes is still applicable today. "Eleven o'clock Sunday morning is still the most segregated hour in America." Even worse;

The Most Segregated School In America; Is Sunday School.

– C.B. Clayton, Sr. -

In your new neighborhood, afterward service you meet other churchgoers and the pastor. The whole experience is rewarding and brings you a sense of community. Until later on in the week, you talk to an Asian neighbor and you find out that they had also attended the church when they moved in and noticed the lack of diversity. After your neighbor visited the church, he mentions having stopped for something to eat and heard two other Caucasian neighbors with their families from the church sitting behind them talking. They were unaware that the family they were talking about was the same family. They were discussing the Asian family that came to church and stated how hard it is to act like you are welcoming towards someone that you know doesn't belong at your church. Their comments ended with, '*Oh well, we can tolerate anyone, it doesn't mean we have to like them or welcome them, does it?*' In essence, they were merely 'putting up' with you and your family.

Reflective Questions

- How would you feel?
- Would you go back to the church the following Sunday?
- How would you feel about your neighbors?
- Would you think of them as welcoming?
- How would you feel about your community?
- Is tolerance just prejudice in its best dress clothes?

This example happened to me and my family. I am certain that it has happened in towns across the country. It creates divided communities, with insular thinking that leaves them devoid of new experiences and ideas.

Replace the church with a new office and the problem leads to a similar level of division. This leads to low levels of motivation and therefore, lower levels of production. The impact is felt across the organization and in particular within the Talent Management team who will struggle with the high turnover this will inevitably create.

Now imagine the difference with this example, if when you joined the church, the other church goers actually, earnestly accepted you and your family, respected you all, and had plans to actively include you. Would you go back the following Sunday?

PERSONAL EXAMPLE: *I recently went to Boston to conduct a workshop for executives in a pharmaceutical company. While staying at a four star globally branded hotel, I went into the restaurant lobby to order a couple of appetizers to take back to my room. There were three servers and less than 5 customers. After 15 minutes of waiting, three attempts to try to get someone's attention even though they walked right by me, I was preparing to go back to my room to order room service.*

Unfortunately, incidents of this sort still happened way too often. Before I could leave my seated area, another customer came over to me and said, I've been watching how difficult it's been for you to even get someone to bring you a glass of water. This is unacceptable! As soon as she raised her hand in the air to try to garner attention all three servers came to her immediately to see how they could help.

Her comment was encouraging. She questioned why no one had stopped to assist me, but all three came to assist her. Each of them blatantly said they never noticed me sitting there. I'm 6 feet 4 inches tall and 275 pounds; I wear a cowboy hat most of the time even in Boston! It's kind of hard not to notice me.

I thanked the customer who spoke up for me, but there was no way I would order a drink or food from any of these three not knowing what can happen when they are around the corner out of sight before bringing the items that I have ordered. I left and went to another hotel, even as it was pouring down rain, rather than order anything at the property where I was staying.

> *"Inclusion is not a matter of political correctness. It is the key to growth." - Jesse Jackson*

At the beginning of this book, we talked about passing on the baton from tolerance to inclusion. If we think of this as a relay race, when the last athlete takes the baton and runs the last leg of the race, they can only do this if the other athletes have run their legs. Tolerance and inclusion can be seen like this. Before inclusion is possible, we need to be tolerant, but we must not stop there. We need to run the leg of the race that is tolerance and then move on and complete the race by running the leg of the race that is inclusion. If we stop the race at tolerance, we will definitely not register as even having finished the race. Coming in second, third, or even forth is not possible, nevertheless winning the race. We cannot stop!

If we say we are tolerant of something, what we are saying is that we passively acknowledge that something exists. It says nothing about whether or not we have accepted it, or if we have taken steps to understand it. While it is possible to tolerate something without understanding it or accepting it, and vice versa, this is not the ideal position to be in. We can function by just tolerating the world, but to be truly successful, we need to understand the world around us. Moving to inclusion, as it will be shown in the following sections, is impossible without this level of dealing with differences. The unwillingness to embrace and understand those differences is like having an institutional blind spot.

Aunt Suzie's – Apron Wisdom

"When One Fish In the Pond Dies...

The Problem Is The Fish

When Half the Fish in One Pond Die.

The Problem is The Pond Water

When Half the Fish in ALL The Ponds Die..

The Problem is The GROUND Water

The ground water is what feeds ALL the ponds. The ground water is indicative of 'institutional' blind spots, biases, and counterproductive behaviors.

The Impact of Tolerance on Your Coworkers

Before we start with this section, I want you to think about the issue of inclusion in relation to one of the biggest and most successful companies on the planet – Google Inc. Now I would like you to guess, as a percentage in 2019, how many of the technology employees working at Google are women. Write it down. I would like you to also guess how many of its employees are black and how many are Hispanic. We will return to this at the end of the section.

- Back to the topic, why do we want to move from tolerance to inclusion?
- Is this just another social justice issue to apply to organizational policy?
- Is it really something that organizations need to pay attention to?
- In previous sections, the link between inclusion and profitability was mentioned; so how do we know this is true?
- The biggest question to ask is what is the impact of tolerance on your coworkers?

I served, for over 20 years, as the Director and Diversity Strategist with the University of Houston's International Institute for Diversity and Cross-Cultural Management, located in the C.T. Bauer College of Business. In that capacity we conducted a longitudinal case study to measure the degree to which organizational culture impacted an organization's ability to increase the number of high performing work groups within the organization[22]. That is, we researched whether or not there was a correlation between inclusive workplace behaviors and organizational growth as measured in terms of the top line (revenue growth), the bottom-line (cost reductions) and the pipeline (recruiting, retention & talent management).

In the case study, titled "A Quantitative Analysis of the Consequences of Derailing Behaviours on Employee Commitment and Corporate Culture", over 10,000 respondents from 13 different companies were involved. It provided a foundation for linking inclusion and equitable human capital management processes to the top line (revenue growth), the bottom line (cost reductions) and the pipeline (recruiting, retention and talent management.)

The study aimed to see what effect diversity management had on profitability and provided a process to frame this relationship. The goal of most publicly traded organizations is to increase profitability. For government, non-profits and associations; they may not have the goal of increasing revenue, but they all have a concern with holding the line on costs.

Human capital productivity factors have long been linked to high performing work teams (HPW). HPW teams are those that through their composition outperform other work groups, when all else is equal. Their productivity, quality, and enthusiasm are normally measurable. They are found in workplaces with high levels of motivation and retention. They also have higher levels of employees willing to give their discretionary effort on a consistent basis. Discretionary effort is defined as follows: When an employee's full capability exceeds the minimum requirements for the job, it is at their discretion to give that 'extra' effort on a consistent basis. If they choose NOT to give that extra effort, there is little the organization can do, as long as the effort given meets the

---

[22] Clayton, Craig. B. Sr, 2010.

job requirements. When a high percentage of team members possess more skills than the job requires and choose to give that effort, that is when you have a high performing work (HPW) team. That is when one plus one equals three!

"As a society, we've learned that we're all better off when everyone is included in the opportunities of this great nation." - Ted Kennedy

---

In the case study, respondents were asked what percentage of their best efforts they gave at work on a regular basis. Only you know what your best efforts are. Surprisingly, 57% stated that they give less than 100% of their best effort on a regular basis. So not only was there no discretionary effort, but the majority of respondents were also working well below the minimum required for their role. When asked what would cause these employees to put more effort in their work, the number one response was not more pay, perks or benefits; it was having a manager that treated them with dignity and respect. This is beyond being tolerant of someone.

The respondents were also asked if they had witnessed or experienced derailing behaviours in the past twelve months. Seventy-one percent (71%) had witnessed on average four derailing behaviours in the past year.

When asked what they believed the basis or foundation for these behaviours were, two thirds of these were perceived to be based on differences associated with race, gender, age, religion and sexual orientation. From the study, these derailing behaviours affected many different areas including:

- The levels of discretionary effort in the organization were lowered.
- Number of sick days taken, absences, and consequent organizational medical expenses.
- Frequency of safety incidents increased.
- Turnover and retention of employees increased.

- Higher levels of "Turn Under ™" – rather than quitting and leaving an organization, employees quit and stay.

- Lower levels of employee creativity including innovation and ideas.

This is by no means the only study that demonstrates the financial benefits of inclusion strategies and the impact on ROI. From a sample of the research on the relationship between inclusion and the bottom line:

- Bersin completed a two-year research project in 2015 that demonstrated that companies with inclusion processes were the highest performing.[23]

- Research by another organization, Catalyst, demonstrated that organizations with more gender diverse boards outperformed their competitors.[24]

- McKinsey demonstrated that companies that are gender diverse are 15% more likely to perform better than their competitors. For companies that are ethnically diverse, the likelihood of outperforming competitors rises to 35%.[25]

- In research conducted by Deloitte Australia, inclusive teams during team-based assessments, outperformed their competitors by 80%.[26]

- In another case study, Opportunity Now, found that inclusive leadership within organizations leads to companies being more likely to increase their market share by 45%. Capturing new markets jumped by 70% with the addition of inclusive leadership.[27]

---

[23] Deloitte, 2017.
[24] Catalyst.org, 2007.
[25] Hunt, Vivian, 2015.
[26] Deloitte, 2013.
[27] Churchard, Claire, 2014.

It is not just research that proves the link. Ernst & Young in a global survey, demonstrated that 84% of managers questioned on inclusive teams, agreed that future competitiveness depended on inclusive management competencies. Eighty-five percent (85%) also agreed that improving performance was only possible with inclusive leadership and with all employees able to have and express different opinions and perspectives.[28]

Notice that the focus of all of these pieces of research is inclusion. There was recognition in all of them that while valuing difference can create innovation in organizations, the real benefits emerged when inclusive management competencies were introduced.

At the beginning of this section, I asked you to take some guesses at what inclusion looks like at Google in 2017. So, do you have your answers? Here are the real results. Of the 56,000 technological employees at Google, only 19% are women, 2% are black and 3% are Hispanic[29]. How were your guesses? Did you come close?

The problem has recently been acknowledged specifically by the infamous memo of a Google employee who wrote a misogynistic article that did not reflect the principles of the company[30]. Google has launched an inclusive initiative as an awareness of the potential impact that this lack of inclusivity has on its bottom line.[31]

If you read about Google's attempt to address this, there is one clear part that sticks out. The policy focus, as of 2017 was on diversity; the focus is still on an objective measurement of how many people have been invited to the dance.

To become best practiced, the emphasis has to shift to becoming inclusive and not just diverse. The key for any organization is to create a culture that values all attributes of difference.

---

[28] Beacon Institute, 2017.
[29] Google, 2017
[30] Bergen, Mark and Huet, Ellen, 2017.
[31] Google, 2017.

The Range of Respect Continuum

In managing differences in our personal lives and at our workplaces, we have a number of choices with how we navigate these challenges, tolerance being one of them. As discussed in earlier sections, tolerance in some ways is not the best tool for this particular problem. There are a range of ways to understand how we approach differences and one way to look at them is to view them as a continuum of respect.

The figure below demonstrates this continuum or range of respect. This range of respect provides insights about the variations between what it means to be tolerated versus respected. Similar to conflict resolution, the range moves from avoidance of the issue to respect and finally inclusion.

Range of Respect - R^2

CONTINUUM OF HOW DIFFERENCE ARE VIEWED

Tolerance   *Acceptance*

Avoidance   *Respect*

"Respect yourself and others will respect you."- Confucius

With issues such as diversity, we are challenged to react to circumstances that require us to change our ingrained perspectives. How we react depends on many factors and it can remain constant at times and then change at others. As we understand a particular issue more, we move along the continuum.

To use a specific example, when women first entered industries that were dominated by men, they often faced resistance. To begin with, the problem was ignored and some men in these workplaces avoided interacting with women.

Avoidance: With this part of the range there are low levels of cooperation and low levels of assertiveness. The issue is well known, but it is not spoken of; it is ignored, and nothing is done to address it. Even worse, in some organizations, dealing with the issue is delayed and evaded. The main goal with this is to avoid the conflict instead of dealing with it. Introverts on the Myers-Briggs indicators are often the types of employees who will avoid issues and conflict.

To address the problem, organizations developed policies that made sure women were treated like everyone else in the organization; women were tolerated. This was the move from avoidance to tolerance.

Tolerance: As we discussed in the sections above, at this stage, the issue is acknowledged. Just because the issue is acknowledged, it does not mean that it is addressed or that people with differences are accepted and, in many cases, people are tolerant simply because they feel they have to be.

As time went on this should transform into acceptance as work policies change to reflect changes in the way the problem of inculcation was seen.

Acceptance: At this stage, organizations reach a place where they understand the value that every employee adds to the organization. There may be active ongoing policies established to develop processes around this.

Lastly, through changes in research in the field of organizational psychology and as our attitudes changed; some people began to move to a position of respect and inclusion.

Respect: At this stage, all coworkers are valued contributors; their input and capabilities are not just accepted but also admired and valued. All employees are seen as having skills, traits, and attributes that are crucial to the organization's success.

Inclusion: This last stage is not an end stage, but it is a process. Organizations that are inclusive actively seek to continuously evaluate whether or not every employee is respected and included in every part of the organization. At this stage in the Range of Respect Continuum, organizations have intersectional inclusion that is viewed as a progressive process rather than a static tool. It is in vast contrast to static and conservative nature of tolerance.

These changes can lead to many questions you can ask yourself:
- Where are you on this scale?
- How do others view you on this scale?
- As a leader, how are you leading this process?
- Have you discussed any of these with your coworkers?
- Have you discussed any of these with your friends?

The change created with this specific example, gender differences in the workplace, took a long time to create and it is an ongoing process that is nowhere near completion. The journey from avoidance to inclusion is a long arduous one and one that requires effort and commitment from leaders.

However, the journey cannot be avoided; our communities are reflected in our workplaces and vice versa. Inclusion as a necessity for successful organizations will only become stronger as our communities become aware of the benefits of valuing differences, respect and the processes of inclusion.

This is not simply powered by moral values or by idealistic principles. As subsequent sections in this book will illustrate, organizational inclusion creates effective and capable people both in our societies and at our workplaces. It is good business to be inclusive and the more successful a business becomes, the more important that is has and maintains inclusive policies.

"Our premise is that inclusion leads to growth. So for those who are locked out, they lose development, and those who are in power lose market and growth." - Jesse Jackson

---

Examples of Coworker (Tolerance Based) Behaviors

The behavior of feeling avoided precedes feeling tolerated. Yet the two can sometimes overlap. When someone's default mode is to avoid the person that is different from them, in the workplace, inevitably they will have to interact in some capacity or another. They are forced to move from a position of avoidance to one of tolerance. So, for example, if a coworker was using the behaviors associated with avoidance in a meeting, these would be immediately perceived by coworkers and others. In these settings the behavior of tolerating the person would be the next step in the interaction.

Many times, tolerating behaviors directed towards the person being tolerated include but are not limited to:

- **The Cold Shoulder**: This behavior basically conveys the persons feeling that they really don't think you add any value. They think your input is not worth listening to, so they put you on 'channel ignore'!

- **Challenge Everything You Say**: This behavior normally doesn't come from your boss. This normally comes from a co-worker or a peer. No matter what you say, suggest or add to the meeting, they find ways to take your ideas and/or comments apart. Their message is clear. Your thoughts don't count, and neither do you. They are also telling you that they are just putting up with you being here.

- **Constant Interruptions**: It's one thing to discount your input or opinion, it's another thing to not even allow you to finish your thoughts or statements. Have you ever had someone who keeps cutting you off, who interrupts everything you try to say? After a while you just want to stop trying, stop talking; after all they aren't listening and could not care less with what you have to say. They are merely tolerating you.

- **Condescending Co-Workers**: This is behavior used to talk down to someone as if they are stupid. It clearly indicates that that you are 'putting up' with them because they are beneath you.

- **Bad Body Language**: This is behavior that may or may not be obvious to everyone. This involves someone who makes eye contact with everyone else but fails to even look in your direction. Sometimes they will even go as far as rolling their eyes at you, mocking you or sneering at you. They will show warm body language to others, (micro-affirmations) but they will reserve bad body language for just you (micro-aggressions).

DEFINITIONS:

- Micro-Aggression: an everyday exchange that cues a sense of subordination based on any one of a number of social identities, including: race, gender, sexual orientation, socioeconomic background, nationality, religion, and disability (see Sue, 2010a, 2010b; Sue, Capodilupo, Torino, Bucceri, Holder, Nadal, & Esquilin, 2007).

- Micro-Affirmation: **Micro-affirmations** are subtle or apparently small acknowledgements of a person's value and accomplishments. They may take the shape of public recognition of the person, "opening a door," referring positively to the work of a person, commending someone on the spot, or making a happy introduction. (see Rowe, Mary, "Barriers to Equality: the Power of Subtle Discrimination," The Employee Responsibilities and Rights Journal, June, 1990, Vol. 3, No. 2, pp. 153–163)

All of these behaviors can quickly add up and leave you feeling as though you are not valued, have nothing to offer, and really should not even be on the team or in the organization.

For many people conflation of the terms tolerance and diversity is also very common. While the two concepts are intertwined, they are very different. Diversity is a term to describe the difference among a group of people. This may include differences in background, race, ethnicity, disability, class, religion, sexuality, gender, or age. This is not a conclusive list and diversity can include many other differences. Most organizations talk about **Diversity Management**, the processes and tools used to manage the differences found in the organization and to ensure that these differences are tolerated.

There are definitely benefits to being tolerant and this book is not suggesting that we throw away the entire concept. In some ways, tolerance is a beneficial tool in managing differences. We're not born with a chip on our shoulder but as we're exposed to society's norms, we develop our own opinions, idiosyncrasies, and beliefs that don't always fall in line with that of our colleagues. These differences have the potential to get in the way of establishing and strengthening relationships in the workplace. In some cases, disagreements arise and escalate, when they could have been avoided through a more strategic form of conflict management.

On the flip side, when we adopt an attitude of tolerance, we open up a world of possibilities. Think of the benefits that come with a conscious adoption of tolerance including:

- More open and honest communication.
- Creativity fostered by an open exchange of ideas from across a broad spectrum of expertise.
- Respect and trust between individuals.
- Teamwork, cooperation, and coordination among professionals in the

workplace.

- Loyalty and productivity, both of which are crucial for organizational efficiency.

In this way, tolerance can be seen as a method of conflict resolution. But is it the best method available?

Tolerance is positive when it asks us to acknowledge diversity and embrace coexisting team members. However, it becomes problematic because it does not ask us to accept, understand, or embrace differences in ways that can build our communities and organizations. This is the fundamental problem with tolerance. As a result of this negative part of tolerance, being tolerant "reinforces instead a set of passive, condescending, and counter-productive attitudes and practices that work against the very goals we have pledged to pursue."[32] So instead of being a tool that helps organizations to understand and develop from diversion, it can achieve the opposite.

Perceptions Linked to Tolerance In The Workplace

In 1990 Roosevelt Thomas published an article called "From Affirmative Action to Affirming Diversity" in the Harvard Business Review. It soon became one of the most popular articles on diversity management and helped to move the focus of organizational culture from Affirmative Action to diversity. It was an important article and ushered in a new way of thinking about organizational culture. While it soon became apparent that diversity was not enough and in reality, organizations need inclusive competencies, this article was very important in determining the perceptions of leaders in workplaces. It defined an era of organizational culture change.

Nowadays, the sources of information available on organizational culture are many. While the Harvard Business Review is still regarded as a primary

---

[32] Jacobs, 2011.

source of information, organizations and individuals are just as likely to get their information from social media and the internet. This has implications for perceptions in the workplace around tolerance, differences, and inclusion.

While many organizations are moving towards an understanding of inclusive competencies, there are still perceptions of the workplace that are stuck in the avoidance stage. Take for example gender diversity in the workplace. There are still many people who feel that women should not work and if they do, they should not have senior positions in organizations. Some people think that women should only participate in certain careers and industries. They feel that women should not be law enforcement officers for example, or work in the intelligence community, military, or other roles.

If women do end up in organizations with this type of limited culture, they face treatment that specifically intends to take away their dignity and self-esteem and cause them to question their capability. The ultimate goal of those targeting women with this behavior is that they will ultimately quit and prove to those in human resources and leadership that women could not cut it.

This behavior of 'denial and disrespect' is not just targeted towards women. It also is often directed towards immigrants and People of Color. In some organizations, it is also exhibited around non-visible aspects of difference.

An example is when you have a team of people who all grew up together working together and someone comes in who is new to the area and as a result not known by the team members, is added to the team. Feelings of rejection can often easily manifest.

In these situations, it would be advantageous to begin with encouraging the team members to feel as though there is an effort to be tolerant of the differences represented by the new team member. Tolerance is infinitely better than avoidance. But it should not be seen as the desired place to be as an individual, teamwork group and/or organization. It is only the beginning.

This narrow-minded perception, that can create derailing behaviors, is in the minority but it still exists and through social media, for example, it can easily spread. This can then increase the negative and limited perceptions. Ultimately, without inclusive competencies to demonstrate to all workers the value of inclusion, limited views such as the ones mentioned above will continue. Developing inclusive practices that are tied to ROI and the bottom line can lead to improved perceptions in the workplace and **in our communities.**

Aunt Suzie's – Apron Wisdom
"Going Back to Open Racism in Society,
Is Not That Long of a Walk!

Looking in the Mirror Isn't Easy

Some organizations conduct training and workshops to help people become more tolerant and accepting of each other. While this is clearly beneficial, especially when compared to the feeling of being avoided, it falls far short of the goal of being accepted or respected.

When people are confronted with the awareness that they have treated someone in a way that left them feeling tolerated we sometimes justify our behaviors by saying things like "I didn't know that someone felt that disrespected by what I said or did."

The feeling of being tolerated can often lead to a reaction that starts with discomfort ("I don't like the way this feels!") and can quickly escalate into anger ("Why are you treating me this way?"). Most of us have had some occasion where we felt like we were being avoided by someone in the workplace. It's not a good feeling and it certainly doesn't cause us to give our best efforts in the workplace. Some of us may also have had occasions to treat people in ways that left them feeling less than valued in the workplace. When we are faced with having to own up to this it is a difficult task; looking in the mirror means having to take responsibility for your behavior and forces you to question your actions.

Questions In The Mirror

Why does the issue of moving beyond tolerance matter? Being tolerant is a feeling of being put up with and for most people it is a negative experience.

- Have you ever felt as though someone was tolerating you?

- How did it feel?

- Have you ever 'tolerated' someone else?

- How might it have impacted them?

"Life is a mirror and will reflect back to the thinker what he thinks into it." - Ernest Holmes

---

The following case study offers an example of how this plays out in an organization:

Case Study: Technology Company. A technology company that was formed many years ago is made up mostly of men; most of them are engineers, others are managers. Recently they hired several new employees who were recent college graduates. Included in this round of recruitment were a number of women. One of them, Sally, was valedictorian of her class and conducted cutting edge research. She was an expert in her area and so had many offers from different organizations for different types of jobs. She chose this specific technology company as she thought they had the best offer and the best role, and she thought that the organizational culture best suited her.

When she started at the company, things went well, and she enjoyed her work. She got along with many of the other workers and felt as though she was achieving things in her role. She was not sure if she was valued in the organization but thought that after a while this would happen. At a monthly meeting, Sally noticed that none of the other female staff were asked to speak. They often had things to say and would try to get their points across but they were interrupted and ignored. After being at the company for two months, Sally attended a meeting where again the female staff were not allowed to speak. At that meeting she overheard one of the male engineers whisper to his colleague: "I told you that women should not have joined; they just can't do the job." After the meeting she spoke to two of the other female staff members and they discussed what to do.

They decided to go to their team leader and report what Sally had heard. They also discussed other ways in which they felt that there had been micro-inequities directed towards the female staff in the company.

Luckily, the management at the company was responsive to their complaints and agreed to do something about this. They called a meeting and made it clear that the company would not allow any behavior that did not value all staff in the organization. Sally and the other staff were pleased with this. After the meeting, Sally walked past the coffee break room. As she walked past, she overheard a group of the male staff talking about the meeting. They all agreed that they could not get the company to change their decision about hiring female staff, but they couldn't be forced to make the female staff feel welcome. One of the men there disagreed with what they were saying but was convinced to go along with the other men. Sally walked into the break room intending to challenge the men about this but as she walked in, they all walked out. After that most of the male staff ignored Sally.

They never said anything disrespectful to her, but just refused to engage with her. They put up with her but did not make her feel welcome. Soon Sally questioned whether or not this was the right organization for her and questioned her decision to choose this technology company over the many offers that she had received. During a visit back on campus to see some friends, some of whom were thinking about applying to Sally's company, Sally told them about the company and told them that she thought as women, they would not be welcomed in the organization. Her friends suggested that she report the company for harassment, but Sally said that as no one had said something specifically to her, she had no real evidence that could be used in a legal case. Sally said that she was going to hand in her resignation and look for a new job. She said that if she was asked about why she wanted to leave she would tell them it was because the company did not value female staff and that she would tell others about the way she had been treated.

- What questions would this company need to ask itself in this situation?
- What questions would the organization need to ask the men in this situation?
- How could the organizational leaders create a learning exercise out of this?
- How could this situation be helped with a learning and training exercises?
- How could this problem be addressed in an effective way?

The next section looks in more details about how reflecting on the status quo or asking questions in the mirror can help organizations understand where they are on the Respect Continuum and so understand what work needs to be done to become inclusive.

"Even a mirror will not show you yourself, if you do not wish to see."

- Sam Toyama

Unconscious Bias & Blind Spots

Unconscious biases are stereotypes that occur when we quickly make judgements about situations and people without even realizing that we are doing it. This happens outside our conscious awareness. There is no escaping the unconscious biases that we all hold; and we all hold many. There is a misperception that having a bias is something that someone chooses to do with the intent on slighting someone. We form them unconsciously and often without realizing. We may form them about different groups or people, or individuals and they come from the fact that our brain is constantly trying to order the world. It is important that we remember bias is not something that is solely based on issues of race and/or gender. Bias can be rooted in many aspects of difference, including age, religion, sexual orientation, weight and more.

Go back to the thinking slow, thinking fast idea. If we think of unconscious bias as part of System 1 thinking, then they are an efficient (but not necessarily good) way of understanding the world; we quickly judge certain situations and form opinions to make quick decisions. The driver at the stop light described earlier in the book is a good example of this quick judgement. We will roll down our window to a stranger based on quick unconscious biases we have. We use this to judge the situation and to make a decision. How we develop these biases depends on our personal experiences, our cultural environment, and our background. These then form the basis for our stereotypes and then perpetuate our unconscious bias.

Our unconscious biases can become so effective at stereotyping the world around us that we fail to see them. When this happens, blind spots are created; these are hidden biases in our unconscious mind that we then use to guide our decision making and behavior. They are often towards groups who we are less familiar with or with things that are unknown. It is why, for example, it is common to hear the strong bias that "math is hard"! (Yes, some parts of math is hard but with enough practice most high school math can easily be mastered.)

"But I think that no matter how smart, people usually see what they're already looking for, that's all." -Veronica Roth, Allegiant

Inherent in decision making processes is an opportunity for these processes to be negatively impacted by cognitive bias and there are literally dozens of cognitive biases that manifest at a subconscious level. These blind spots impact every aspect of how we do our jobs. These unconscious biases and blind spots can include:

The Halo Effect

The Halo Effect is often considered a form of positive cognitive bias. For example, if a Talent Management professional is told that people who are more attractive make better candidates, they are more likely to hire more attractive candidates without questioning the rationale behind this statement. This is a powerful bias as it is reinforced in everyday life in many ways. It is a real, quantifiable and most importantly avoidable effect.

In-Group Bias

People instinctively tend to cluster in groups. This occurs at social gatherings, before a meeting starts, and in most social situations. This bias manifests itself into certain attributes. People tend to not only congregate in like groups, they also reach judgements based on those groups. They view their collective group as better than the other groups, and they tend to view the outside groups as inferior. When done at a subconscious level it can result in treatment, judgement, assessment, and valuations linked to someone's group identity and not their ability. This is In-Group bias and it can have an incredible powerful negative effect on Talent Management professionals, managers, and leaders.

Confirmation Bias

This is a common bias that occurs in and out of work forces. It is especially dangerous among Talent Management staff as it can perpetuate practices that negatively impact the organization. With this bias, people ignore information that does not match their existing belief systems. Instead, they look at information that confirms their beliefs and hold that as more truthful. This is becoming more and more common with the increase in use of social media. Social media is a perfect communication tool to create confirmation biases as we can select what information we want to consume and so create information bubbles online.

EXAMPLE: I mentioned that I have done work with law enforcement and the intelligence community. Confirmation bias can be particularly insidious in these two fields. Being predisposed to a conclusion, result or suspect, can cause those in these fields to look for fact, datapoint or even circumstances that validate their supposition, instead of letting the facts speak for themselves.

The Mere-Exposure Effect

One of the key successes of international organizations like McDonald's is the reliance on this bias. Wherever you are in the world, if you find a McDonalds you will be able to order a meal that is familiar; you will know what to order, what it costs, and what it tastes like. It draws millions of people in to the restaurant around the world. They have carefully and lucratively relied on people preferring certain things simply because they know what they are. This is the Mere-Exposure Effect. As seen with McDonald's, organizations can use this to their benefit. If you enter a McDonalds in Waikiki, Hawaii you will find spam on the menu because the local are accustomed to having spam as a meat choice. (Thought I don't know why!)

Talent Management can use this tool to enhance Intercultural Agility among the organization. The more that people in the organization are exposed to the ideas behind Intercultural Agility, the more that it will be accepted.

However, this bias can also enhance negative perceptions that exist in the organization and Talent Management and leadership teams have to ensure that this is controlled. We will present more information on Intercultural Agility in subsequent sections of this book.

The Negativity Bias

Have you ever found yourself dwelling on an insult or fixating on your errors or mistakes? Criticisms tend to have a more significant impact than compliments and bad news frequently draws more attention than good. The reason for this is that negative events have a greater impact on our brains than positive ones.

Unfortunately, people by virtue of being people, pay more attention to negative experiences and also give negative experiences more weight. The key to overcoming this bias is to increase positive interactions within an organization.

System Justification

This is a common reason why many organizations fail. The system justification bias is when the status quo is seen as preferable to any other alternative, even if the alternatives are more effective, more legitimate and as better than the existing situation. Obviously, this can be a real threat to innovation, and so can be a real threat for an organization's growth.

This bias is particularly dangerous as it grows when organizations are under threat. This is why in situations when a change occurs, the transition can be very hard to achieve.

The Spacing Effect

Information that is repeatedly provided over a duration of time is often not only retained more, but it is also more accepted. Comparably, information that is given only once is harder to accept.

As indicated in these examples, and as with other forms of System 1 thinking, there can be dangers in ignoring our unconscious bias. If we are dealing with complex problems or complex situations, then our unconscious biases are not very useful. Our unconscious biases also create situations where we develop incorrect understandings of the world. They can stunt innovative ideas, creativity, and limit our experiences.

By understanding our biases, we can overcome them. Becoming aware of the most prevalent forms of cognitive bias, including stereotyping helps us to develop steps and process to identify and mitigate them before they create opportunities to impact our decision-making processes in non-productive ways. Once you realize that in order to do math you need to practice math, for example, you can begin to understand it. Once that happens, you can then see that some aspects of it are a lot of fun, and your unconscious bias towards the subject tends to disappear. In the same way, if we have developed unconscious biases about other cultures, once we understand these cultures, get to know them, and we find out that people all over the world have so much in common, many of the biases disappear.

To make these changes and to understand the effect of our unconscious biases, in most organizations the term unconscious bias has become a routine and is part of the regularly offered training curriculum. The amount of money being spent on bias training has grown exponentially with some estimates exceeding $100 million dollars annually. There are numerous training approaches, concepts and materials that help employees, managers, leaders, and others understand that we all have blind spots.

Linking this to tolerance, treating someone in a way that demonstrates you are 'tolerating' them can sometimes be rooted in conscious or unconscious biases.

The difference though is that the act of tolerating someone is a conscious choice. The reason behind why someone feels it is acceptable to make that choice, can be rooted in an unconscious bias. Someone who was reared in a small rural town, with little exposure to people from different cultural backgrounds can find themselves serving in the military with people from every cultural background imaginable. If they are transferred to a new country with new cultures, they will be exposed to even more unique cultures. To expect that person to automatically go to the default position of acceptance and/or respect when interacting with these new cultures might be unrealistic.

In this example, it is common for the person to move from a stage of avoidance (when they lived in a homogenous culture), to tolerance (before they have understood the culture), and then to acceptance (to when they understand more about the other culture and their own unconscious biases). This is an ideal situation, and in the situation of being immersed in another culture, the move towards acceptance, ideally is quick.

"No culture can live if it attempts to be exclusive." - Mahatma Gandhi

Examining Bias & Tolerance

Unconscious biases can impact how people in workplaces interact. It can have a higher impact if the people in the workplace have limited shared personal experiences. It is common that in most workplaces, there would need to be a maturation to take place for change to happen, as moving from avoidance to tolerance and then to acceptance has to be a conscious effort.

The first step in clearing your lens of bias, is understanding that you have them. The next step is to make a conscious effort to move from awareness to owning the process of improvement and change.

There are many different tools available that help you to determine what biases you may have. Harvard and Yale have conducted a tremendous amount of research in the development and deployment of what is called the Implicit Aptitude Test (IAT). These tests help assess unconscious biases based on age, race, sexuality, disabilities and religion. They measure the beliefs and attitudes that we might be unable or unwilling to report.[33] The tests do this by measuring the strength of associations that we have between concepts (such as race or gender), and evaluations (such as good or bad) or stereotypes (descriptions such as athletic or clumsy).

Aunt Suzie's – Apron Wisdom
"How can you defeat something
You won't even admit belongs to you!!

When completing the tests, you have to quickly classify different words into categories that are either on the right or left of the screen. The test then measures the strength of your associations between different evaluations or stereotypes and concepts. The idea is that the more we associate things, the faster our response is with the test.

So, if you have an unconscious bias such as believing older people are smarter, then you will react faster when these associations are made. While no test can be perfect, and they do encourage that people take the test more than once, the test has been validated as a very good measurement of implicit attitudes and values. The most important part of our unconscious biases and blind spots is that by identifying them and understanding them we can minimize their negative impact.

---

[33] Harvard University, Implicit Attitude Test, 2011.

Changing Your Self Tape

Once we realize what our biases are and how they might be impacting our ability to interact with people who are different from ourselves, the challenge is to begin to modify those debilitating biases. While it is not possible to completely remove all of our unconscious biases, we can make steps to reduce our blind spots.

The input we receive from others has a significant impact on our self-perception. If someone consistently hears that they cannot accomplish something, they will begin to question whether or not they can.

The voice that most of us hear more often than any other, is also the voice we have the most ability to change and/or modify; our own. We spend most of our time listening to the voice inside our head. Sometimes we are so accustomed to our inner monologue that we don't always realize the tone and tenor of what that voice is saying.

Eliminating unconscious bias is strongly connected to getting attuned to what we are saying to ourselves. This includes what we are saying about ourselves as well as what we are saying to ourselves about others. Understanding the way we view others, especially those who are different from ourselves, starts with analyzing what our self-tape is saying about those who differ from us.

Changing your self-tape requires you to:

- Note the themes and tone of your inner voice.
- Decide what, if anything, needs to change.
- Don't allow the negatives to dominate your inner voice.
- Focus on the positives and FEED those thoughts!!
- Start off small and take little steps.

Additionally, we can take many other steps to work towards reducing our unconscious bias. We have no idea how much of our conscious brain we are using. Most of our brain processes are internal unconscious processes of which unconscious biases are a part. As a result, we need to make sure that as much of our conscious thinking is focused on reducing the System 1 thinking that creates our blind spots.

Courtney Seiter summarized seven key steps to reducing unconscious bias as follows:[34]

Using Inclusive Language.

In many workplaces, the use of email means that most of our communication is written. When we do use written communication, we can consciously decide to make sure that whatever we write is as inclusive as possible. We can refrain from using language that could exclude some groups in your office. Seiter gives an example of refraining from using the phrase "you guys." While it is meant as an inclusive term in most cases, it could be misconstrued as an exclusive term. In the same way, using the phrases "boys" and "girls" can also be seen as being filled with unconscious bias so they can be avoided. When we speak face to face, it can be harder to double check what we say but training workshops can easily be set up to try to provide inclusive communication skills in the workplace.

Use Counter-Stereotyping Images.

The first step with this is to find out what are the main unconscious biases in your workplace. This can be simply achieved by getting your employees to take the IAT discussed in the previous sections. Once this has been completed, you can ask the IAT assessors to provide you with an overview of the results (although ethically they will not provide the specific results for individuals, they can provide an overview). This will give you an idea of what unconscious biases are in your workplace and so what you need to focus on. Once this has been

---

[34] Seitner, 2015.

established, you can then use counter-stereotyping imagery in your workplace to counter act this.

So, for example, if the IAT comes back and there is a high unconscious bias against older people in the workplace, you can then use images of successful older people to counteract this bias. In this way, the unconscious bias can be subtly challenged. The imagery selected needs to be carefully selected to sufficiently challenge the biases while not creating additional unconscious bias. Seiter describes a "drawing from a New Yorker magazine cover, of a construction worker with hard hat on, breast-feeding her baby" as a great counter-stereotyping image to use in any workplace.

Work On Your Interior Design

This suggestion was one which demonstrated how deep our unconscious biases go. In a study by Sapna Cheryan at the University of Washington[35], it was demonstrated that by adding more gender inclusive furniture, inclusive associations rose. So, in a computer science classroom, they changed the furniture to be more gender neutral and things considered less stereotypical of computer science. The positive and inclusive associations of the participants rose as a result. Adding more plants, more decorations, and more accessories in your workplace can mean that it becomes a more inclusive place reflective of everyone in the office. Our environments are like gatekeepers, they determine if we feel comfortable in them or not. To demonstrate this, think of the last time you were in a room and felt uncomfortable.

- Why were you uncomfortable?
- How did you feel?
- What did you like and dislike about the room?
- Now think about the room that makes you most comfortable. What do

---

[35] Cheryan S., Plaut V. C., Davies P. G., Steele C. M., 2009.

you like about it?

- How does it make you feel?

Now think of the difference between the two and it is easy to understand how important our environments are in making us feel inclusive.

Create and Empower Mentors In Underrepresented Groups

If you turn on social media or pick up a magazine and have a look at who are the successful people, they often do not include people from diverse groups. The same is true in our workplaces. Think of this example, which I observed in a workplace. A manager had to choose between two people to send to management training, and so give them a promotion after they completed the training. He had to choose between a black woman who had a college degree and a white man who graduated from high school. He chose the white male. I asked him why he had chosen the white male. He told me that the white male reminded him of himself when he was first starting out, so he wanted to give him a chance. He added, "He just looks like a manager." If we were to go through the manager's life and see the examples of successful people he had seen in his life, I would not be surprised if it was devoid of People of Color and women.

If someone in his workplace who was for example, a black woman, was given a mentor position and asked to mentor other people on the team, then the idea of what a successful person looks like could change. Importantly, this would not just affect the images that white male had; importantly it would also provide other black women a more positive self-image as their views on what success looks like. The campaign "Black Girl Magic" is based on this exact psychology. The activists who started this campaign started from a realization that there are few role models for young black girls. They decided to highlight as many as they could to demonstrate that they were out there but just not highlighted in the media and elsewhere.

Using Social Media to Amplify New Voices

If you have a Twitter account, one of the interesting things you can do is have a look at your analytics section. From there you can see the details of who you interact with. For example, you can see what genders follow you. You cannot break it down beyond that on Twitter (although there are other apps and software products that can analyze your social media in more detail) but it does raise the question of who dominates social media and what unconscious biases are perpetuated by those who have more of a voice across the platforms. One exercise which is common on Twitter is for some accounts to decide to only retweet and like posts by women or posts by People of Color. I have often decided to only interact with people outside of the United States so that I can get interact more with people from different cultures.

Find diverse people that you admire

Similar to finding role models and empowering mentors in the workplace, this involves finding people you admire outside of work. Once you have found a bias in your IAT, you can then use that to find role models of people you are bias against and then learn about them, read about them, put up posters of them, and discuss them with others. This can be replicated in the workplace as well.

Counterprogram your brain

This last exercise is a simple yet effective way of reprogramming our subconscious thoughts. Say for example you find out that you have an unconscious bias that men are smarter than women. Take some time by yourself or with others to write up a list of attributes of what a smart woman would look like. Describe the smart woman and why she is smart and capable and what she has achieved in her life. Ignore her physical attributes and focus on her characteristics.

If you do this as a group you can draw the smart woman, and then as a group list what makes her smart. Something this simple and creative reduces our unconscious biases and stereotypes.

These are all simple ways to reduce the effects of unconscious bias, but nothing is more effective than leaders with purpose. If you set out to lead by example, you will encourage others to challenge their bias more, but if you address this issue with purpose, you will enable your employees to change in positive ways. Section 2 will show you how you can achieve this.

"Where there is no vision, the people perish." — Proverbs 29:18

How to React to Unconscious Bias

Just being tolerated or being treating negatively because of unconscious bias, can make you feel pretty low. You cannot blame yourself for feeling this way; the person who treats you negatively is at fault. However, you can control the way you react to this behavior. You can choose whether or not you let it get you down.

What is the best way to react when it happens? In many cases, the behavior comes as a surprise. It is shocking and leaves us wondering, "what happened?"[36] Let's take a very common example of biased behavior that most of us have probably seen. A woman who you work with is assertive and because of this, she is labeled as angry. Another coworker who is male, behaves the same way but is seen as a strong team player. In moments like this, we need to decide whether or not to stand up and say something or be quiet. Should we rock the boat, or

---

[36] Judith Honesty, David Maxfield, and Joseph Grenny, 2017.

should we keep the peace? How do we set rules about this? It is something so small and yet it has such a big impact. How do you create ways to limit the effect of this type of behavior?

In their study on workplace bias, Honest, Maxfield, and Grenny started out by trying to rate bias among their respondents. They asked how permanent, pervasive and controllable the bias in their workplace was. The results were as follows:

- 49% of the respondents reported that bias is an "enduring part of their workplace and happens regularly and routinely."[37] In this way the bias was **permanent.**

- 66% of the respondents said that it impacts "all aspects of their engagement, morale, motivation, commitment, and desire to advance in the organization."[38] In this way it was definitely **pervasive.**

- 60% of the respondents said that they don't feel that they could "master incidents of bias in the moment or prevent them from recurring in the future."[39] In this way they were **uncontrollable.**

When asked if the bias they experienced was a combination of these three features, 27% said that what they had experienced was permanent, pervasive, and uncontrollable.

It demonstrates how difficult it can be to then respond to bias. Honest, Maxfield, and Grenny summarize the skills necessary for dealing with bias as follows:

---

[37] Ibid, 2017.
[38] Ibid, 2017.
[39] Ibid, 2017.

Personal Methods of Dealing with Bias

1. **C.P.R.** The first way to address bias is to look at the three levels –
    Content, Pattern, and Relationship. The content is what happens in that
    particular incident. Pattern is looking at the details of a number of
    incidents. Relationship is when the pattern impacts on whether or not
    you can work with others or not. If we use the example above, if you
    notice someone being bias to an assertive woman just once, you can use
    a conversation about content to solve the problem. If you see this
    happening on a number of occasions, then you will need to focus on
    the pattern of behavior. Lastly, if it starts to affect how people work
    then you need to start to look at the larger impact on self-esteem,
    corporation, and trust.

2. **Know Your Goal.** Before doing anything, think about what you want
    to achieve. Before you act, think about what you want to change.

    *   Do you want some form of apology or punishment?
    *   Or do you just want the behavior to stop?
    *   What do you want afterwards? The clearer the goals the better
        chance you have of achieving them.

3. **State Your Take**. The better you have described what happened, the
    easier it is to address the behavior - really describe what happened. What
    time was it, when was it, what was said exactly? This also need to be
    objective so no apologies, no accusations, just clear communication of
    the detailed facts.

4. **Make it Safe**. One of the most important things to recognize is that we
    all use unconscious bias at some point. We are human and this is what
    causes us to have unconscious biases. Regardless, when we bring up the

flaws of others, it is natural for them to feel as if they are being attacked. The best way to deal with this is to start the conversation by making them feel safe. Saying things like "I doubt you realized that…" can help to make it safer.

Organizational Methods of Dealing With Bias

1. **Set Challenging Goals.** This was discussed in an earlier section of this book - setting challenging goals can provide motivation for people to try to achieve them. Setting goals around bias behaviors can help to reduce them if they are challenging and if the results are tracked. Some goals can be related to objective measures such as the number of women in certain departments. You can also include subjective measures to help change behaviors. You could measure perceived levels of bias and monitor the change in this. More on the types of measures and metrics are covered in the organizational section of this book.

2. **Identify Crucial Moments and Act!** Keeping records of when and where incidents occur can help to analyze when they are most likely to occur and where improvements need to be made. These can include when harassment occurs, when there are problems with managers, when behavior comes from one person, and when the behavior follows a pattern.

3. **Combine Solutions.** Normally when we think of a solution to bias or tolerance, we think of one event that will fix the problem. We will run one training course and think that will solve the problem. Bias is so deeply rooted; it is a stubborn problem that one training session cannot solve it all. To address it, we need to use many different solutions and we need to use them often and frequently.

"The eyes only see what the mind is prepared to comprehend."

- Robertson Davies

Bias in Talent Management

In Section 2.4, I gave the example of the Google worker who was fired for writing a misogynistic memo. What struck me as pertinent to that case was the fact that Google would have hired someone like that in the first place. When you look at the gender and ethnic statistics in the tech industry in general, it is clear that they do not focus their Talent Management practices on hiring representative of the communities they are located in; but when you examine the "memo incident", it is also clear that their Talent Management is not focused on inclusion. The next three sections of this book will look at how teams, leaders and therefore organizations can become inclusive places to work. A significant part of this includes creating an inclusive mindset for those with talent management responsibilities.

Some examples of how bias manifests in Talent Management include:

- Resumes with typically WASP (White Anglo-Saxon Protestant) names receive 50% more requests for phone interviews than those with stereotypically black sounding names.

- With everything else being equal; male applicants for scientific jobs and technology jobs are more likely to get interviewed, hired and to be treated as having higher qualifications.

- In interviews, interviewers typically sat further away from black applicants than white applicants and ended the interviews much sooner.

- More than 60% of all CEOs in America are 6 feet tall or over.

- The salaries of brunettes and redheads are 7% less than blond haired women.[40]

How can we address this? What steps can we take to reduce these biases? Once you have read through the rest of this book, you will understand that the answer to this is a holistic one that relies on leadership leading with purpose.

However, specific tools for Talent Management are available that can help to reduce the biases in recruitment. Many of them we have discussed but they are worth repeating:

Develop and maintain Employee-to-Employee learning programs.

These tools such as one-to-one mentoring, teaching courses, ad hoc workshops, training sessions, talks, and learning games help organizations to stimulate curiosity and thought. Specific topics that are uncovered in IAT tests can be covered and then organizations can improve soft skills in their organization. These can then be used specifically to train your Talent Management employees to focus on working towards inclusive techniques.

Talent Management employees can also run training on specific techniques such as interviewing, writing job descriptions, being inclusive in Talent management, and so on.

Shape the Candidate Experience

Imagine you apply for a job and it takes six months for them to invite you to an interview. Then at the interview they are late, and they forget to ask you some very basic questions. It then takes them another two months to offer you the job and you then have to wait another month to start. How do you think your initial job satisfaction would be? Driving a positive candidate experience helps you to

---

[40] O'Toole Murphy, Erin, 2016.

attract and recruit the best and in turn increases your ability to promote inclusion.

Hire by Committee

This sounds like an obvious tool to use but you would be surprised by how few organizations use this tool to promote inclusive Talent Management. The premise is simple. As we all have different biases that manifest in numerous ways, if a group of people that are diverse are asked to recruit and interview an individual, they are more likely to be inclusive. They are more likely as a group to overlook their gender bias for example and hire the most qualified candidate regardless of their gender. In this way they reduce unconscious bias on an individual basis, and the decision as it is discussed by a group of people is more likely to be based on System 2, slow thinking that is more analytical.

Use Structured Interviewing

This is another very simple tool that is often overlooked. Structured interviews are based on utilizing the same methods. This means that each candidate gets the same questions and techniques and is then graded using specific criteria and the same scale. This means that the decision is made in a consistent way and it can help to reduce biases.

Create Objective Job Description

Job descriptions will be the first time that a potential employee sees what your organization is like. What this looks like, largely determines the quality of who is going to apply to your organization. Unconscious bias in job descriptions is extremely common but most organizations do not even know that they are doing it! Take the following job description. Can you spot how this is a bias job description?

Job Description
We are looking for an independent assertive Python programmer who will apply their analytical skills to our software projects. We are building a committed team to work on our various software projects that include database management, gaming, and cloud computing. The successful candidate will be a coding ninja and have experience in a similar role and will have worked on similar collaborative projects.

While legally, job descriptions cannot discriminate or condone harassment, we all unconsciously include biases in these documents. Can you spot which words have an unconscious bias?

- The unconsciously (traditionally) feminine words include **collaborative, supportive, and committed.**

- The unconsciously (traditionally) masculine words include **ninja, independent, assertive, and analytical.**

Without fully understanding this, your job description could be deterring women from responding or it could be deterring men from responding. One way to avoid this is to use a mixture of so it is balanced out. There are software programs that you can use to determine whether or not your job descriptions are biased, and these are well worth the investment. They can be used across the board to determine where unconscious biases exist in other areas.

Review Resumes

We have all been in that situation where you have 100 resumes to get through and it is 5pm and you want to just wrap things up. To give you an idea, Google reviews 3 million resumes a year.

That is a lot of resumes! It can be tempting to come up with methods to quickly assess each resume so that you can "skim" through. Unconsciously, we will already have bias against many different parts of a resume – parental statues, race, employment, school, names, clubs and even addresses can be used to form a prejudicial opinion leading to an incorrect assessment of the candidate.

While you do need a way to go through resumes efficiently, there is also the need to be careful to not let your unconscious bias guide this process.

The best way to narrow down resumes efficiently while reducing bias is by using categories intentionally. Three examples?

1. **Attention to detail.** Are there grammar mistakes? Is it consistent? Is it formatted?

2. **Accomplishments.** Does the resume demonstrate quantifiable achievements?

3. **Experiences.** Are the experiences demonstrated clearly? Do they have experiences linked to the position?

By deciding on specific criteria to judge resumes coming in, anyone who is tasked to review resumes will be using the same judgement for the candidates. They will also eliminate their own unconscious bias as much as possible.

Educate. Educate. Educate.

In earlier sections of this book, I discussed some of the psychological reasons behind our behaviors related to tolerance and inclusion. One keyway to address the problems relating to these two issues is to understand them. It is important that a deep level of understanding is across the board by educating your team about this. Additionally, as we learn to understand our own biases, we actually become less attached to them and so can change our own behavior. As mentioned earlier, getting your entire team to take the IAT test from Project Implicit is the first start. Training your teams further is the next step. This training and understanding needs to be continuous; repeated timely and its impact monitored.

Partner with Others.

There are many organizations that specialize in understanding inclusion and that help to build Talent Management around inclusion partnering with organizations with these specialties can help with finding candidates that have inclusive skills.

Build Inclusive Culture.

Inclusion begets inclusion. The more inclusive your business culture, the more likely you are to recruit inclusive candidates and the more inclusive your business culture will become and so on. This is more than just recruitment though; to have a truly inclusive culture, diversity needs to exist at all levels including senior management and the board, and key employees of all types, need to be retained and valued.

What goes on outside, affects what goes on inside.

Our organizations do not exist in a vacuum. What happens in our communities has an impact on what happens in our organizations. The conversations of the latest news story, the latest hard topic, the latest hushed topic, take place in our offices perhaps more so than anywhere else. They cannot be avoided. If you ignore them, you will not understand them, and you will not be able to use them to create inclusive organizations. By talking about them, understanding them, using them to allow your employees to understand their unconscious biases, and helping your employees understand how you can increase the success of the organization by being more inclusive is a vital part of building inclusivity. Keep in mind, these conversations are going to happen, whether you do anything about them or not. It is much better to use them as learning experiences and guide the outcomes.

In the sections that follow on teams, leadership, and organizational culture, all of these will be explored in more detail and we will look further at how these tools enhance your organizations purpose and success.

---

*"I speak to everyone in the same way, whether he is the garbage man
or the president of the university." - Albert Einstein*

Moving Beyond Tolerance Takes Courage

Courage in the workplace is a requirement to achieve the levels of workplace respect and teamwork that best-in-class organizations strive to achieve. Courage in the workplace has been defined by James R. Detert, the University of Virginia's Dean of the Darden School of Business as:

"Acts, related to one's work that are done for a worthy cause/reason, despite perceived risks, threats or obstacles to the self."[41]

Their research coined a unique phrase. Courageous leaders exhibited behaviors that were called *"**voluntary vulnerability**"*. Examples of these behaviors included leaders who:

- Admitted they did not have all the answers.

- Demonstrated emotions, including fear and/or sadness.

- Apologized publicly when they were wrong.

Courage to be vulnerable, is what true leadership is all about. With workplaces changes and people from different background and experiences becoming more prevalent; the likelihood of people feeling tolerated and/or avoided is real.

The success of most organizations depends on the ability to get the best efforts from all stakeholders on a regular basis. When people feel disrespected in the workplace there are many ways that their efforts at work are impacted.

---

[41] Detert, James R., 2017.

Derailing behaviors are happening in all organizations in increasing levels and these have a negative impact on success. It takes courage to step up to these behaviors and change them. Consider this case study:

A Health Care Organization.

This organization focuses on providing health care and uses the motto: "Where Compassion and Healing Unite!" During recent meetings, several physicians told the hospital administrator that the providing compassion should come from nurses. The patients were giving the doctors very good feedback when it came to providing care, but they were seen as lacking empathy and emotional intelligence.

These ratings were having an impact on the hospital's performance and subsequently the performance-based compensation for the institution as well as all staff.

During the meeting with the physicians, the hospital administrator chooses to share a story about his daughter's experience of suffering terminal cancer and being hospitalized. He told them that he was an intern when his two-year-old daughter was diagnosed with an aggressive and rare form of brain cancer. It devastated his wife, and they could not understand why this was happening to them. His wife and he had both dedicated their lives to the well-being of others. He told the physicians that the only thing that kept them going was the caring and compassion they received from the pediatrician throughout their daughter's illness. Due to this compassion, they were able to focus on their child during the short and painful disease.

After the meeting, several physicians approached the hospital administrator and asked for coaching on how to improve their emotional intelligence. His vulnerability and courage to share his personal story changed their conception of courage and compassion. This was an example of 'voluntary vulnerability' and unfortunately is the exception and not the rule in many organizations. This example demonstrates that leaders need to be courageous or no one will follow by example. Leaders need to set the stage and by being courageous, they promote courage throughout the organization.

"Men make history and not the other way around. In periods where there is no leadership, society stands still. Progress occurs when courageous, skilful leaders seize the opportunity to change things for the better." —Harry S. Truman

---

From Avoidance/Tolerance to Respect/Inclusion

THE EXTRA DEGREE: As with the personal journey that requires you to stretch your cultural comfort zone, moving across the Range of Respect continuum can be seen through the analogy of water in its three primary forms, ice, liquid, and steam.

In the first stage, avoidance is like frozen water. It has limited uses for the average person. It helps to make drinks easier to digest, but it is the least use form of water. It has benefits when applied to an injury, but only on a temporary basis. Avoidance has often been referred to as giving someone the cold shoulder. When this behavior is exhibited in the workplace it can place a chill on relationships on the team and in your workgroup. There are legitimate reasons to avoid some people. There are people who always seem to have a negative outlook. It's hard to be around people like that without it impacting you. The instances where that avoidance is based on categories of difference such as age, gender, religion, sexual orientation, or ethnicity is more than eliminating discomfort it becomes an issue of discriminations. This form of avoidance is often rooted in prejudice. Avoiding those we differ from does not enhance our opportunities to understand each other. In fact, it only enhances the likelihood that we will reaffirm our prejudices or our rationale to continue to avoid someone. Part of the reason we avoid people is a general perception that we have nothing in common or an overriding distain for someone based on the categories of difference we have been told about. Once we get a chance to spend time with and get to know people, we often find that we have more things in common than ways we differ.

> *Our Similarities Are The Bridges That Allow Us*
> *To Cross Over The Walls That Divide Us.*

In physics it takes 80 times more energy to move water from a frozen state to a liquid state. As the freezing water of avoidance thaws with the acknowledgement that we actually are not as different as we have been led to believe, we move into the liquid state of called water. In this state, there are many uses for water. It can become easy to become complacent and assume that water in its liquid state is the best we can hope for.

After all we can not only put it to great practical use. Man has harnessed water for domestic, agricultural, industrial, and recreational purposes. We have even found ways to generate hydroelectrical power from water; what more could one ask? It is easy to see how in this analogy the state of liquid water, tolerance, seems to be more than acceptable.

The next state is when you continue to heat water. When you apply heat to water it maintains its watery state even though the temperature of the water may rise. As it rises it can become comfortable for a while. As the temperature continues to rise it quickly becomes uncomfortable. The longer one is on the receiving end of tolerant behaviors, the more awkward it feels. As the temperature escalates the heated water can create a state of unrest. When water is at a temperature of 211 degrees Fahrenheit, it is still in its liquid form. Though unbearable, it is still a liquid.

Once the water temperature rises one more degree to 212 degrees Fahrenheit, it takes on a completely different form and changes into steam. In this state, its capabilities, uses, benefits, and applications change dramatically. When water reaches 212 degrees, in the form of steam, it can now power a moving engine. It goes beyond hydropower generation, which is stationary. It now has the capability of reaching any location, it can transport and change a society, move goods across landscapes including mountains and oceans.

The Extra Degree!

In this analogy, respect and inclusion are that steam. It takes effort to exceed the 211-degree threshold, but it is worth the effort. Sometimes we find ourselves at the edge of making a breakthrough; a step away from exceeding our expectations; a degree away from changing from a liquid state to steam. On the verge of moving from the uncomfortable state of hot water to the society changing state of steam.

That extra degree, that extra effort may be out of your reach, but it doesn't mean we shouldn't try. The importance of being willing to stretch your cultural comfort zone means sometimes having to try something different.

This extra degree is what separates the best practiced organizations from the best-in-class organization.

Best Practiced or Best in Class?

For most executives the key has always been to lead and not follow. The goal of organizations is to be best in class and not just best practiced. Best practice means you are doing what others have found to be successful. Best in class means that those engaged in best practices are following you! I once had a poster in my dorm room in college. It showed teams of sled dogs pulling the bobsled across the frozen tundra two-by-two. The caption under the photo said the following:

If You Are Not the Lead Dog... The View Never Changes!

When looking to create inclusive respectful teams you have two choices. **BE** the lead team or **FOLLOW** the lead team.

As we are changing states, the laws of physics tell us that this takes a lot more energy. Moving from avoidance to tolerance to acceptance and ultimately respect & inclusion can be exhausting in itself without a roadmap or a path to follow. This book will provide the roadmap to help on that journey, but it will take effort. Sometimes you may be one degree away from seeing the difference. Don't let that stop you from trying. You have to have a goal, a purpose or you are simply existing and not living.

Remember: If You Aim At Nothing You Will Hit It Every Time!

Most importantly, as an analogy, this provides a good way to look at the effort required to move from tolerance to respect.

The difference in the states is clear in the way that it makes people feel. If you have ever been avoided or simply tolerated, you are aware how negative this can be. It can make you feel as if you have little to no value. If things change and you are respected and then included, how you feel changes dramatically. Your self-worth and self-value is raised and you now see yourself and your capabilities in a much more positive light.

If this happens as a single event in an organization, this is short lasting and will have little impact. To have a larger impact, to change the state within an entire organization, everyone within the company needs to be involved and this requires a lot of effort. Rather than simply developing an inclusion policy, organizations need to develop and continuously manage and monitor an inclusive culture in order to achieve the real success.

Returning to the earlier discussions on thinking fast and thinking slow, what we see is that moving from tolerance to inclusion takes effort because of the way in which our brains think. It also shows that maintaining an inclusive culture also requires effort. In Kahneman's research on how we think and when we use System 1 and System 2 thinking, he discovered something very interesting. When we frown, we have normally activated System 2 thinking. Additionally, when we are using System 2 thinking, our pupils dilate[42]. Biologically, System 2 thinking requires more energy in many ways. Just like moving from ice to liquid to steam takes energy, so does changing our thinking systems. System 2 is more deliberate and more rational but as it uses so much energy it can also be tiring.

It takes concentrated effort to use this type of thinking and also **to maintain** this type of thinking. This is why System 1 thinking is more common; it is easy to use and easy to maintain. If we have problems in our lives it is hard to use System 2 thinking as we tend to use more energy to focus on our existing problems and on survival. In order to develop and maintain System 2 thinking, we need to have stable environments. Only then can we move from System 1 thought towards System 2's more organized thinking.

Being Inclusive: Treat Others How They Want to be Treated

How many times have you heard the phrase "treat others the way you want to be treated?" It is a saying that it is more than 3,000 years old so there is no wonder we don't question the saying. For many we know this as the golden rule. It has become a cultural meme.

- But does it always work?
- What happens when you have different styles of conflict resolution?
- What if you like to resolve conflict by talking about it whereas someone else needs to analyze it independently?
- If you treated each other how you wanted to be treated in this situation would this be the best solution?

---

[42] Kahneman, 2011, Pg. 152

In truth, most of the people you meet will have different preferences, different needs, different wants, different backgrounds, and different areas of development. If we walked around really treating everyone how we like to be treated, we would be in constant chaos!

Instead, we need to treat people how they want to be treated. This is called the platinum rule. Consider how this works in the workplace. You have a new employee coming in to work. You will be managing them. You like to work with a clear strategy, but you are flexible with how the work gets done. Your aim is to focus on flexibility and innovation, so you give your employees freedom. When your new employee starts working, you assume they also like to work like this and leave them to their work. After a while you notice that they are spending a lot of time on planning documents. You ask them why they are doing this, and they say that it is because they don't seem to have clear targets, and they found this disconcerting. Before they could start work, they needed to organize a plan like they had done in all of their previous roles.

One keyway to have avoided this would have been to set up a meeting with the new employee before they started and ask them how they work when it comes to strategy and planning. Together you could develop a way to work together. In this way, you would be treating your new employee how they wanted to be treated. As a tool for inclusion, this is immensely powerful as it demonstrates how much you value that particular employee. While it may not be possible to make all decisions in this way due to time constraints and other considerations as a foundation to inclusive culture, this is extremely effective. For developing inclusive cultures, the "Emotional Quotient" or EQ, is just as important as "Intelligence Quotient" or IQ.

In his New York Times best-selling book, "First Break All the Rules", Marcus Buckingham built the book around Gallup Research involving 80,000 managers in different industries documented the fact that great managers attract, focus, hire and retain great managers by following several key concepts. One of the core concepts revealed in their research was that Great Managers treat each employee as a unique individual!

They also found these managers set outcomes and didn't focus on the steps to reach those outcomes. The end is established and standardized, but the employees' approach to reaching those goals may be completely unique and separate from others in their effort to meet or even exceed the goals you have established.

The logic of treating people the way they want to be treated is also a key precept behind the many different personality and behavior assessment models. Once you know your preferred method of communicating, or your default mode of thinking, you then have the ability to flex your style to that of your team members to increase productivity and or engagement. This only further validates the importance of the Platinum Rule.

Intersectional Inclusion

The term intersectionality was first used in 1989 by Kimberlé Crenshaw in legal research exploring violence against black women. Crenshaw developed the term as a way to explain the intersections of race and gender that affect the way some groups are excluded and marginalized because of the way that these characteristics intersect. The idea is a powerful way of understanding how we interact with each other in the workplace. When we come to work, we have multiple personalities. We are mixture of our ability/disability, social-economic class, age, sexual orientation, gender, race and more. You can be a white disabled man, or a black lesbian woman or even a wealthy older white man. These are not "additive" identities, but they are who we are as a whole. This is intersectionality.

Our identities are complex in nature and this is what allows us to bring something to the garden salad that is inclusion. A 65-year-old white gay man will bring a different experience than a 22-year-old black gay woman. Their identities may intersect in some ways, but they will still have very different perspectives because of their intersectional identities.

As we are multi-dimensional individuals, when we are examining inclusion, we need to look at how these dimensions affect inclusive workplace, workforce and marketplace practices. We also need to be aware that only looking at issues in terms of just one dimension of difference, falls short in allowing an inclusive mindset to truly reflect our communities, our team members, and our broader society.

Determining the intersectional identities in your organization as part of your inclusion journey has to be part of having an inclusive mindset. Teams need to come together to understand how intersectionality, power, privilege, and bias are being played out in your organization. These discussions can include dialog on how overlapping forms of bias affect employees as well as the connections that have been made based on intersectional identities. Using open discussions allows the complexities and nuances to emerge. This is a difficult thing to do and the importance of inclusive leaders who are able to coach their peers and facilitate these types of discussions cannot be underestimated.

The idea is not to target people but instead open up the discussion to allow all employees to participate.[43] Organizations can then develop an intersectional strategy as part of their overall inclusion strategy. The benefits of addressing intersectionality are felt in the same way inclusion strategies are. Organizations can become more competitive by focusing on the positive impact of intersectionality and inclusion. Intersectionality, additionally, is a very good tool in addressing the needs and wellbeing of employees. It creates space for leaders to be compassionate. It also identifies the potential areas where there may be a need to focus on emotional intelligence as a key quality of an inclusive leader. It lets employees know that their wellbeing is important and that their identity as a whole, and not just as additive parts, is a crucial part of their value and therefore inclusion.[44]

[43] https://www.goodcall.com/news/intersectionality-workplace-011486
[44] https://dupress.deloitte.com/dup-us-en/topics/talent/multidimensional-diversity.html

Organizations can also use this approach to inclusion to help them understand the positive aspects of intersectionality. It can be used to help bring people together because of shared connections. Our multiple identities allow us to connect with people in different ways and this is an asset when building inclusive organizations. This will be discussed further on in this book, but intersectionality is a vital tool for innovation and creativity as we can use shared connections to think about problems in new ways.

In the USA, intersectionality has an impact on the way in which US-EEOC (Equal Employment Opportunity Commission) requirements are managed as every single team member will be affected by multiple classes. A disabled black man who is a veteran for example, will be covered by multiple EEOC classes. Organizations will have to think about how to provide resources to employees that cover different intersectional identities.

Intersectionality in the workplace is more than just adjusting to EEOC requirements. Consider the fact that women receive higher levels of workplace bullying than other groups, alongside the fact that women of color are most likely to be denied a promotion. LGBTQI employees are also increasingly on the receiving end or derailing behaviors in the workplace. What does this then mean for a queer, woman of color working in your organization? The intersections of their identity will affect whether or not they feel included in a much bigger way than other employees.

This also has implications for inclusion strategies. How do we introduce practices and processes that allows engagement, empowerment, and enablement to incorporate intersectionality? If we are building inclusive organizational cultures, do we automatically address intersectionality? To move towards inclusion, organizations will have to create inclusive strategies that are unique to their particular organization with the aim of valuing every employee. To do this, organizations will have to actively embrace all aspects of someone's identity. Using intersectionality as the framework allows organizations to address the negative impacts of intersectionality but also brings positive benefits from connections made through intersectional identities.

Disrupting the Status Quo with Purpose

How does all of this fit into your own purpose and meaning in the workplace? And does your purpose and meaning in the workplace matter?

More than 70% of the American workforce dislike what they do for work. That is 7 out of 10 Americans who are going to have a large impact on the productivity of those people in the workforce and this means that the majority of Americans are not working to their full potential. It is estimated that it cost $550 billion a year in lost productivity. That is a lot of money that could have been pumped into the bottom line and into our economy.[45]

At the same time in a recent study it was found that 75% of people who were said to be happy at work reported that they had little meaning in their job.[46]

By focusing on making workers feel happy, their productivity increases but if we then add purpose, we get can get additional boost in productivity.

Finding meaning in our work gives us loyalty to the organization, promotes engagement, and also drives us to achieve more for the organization. Finding purpose matters.

On a personal level, as part of your personal journey, finding meaning helps to give your life more clarity. You can also feel more passionate about your own life goals and you can gain more satisfaction when you achieve life goals alongside professional goals. The gratification from this can drive you to achieve more and have a bigger positive impact on those around you. Your life can become one based on values rather than just your paycheck. You too can start to say, this is not what I do, this is who I am when you discuss your work and profession.

Do you know your life purpose? Do you know your professional purpose?

---

[45] Farmiloe, Brett, 2017.

[46] Amortegui, Jessica, 2014.

Do you know how to go about finding them?

Our life purposes depend on our many value systems and also on our individual spirituality. This is something that is a subjective journey that is not the focus of this book.

Our professional purpose can be found by examining some simple attributes and characteristics of who we are. Ask yourselves these questions[47]:

- What is your craft?
- What is it that you can do that is your passion?
- What is it that you do for fun?
- What is it that you are always trying to perfect?
- What skill do you have that you enjoy the most?

The answer to these questions may be many things, but these questions can help us to hone-in on some skills that link to our meaning and purpose at work.

To better understand our purpose:

1. Move away from WHAT and look at WHY.

    *Instead of goals that focus on being the most successful at something, you can look at goals that focus on being the most successful **for something**.*

2. Other people matter. In a book published by Bronnie Ware, a nurse who worked on a palliative care unit, she described what the five most common regrets of the dying were:

    - I wish I'd had the courage to live a life true to myself, not the life others expected of me.

---

[47] Ibid. 2014.

- I wish I hadn't worked so hard.

- I wish I'd had the courage to express my feelings.

- I wish I had stayed in touch with my friends.

- I wish that I had let myself be happier.[48]

Do you notice that none of these include work goals? All of them are related to our relationships with other people. This is true of our workplace relations and it is how we find meaning in work. That is what matters and that is where we can find purpose.

> *"There's no greater gift than to honor your life's calling. It's why you were born. And how you become most truly alive." – Oprah Winfrey*

Making It Stick

1. Remember a time in your personal life or professional life where you felt valued, respected, and appreciated. Write down three words that describe what it felt like when you were treated in this way.

    a. _____

    b. _____

    c. _____

2. Remember a time in your personal or professional life where you felt devalued, disrespected, or unappreciated. Write down three words that describe what it felt like when you were treated in this way.

    d. _____

    e. _____

---

[48] Steiner, Susie, 2012.

f. _____

3. Think about the impact on performance, engagement, teamwork, and safety when employees feel disrespected in the workplace. If their emotions are described the way you answered question number two, how effective would that organization be? Why is it important to understand dignity and respect in the workplace?

Reflective Questions

- What areas of your life do you just tolerate the way things are going?
- When you acknowledge this, how does it make you feel?
- Does it bring you joy or wellbeing to be tolerating these things?
- Do you think it helps you to lead a fulfilled life?
- How does it impact your relationships with the people around you?
- Do you think it is possible to change this?
- What can you do differently to change this behavior?

Questions In The Mirror

Why does the issue of moving beyond tolerance matter? Being tolerant is a feeling of being put up with and for most people it is a negative experience.

- Have you ever felt as though someone was tolerating you?
- How did it feel?
- Have you ever 'tolerated' someone else?
- How might it have impacted them?

Purpose Questions

- Do you know your life purpose?
- Do you know your professional purpose?

- Do you know how to go about finding them?

Our life purposes depend on our many value systems and also on our individual spirituality. Our professional purpose can be found by examining some simple attributes and characteristics of who we are. Ask yourselves these questions[49]:

- What is your craft?
- What is it that you can do that is your passion?
- What is it that you do for fun?
- What is it that you are always trying to perfect?
- What skill do you have that you enjoy the most?

---

[49] Ibid. 2014.

Chapter 3

The Team Journey

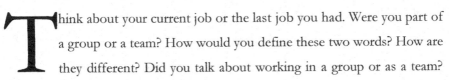

Think about your current job or the last job you had. Were you part of a group or a team? How would you define these two words? How are they different? Did you talk about working in a group or as a team? Why do you think you considered yourself as part of a group? Why did you think you considered yourself part of a team?

> *"Good teams incorporate teamwork into their culture, creating the building blocks for success." – Ted Sundquist*

In many cases, people use these two words interchangeably. But they are very different. Here is an example: William works in a large company as a salesperson. He manages four salespeople and is a senior manager. He respects the four salespeople he manages and always asks them for input on his decisions. They set their targets together and work to help each other when they don't meet them. Their performance is high, and they enjoy very good bonuses as a result. Meanwhile, William and the other senior managers have just been told that they will get a new boss. The boss arrives and immediately begins to shake things up.

The new boss does this without talking to any of the managers. They are frustrated by this and dislike this style of management. Their old boss involved them more in decisions and respected them as senior managers. They decide to tell their new boss about this and meet with her. At the meeting she tells them this is her management style, and she will not change this. They leave the meeting having achieved nothing. William does not tell the staff members that are on his team about the meeting and continues to support their work. They continue to perform well regardless of William's problems with his boss.

- What is the difference between William and the four salespeople he leads and the senior management members?
- Which one is a group, and which one is a team?
- Why is there a difference?
- What creates this difference?
- Why don't we say football, baseball, basketball groups? Why do we call them teams?

The main difference may seem obvious but oftentimes in our workplaces, we fail to acknowledge this. Very simply, this is the main way to distinguish between the two:

- **Groups** are individuals coming together for a cause or a reason.
- **Teams** are qualified people coming together to achieve a goal.

A team's strength therefore relies on whether or not the team is connected and can work together and also if they all believe in their goal. A groups success often comes from having a large enough number of people to carry out their tasks. When we place these definitions into our workplaces, we get a similar scenario. If we are part of a **work group,** then we are independent in our main goals and come together to work on a specific task. When we are part of a **work team,** we are working together with others towards achieving some unified goal.

When we work in teams or groups, the leadership style changes. Groups are dominated by a leader who normally has a more controlling style. The group leader will conduct meetings and assigns the tasks to the members of the group. In a best-case scenario, the team members will normally agree how to approach the task, they will often discuss things together and there may be more than one leader. The key goal with teams is to achieve their goal; anything other than that is a distraction.

In the example above, William runs a team of salespeople, but his boss runs a group of senior managers. The difference in this scenario is the focus on the goal. There is also a difference with William's leadership style and with the collaboration displayed by the sales managers. They are working together to achieve a goal.

- What difference does it make?
- Does it matter if you have a group or a team?

This section will explore these questions by looking at which set up produces the most opportunities for equity and inclusion and by doing so produces more successful organizations.

"None of us is as smart as all of us." – Ken Blanchard

The Workplace is Changing

Working in a group has obvious advantages; work can be done faster, and a group can be used to maximize expertise. Individuals working together on a specific task as a group can focus their skills on that specific task. A group of accountants working together can solve an accounting problem faster than one accountant working alone. As the saying goes, two heads are better than one. With groups though, the disadvantage is that the organization's goal or purpose is not as important as your own personal targets. In some cases, when working in a group, employees can forget about the organization's goals and purpose. This seems strange but it happens more often than you think!

Working in teams can mean that individuals work towards their own goals

and the organization's goals.

Working as a team takes the functions of groups and adds efficiency and gives the group a purpose. Teams work towards a specific goal together as an interdependent collective where they will have different expertise that are drawn together to reach the specific goal. Efficiency is achieved through this leveraging of the expertise from many different areas. When attempting to resolve an accounting related challenge, a team approach would include people who are not accountants. The team may include members of marketing groups who can provide insight into how accounting affects the marketing groups.

This way the team can solve a complex problem such as reducing costs of advertising. If it was left to the marketing groups alone, they miss an accounting aspect of the problem. If it was just left to the accountants alone, they may miss a marketing aspect of the problem. In this way, teams are more efficient than groups.

Teams need leaders in order to achieve efficiency. Without coordination, teams are not any more effective than groups. It is a common mistake to think that by setting up a team, performance will increase. Team dynamics are much more complicated than this and it involves many different parts, especially with the changing composition of many workforces.

Think of your favorite professional sports team and the coach that leads the team. Think about how much the coach affects the performance of the team. The coach does not work alone and would have assistant coaches, as well as administrative. front office, executive, marketing, sales staff, and much more.

The performance of the team is linked to the head coach, assistance coach, conditioning coach, strength coach, nutritional coach, and everyone involved in all levels of coaching as well as the administrative support staff. All these components will affect the performance of the entire team. As a sports fan, it's frustrating when you have great players but a coach that does not manage the team properly! Equally, we have all seen how a group of players can become champions at the hands of great coaches. It is hard to imagine a group of athletes trying to succeed without effective coaching.

Teams in the workplace, similarly, have this problem. With a good coach, i.e. a good manager who coordinates the team, they succeed. Without good coordination and management, they do not perform to the best of their ability.

Not only does teamwork matter but managing teams matter. The Equitable Workplace Institute found in numerous studies that when employees were asked what would incentivize them to give more of their best efforts at work, the number one answer has consistently been, *"Having A Boss That Treats Me With Dignity And Respect."*

This is especially true with teams. Without effective management of teams, they become ineffective and they can reduce morale **instead** of increase efficiency. In the book by Marcus Buckingham, mentioned earlier, he said their research found that while people join companies, ***they normally leave managers!*** Some degree of turnover in an organization is healthy. The turnover that most regret is when that turnover includes an increase in regrettable losses. By definition, regrettable losses are those employees often considered high potential. Their loss has a significant impact on the teams' mission.

The bigger challenge for many organizations is not managing the costs and productivity loss when acceptable voluntary turnover occurs. This is when people quit and leave that are not regrettable. That turnover is deemed the cost of doing business. Regrettable loss can also have a significant impact on a team or organization. Even more impactful than regrettable loss and voluntary turnover is a term we have coined called turn-under™.

Turnover is when people quit and leave
Turn-Under™ is when people quit...and stay!

There are significant number of employees in organizations who are being disrespected, tolerated, even avoided in the workplace that have already quit. They just haven't bothered to tell you they quit. Instead, they come in and collect a paycheck every day and only do what they have to do to avoid being seen as slacking off.

The success of any business cannot be guaranteed simply by getting a forward-thinking CEO; there needs to be teamwork. Without teamwork, even with the best CEO or the best set of leaders, the business will not be as successful as it can be. The goal of the leaders who want their organization to succeed should be to create a team that can survive without them. They should be aiming to create a team so strong that their departure will not fragment the team. Strong teams survive any change both externally and internally and therefore create the most successful organizations.

The workplace is a constantly changing place. The idea of working in teams instead of groups is not new. Groups are more hierarchical and come from an era of top-down management "knowing best" and of a time when creating inclusive cohesive teams was not considered important. When homogeneity was more important than allowing people to bring their whole self to the workplace, acculturation was not a term being discussed.

If you want your organization to be moved forward and become a successful inclusive organization, teaming together cannot be ignored.

"The best teamwork comes from men who are working independently toward one goal in unison." – James Cash Penney

---

Teaming together matters for these four main reasons[50]:

1. **Motivation:** Hopefully, we all know what it is like when we get a boost from working in a team. In successful teams, achieving goals together with teammates is a lot more satisfying. We have shared goals, we can share our problems, and there is a healthy level of competition.

---

[50] Nandagopal, Amrita, 2017.

Motivation grows as well because if we don't do our best, we don't just let ourselves down; we also let down our team. Working in a team can be helped by organizing team bonding activities.

2. **Faster Learning:** When you are working alone and you come across a problem, you have to solve it alone. There is an obvious benefit of working in a team; problems can be solved faster.

    However, there is a less obvious advantage. When we work in inclusive teams, we also learn faster because of the interactions we have. Not only do we learn from the other people on the team, but we also learn from team activities such as brainstorming. We learn different ways of thinking about a problem and different ways of solving problems from the way in which monolithic teammates might approach the challenge.

3. **Increased Interpersonal Skills:** Working on an inclusive team requires a certain set of skills including assertiveness, communication, confidence, patience, and other social skills. Working on a team also boosts these skills and improves interpersonal skills. Healthy inclusive teams are often places where we can accept constructive criticism and work on our faults. In these setting we tend to share our opinion more openly and develop good working relationships based on common goals and solving problems together. This is invaluable for the continued growth and success of organizations. It becomes a very effective and efficient way to develop individuals and is very cost effective. The more teamwork you have, the more successful individuals in your organization will be!

4. **Increased Efficiency:** Imagine you have five people who want to make paper airplanes, but they only have five minutes to make as many as they can. Each of the five set out and they all make as many as they can within

the time limit. Now imagine if the same five people decided to work together as a team. Instead of each person making a whole paper airplane, each person was assigned a specific role. Person one folded the paper in half and passed it on to person two. They then added one wing and passed it on to person three. Person three then added the second wing and pass it on to person four. Person four folded the wing to improve the aerodynamics and passed it onto person five. Person five then folds the last part of the wing and the airplane is complete. With this method the five people have five minutes to make as many airplanes as they can.

Which scenario produces the most airplanes? While it seems obvious that the team will make more airplanes than individuals producing their own, this type of teamwork has only really been understood for the last one hundred years. The level of efficiency increases because of the well-defined roles. In more complex teams this also happens, especially as tasks become more skilled and defined.

This is why inclusive teaming matters. In the next sections, how to achieve this will be discussed and specific tools provided on how to move from groups to inclusive teams.

Moving From Being a Group to Being a Team

One of the most amazing things about humanity, is that almost every single major accomplishment we have achieved has been the result of groups working together to achieve a shared goal. That is pretty amazing if you stop and think about it. It also demonstrates how important teams are – working in teams really matters!

If this is the case, why is it so hard to form inclusive teams? Why is it so hard to achieve teamwork? And why is there no secret formula to achieving teamwork? We are complex individuals that shift from System 1 thinking to System 2 thinking all the time. We are unpredictable and complex, and this makes creating inclusive, respectful teams hard. It is not impossible though!

The biggest challenge when moving from a group to a team is convincing the members to cooperate. Groups operate on individual goals, while teams focus on shared goals. Shifting this can be hard as individuals will often ask, "Why should I work with others?" or "What will I get from working with others?" You also have to decide who will be the leader of this newly formed team. This changes the dynamics of the group and can be a tricky balancing act. The new leader needs to be able to lead the team but not manage a group. Finding the distinction is a delicate process. While the new person needs to establish some sort of authority, they also need to be able to get the new team to collaborate and work towards a shared goal. They need the team to communicate effectively and for opinions to matter in the new discussions. If this is not achieved, then the new person could become simply the new authoritarian figure no different from the leader of a group. So, what is needed to move from a group to a team **successfully?**

> *"When the student is ready the teacher will appear. When the student is truly ready, the teacher will disappear." - Lao Tzu*

First of all, we need to look at what are the stages of a team. In the 1970s, Tuckman suggested that there were four main stages when teams are developing:

- Forming – This is when teams meet, and they start to work together.
- Storming – As described above, this is when the leader is decided and when struggles can occur as the team members try to figure out who will lead them.
- Norming – The team members accept their positions along with the

rules that determine how the team will work.

- <u>Performing</u> – the teams starts to work efficiently and start to produce results.

This is an important analysis, and it is important to recognize that the way teams move through these stages depends on the leadership, the tasks or goals, the capabilities of the team members, and the makeup of the team. Importantly, no team can avoid the "storming" phase; teams must prepare for this tricky stage.

With increasing levels of difference in the workplace, the process of successfully navigating to get to the performing stage can be hindered. Adding the multitude of differences that exist in what was previously a homogeneous group can make the process of norming much more difficult and thus delay the performing stage. **The importance of moving from a group that has differences that are avoided or tolerated to a team that respects and values those differences is critical.**

FOR EXAMPLE: In some organizations, there are as many as five generations in the workforce! When taking into account all the attributes of difference that exist, this aspect of difference illustrates the potential misalignment that can exist in values, work ethics, communications, motivation, loyalty, approaches to conflict, collaboration, and more.

Imagine all the disparities that exist due to intersectional differences. This topic will be discussed in more detail later in this book. Intersectionality includes gender, marital status, ethnicity, language, race, thinking styles, communication styles, and much more. These differences must be valued and respected to allow the group forming process to happen sooner rather than later. Without there being respect and value associated with these attributes of difference, the productivity of the group can be negatively impacted.

Since the existence of diversity in the workplace is not an option, the challenge is having leaders that can inclusively and respectfully manage that diversity. Many people cite the existence of a diverse team as the reason for better performance and productivity. The reality is having a diverse team actually increases the level of tension, disagreements, and slows down decision making, especially if the team members feel that they are being disrespected, not valued, or simply being tolerated. What actually leads to increased workplace performance is when the diverse team becomes inclusive.

Having a team leader that provides for the welfare of their team members, regardless of their aspect of difference, and produces an environment where everyone feels their input is wanted and needed, creates high performing teams. This is what drive long term organizational success, even if it takes a little more time in the norming process to occur.[51]

Being an inclusive leader takes effort and requires new skills that some managers do not have in their toolkit. This book also provides some insights about what those specific skills are and provides ways to acquire and develop them.

Teams can sometimes go backwards with these stages; they can, for example, struggle through the norming stage and so revert back to the storming stage. Or they can be at the performing stage and then return to the norming stage.

These stages also demonstrate that moving from being a group to becoming a team **is a process** and even though teams may get to the performing stage, they could fall back to the norming stage if they are not coordinated. They also demonstrate that in order to form a team, a specific strategy and specific skills are needed to guide a group towards achieving teamwork.

Without moving towards forming teams, it is unlikely that inclusive competencies can be developed and entrenched in your organizational culture. Developing and maintaining teams is one of the key first steps towards developing successful inclusive organizations.

---

[51] Dike, P. (2013) *The Impact of Workplace Diversity on Organisations*

As a leader tasked with creating this transformation, there is a success toolkit to achieve this – based on selecting and developing an inclusive leader/coach. This is a simple way to transform groups into teams as a specific inclusive leader/coach can help to lead the process of setting up additional leaders within the team and to simultaneously create teamwork. This person needs to have the inclusive leadership skills to achieve this; they need to be assertive, confident, creative, open, innovative, strong, good communicators, and team players. This person can then guide the team through the process. Having an independent inclusive leader/coach allows disputes to be resolved along the way and it also allows the team to have an expert to turn to as necessary.

Identifying A Inclusive Leader/Coach [52]

Selecting a senior leader to act as an inclusive leader/coach to work with your group, can increase your chances of successfully forming a team. This type of leader can determine whether or not your transformation proves successful or not. Their key tasks can include:

- Selecting who is a team member.
- Identifying roles for each team member.
- Selecting and coaching the team leader.
- Moving the team through the stages.
- Deciding when the team moves through different stages.
- Advising on team rules.
- Put the team at ease when challenges arise.
- Monitoring alliances within the team to ensure they are productive.

The inclusive leader/coach will need to be sure that they operate within their own strengths and weaknesses. They need to outline their expectations of

---

[52] Allan, M., 2015.

what they expect from the team from the start; and they need the team members to do the same. They will need to pay special attention to how the rules and guidelines are formed and provide input into how they are finally agreed upon. These need to be fair and above all, focused on how the team will achieve their goals.

Hold A Forming Meeting

The first meeting of the new team is the first part of the "forming" stage. The inclusive leader/coach plays a key role in this meeting. The meeting can be a difficult balancing act, with members of the group trying to work out where they rank in the group. At this meeting, the inclusive leader/coach will set up the grounding for the team and set out the following:

1. Introduce the team members and explain why they are part of the team.
2. Determine the goal(s) of the team.
3. Define each person's role in the team.
4. Discuss and detail expectations.
5. Develop rules and guidelines of the group.
6. Ensure each team member contributes to rules and guidelines.
7. Decide on how to reward and recognize success. Feedback mechanism can also be included.
8. Define decision making processes.
9. Encourage team members to share concerns.

Lead The Team Through The Storming Stage

This is both an unavoidable and challenging phase. The guidance of the inclusive leader/coach will be tested. The original goals and rules set out in the first stage will be tested as the team tries to interpret these. The inclusive leader/coach will need to guide and support the team through this by helping to select the leaders of the team. They will need to rely on the guidelines they formed in the first stage to get them through this stage. They will have to continuously remind the team of these guidelines to steer them through this stage.

The inclusive leader/coach will also need to rely on their communication skills at this stage. They will need to assertively discuss any problems and also encourage team members to be open. Open communication is the key to surviving this stage; without it, the team will likely regenerate and return to the first stage.

By the end of the storming stage, the team members should be comfortable with their roles but will also have chosen a leader or leaders. They will be able to start functioning and will be comfortable with the way the team operates.

If at any point a new team member is introduced, returning to the storming stage can be useful to reassert the rules and guidelines of the team.

Guide The Team Through The Norming Stage

The turbulence of the storming stage is followed by the acceptance and focus of the norming stage. The inclusive leader/coach will guide the team through this as well, ensuring that rules and regulations are followed and that any grievances that come up are dealt with. The team in this stage will be working towards their goals; focused on achieving these above all else. The inclusive leader/coach can focus now on developing the capabilities of individuals within the team and support the team leader(s) to reach their potential.

Facilitate The Jump To Performing

The next task is to get the team to jump up to the performing level. This can be a difficult thing to achieve. **The norming stage is an enabled team while the performing team is an engaged team.**

The norming stage is comfortable, it is secure, and it is not very risky.

However, although during the norming stage team members might think they are working towards their goals, they have not reached their true potential; they are not working towards the team's goals. The inclusive leader/coach is vital in encouraging the team leader(s) to get the team to this stage by focusing on the teams shared goals. They will facilitate communication and make sure that the team is driving towards their goal.

Each team member will know what the goals are, why they were set, and will be determined to meet them. They will be rewarded for this and the team will grow as individuals and as a group because of this. Once this stage has been achieved, the inclusive leader/coach will then take a less direct role and manage the strategy of the team as it moves forward.

They will also help the team leader(s) to grow by establishing challenges which will help them to increase their own emotional intelligence, vital for the success of their team and for their own development. At this stage, the inclusive leader/coach can also bring in independent outside help to work with the team to achieve their goals. They can bring in leaders to inspire the team or to help build better work environments. They can also bring in outside help to further guide the team towards their goal and towards the organizations purpose.

Lastly, the inclusive leader/coach and the team leader(s) must accept that the team will always be adapting, changing and growing. This is the definition of a team! This should be seen as a success and encouraged. As goals are met and new ones introduced, the team should be rewarded and their achievements recognized but they should also be reminded that they will always have to adapt to change, and they will always grow as a result. The benefits of this are almost limitless; teams allow individuals to grow and by doing so, also increase the success of your organization.

No Time for Tolerance With Teams

Think of an airline like United Airlines. They hire people who have the key skills to be flight attendants, pilots, grounds crew, engineers, cleaners, counter-staff, accountants, project managers, salespeople, marketing experts, managers, and so on. They come from all walks of life and in many cases, they come from many different countries. They bring very specific skills and expertise in order to fulfill the function of their role. They will be a diverse group of people but share one thing – they all are (or at least they should be) working towards the larger goal of the success of United Airlines. They are all working to ensure that passengers flying with United have a safe and enjoyable flying experience. Occasional news stories will highlight when an employee interacts with a customer in a way that is outside the organizational values. It has resulted in situations where passengers have been physically dragged off airlines, only to find it was a bias of one specific employee and not the policy of the airline. In those cases, momentarily, that employee puts the overall goal of the airline as a secondary consideration to their own blind spot.

"Talent wins games, but teamwork and intelligence wins championships." – Michael Jordan

---

One of the most important values a person has is their ability to work on a team. For a team to successfully perform at optimal levels each team member must be willing to move beyond tolerance. Without this ability, the team will never move beyond a group. To develop successful teams that have strong levels of teamwork and are **at the performing stage** requires everyone on the team to move beyond tolerance and towards acceptance and valuing all differences.

Aunt Suzie's – Apron Wisdom

"You Don't Have A Respect Problem..

You Have An Entitlement Problem!"

Derailing Behaviors

Why is moving beyond tolerance so important for teams? Because derailing behaviors are becoming more and more prevalent and are occurring in every organization, in every industry, in every part of the world. These behaviors prevent organizations from reaching their true potential. The goal then becomes how do we change derailing behaviors? In the study by the University of Houston described in earlier chapters, the fiscal impact of derailing behaviors on organizations was calculated. The detail of how fiscally impactful these behaviors are will be detailed fully in the organizational chapter of this book and the addendum.

Workplace derailing behaviors are behaviors that, whether intentional or not, sabotage, undermine, or weaken an employee's commitment, passion or willingness to conduct their responsibilities at their full potential.

The problem is widespread. A longitudinal study conducted by the Equitable Workplace Institute partnered with the University of Houston's International Institute for Diversity & Cross Cultural Management, 2006 through 2014, found more than 71 percent of employees had witnessed on average four derailing behaviors per year.

These behaviors manifest themselves in many ways. The first step in beginning to reduce them is to get some conceptual clarity about what derailing behaviors are, how prevalent they are, and how they affect your business metrics.

The four primary types of derailing behaviors measured in this longitudinal study were:

- Broken Dignity Entitlements
- Micro-Inequities
- Workplace Bullying
- Acts of Incivility/Disrespect

Each of these terms was coined in other studies that began the process of identifying the impact of derailing behaviors. While those studies did not carry their research far enough to fiscally quantify the damage these behaviors create for an organizational bottom line, they provided a useful starting place when identifying these behaviors. Once these behaviors have been identified, they can be addressed, and inclusive competencies can be developed to reduce them.

Let's look at each one more closely.

Broken Dignity Entitlements

This is based on the work of Michael B. Arthur and Denice M. Rousseau. Dignity entitlements are wide ranging but include "the right to be heard, to receive recognition in proportion to one's contributions, to receive fair evaluations based on performance rather than personality style, professional background, race, gender, sexual preference, or some other personal characteristic."[53]

To demonstrate what happens when these are broken, think about this scenario. You have been working in a company for a long time, perhaps a decade. You perform well and you are respected in the organization. The organization brings in new management and so you get a new boss. This boss doesn't respect you and does not value your opinions. The new boss removes some of your responsibilities from your role and then decides to evaluate your performance.

---

[53] Arthur, M. B., & Rousseau, D. (1996). Pg. 28 – 39.

They give you a negative evaluation claiming that you are not innovative, and you do not achieve as much as you used to. How would you feel in this situation? Would you be pleased with the new manager? Would you want to stay in this position? The relationship between power and the entitlement to dignity is clear in this situation.

Micro-Inequities

Micro-inequities are derailing behaviors that are harder to define and therefore harder to find. They are often subconscious, always subtle, and they are used to devalue, overlook, ignore, or discount an individual. The acts are often hard to notice as they are based on gestures, voice inflection, facial expressions, and nuances that are hard to pick up on. This is their power. The person acting out micro-inequities, when they are caught can easily deny that they occurred, or they can say that it was a misunderstanding. There is little evidence of their acts and so it is hard for these behaviors to be caught.

Rowe described them as: "tiny, damaging characteristics of an environment… (that) affect a person not indigenous to that environment. They are distinguished by the fact that for all practical purposes one cannot do anything about them; one cannot take them to court or file a grievance."[54] These actions often occur because of prejudice against someone's characteristics that are not related to work performance such as gender, race, age, religion, nationality or ethnicity but they can also happen for other reasons. They also have a unique feature; they are small actions that are hard to notice. However, their impact is never small. Although they are small, collectively and over time, they can cause a lot of damage. Rowe compares them to the effect of a drop of water; one drop has an impact, but continuous drops can be destructive. It has often been said that a drop of water from a leaking faucet can put a hole in

---

[54] Rowe, 1990. Pg. 153–163.

concrete over time. In the same way, one act of prejudice that is barely visible has a negative impact, but many small acts of prejudice together create systemic prejudice.

Workplace Bullying

This is often the most visible form of derailing behavior. While there isn't one definitive definition, in 2014 a National Survey on workplace bullying defined it as: "repeated mistreatment; abusive conduct that is threatening, humiliating, or intimidating, work sabotage, or verbal abuse."[55] Even with this definition, bullying can take on many different forms aimed at undermining your dignity. There are normally a number of common characteristics of workplace bullying:

- It is negative mistreatment. This can take many forms.
- It is repeated. The negative conduct is more than once.
- It is persistent. It does not stop over time.
- It is intentional. The bully wants you to feel intimidated, degraded, offended, or humiliated.
- It is aggression. It is not assertive, and it is not normal behavior and can escalate.

Bullying can often be difficult to recognize and if you are being bullied you may think it is normal 'aggressive' management culture. Often people being bullied think that if they complain about it, others will see them as weak or not able to do their job. Maybe you fear that someone will say that you are overreacting or not "strong enough" to take on a tough working culture. People being bullied also fear retribution or further victimization if they complain about bullying. Co-workers are often reluctant to act as witnesses as they think that they will be bullied as well for speaking up. Most often the bully is a manager

---

[55] Namie, Gary, 2014.

(70+%) and the person that they target is usually their top producer or performer. This is normally the person that they feel is a threat to their professional standing in the organization.

Workplace Incivility

Like incivility in our personal lives, workplace incivility is behavior that is insensitive, discourteous, inconsiderate, rude, or ambiguous but aims to cause harm. [56] This behavior always displays a lack of regard for others and this conduct is often an understudied aspect of organizational cultures. In a 2001 study, Cortina, Magley, Williams, and Langhout found out that over a period of 5 years more than 70% of respondents experienced some form of workplace incivility. [57] Like incivility in our personal lives, there are many forms that incivility in the workplace can take. These include:

- Disrupting meetings.
- Publicly reprimanding coworkers.
- Putting people down emotionally.
- Refusing to speak to certain people or giving them the silent treatment.
- Interrupting others, not listening to others, speaking in a condescending tone and other negative forms of communication.

Broken Dignity Entitlements, Micro-Inequities, Workplace Bullying, and Acts of Incivility are terms coined in other studies that began the process of identifying the impact of derailing behaviors, but those studies didn't carry their research far enough to fiscally quantify the link to the bottom line, top line, or pipeline. In the organizational section of this book, we will provide examples of just how financially impactful these behaviors are.

Inclusive teams have to move beyond tolerance and have to mitigate or

---

[56] Zauderer, D. G. 2002. Pg. 36 – 42.
[57] Cortina et al, 2001. Pg. 64–80.

eliminate these derailing behaviors. Derailing behaviors are a sign that there is little inclusion in the organizational culture or on the team.

Workplace bullying is devastating for teamwork. If members of the team are threatened or humiliated, they may have little trust in the team. They can be intimidated and become unwilling to function as part of the team. They can be fearful that their actions will be punished, and as a result they may be reluctant to participate in team activities. If the purpose of a team is to build employees, workplace bullying as a derailing behavior is the direct opposite of this goal. Corporate bullying destroys employees and leaves them unable to perform basic functions. If bullying emerges in a team and it is left to fester, the team will very quickly degenerate back to a group. There will be little chance for the team to survive let alone grow. It's the same with other types of derailing behaviors – broken dignity entitlements, micro-inequities, and acts of incivility.

Think of their impact on the performance of a team.

- Is it possible for a team that is at the norming level to advance to the more effective stage of performing if the team suffers from a plague of micro-inequities?
- What would the impact of broken dignity entitlements on a team? If team members are not given the right to be heard, can they actually be part of the team?

One very common consequence of intolerance is workplace incivility. When we are tolerating other people, to return the definition, we are 'putting up with' the existence of something that we don't agree with. If we think about things that we tolerate in our own life, we can see how these can have a negative impact on us. Say for example your significant other is often late in getting ready to go out. Each time you need to go out you end up waiting for them to get ready. You tolerate this behavior, but it annoys you and you don't like being late. What happens in this situation?

Now imagine if there is a similar situation in your workplace when we are trying to form professional relationships. Imagine a coworker who is always late. Or imagine your coworker is bigoted in some way and you tolerate their prejudice.

- *What will ultimately happen in this situation?*
- *What will happen if nothing changes over a month, or over a year?*
- *Can you work in this situation for a decade?*

Our ability to perform is reduced as we focus so much of our attention on these problems, and we lose motivation. The key benefits of working in a team are lost as we cannot grow, we cannot be innovative, we lose open communication, we stop sharing knowledge, and we lose our shared objectives.

Groups that have not started moving beyond intolerance are in danger of falling into this pattern and this is why there is no time for tolerance in teams.

Valuing Differences is More Than Being Tolerant

To get to the last stage of team formation, the performing stage, and to become successful teams, as listed in the tool kit above, teams need to value each member of the team.

Due to this, one core aspect of teamwork is valuing and respecting the differences of team members. It is how teams thrive. The different skills, aptitudes, attitudes and ways of thinking that different team members bring to the team is why teams are more successful than groups. Inclusive teams encourage diverse thinking and rely on all team members as this creates the type of creativity that can lead to effective and efficient work that meets the team's goals.

As discussed earlier in this book, valuing diversity is often seen as being tolerant. In that section, I argued that moving beyond tolerance is vital for any organization. I argued that if organizations are not tolerant, they won't benefit from the different experiences, insights, and expertise brought by their people. Their goals could be impacted, and they may have coworkers who have little understanding among each other. Equally, if teams view tolerance as a way to value differences, the team will struggle with achieving their goals. Valuing difference has to move towards inclusion and towards accepting and valuing every team member as a unique and vital contributor. This is the only way to benefit from each team member and to benefit from the many skills, talents, and experiences within the team.

In the previous section, this was elaborated on when discussing "Treating Others How They Want to be Treated." In that section we looked at the difference between treating people how you want to be treated and treating people with respect and empathy and therefore, treating them how **they** want to be treated. This is a key difference as explained in that section and can be applied here.

Valuing differences is about respecting the fact that other people are different from you and it is about seeing the value in that. It is recognizing that we are all different and ultimately that difference is the only constant that we will face. People around us will always be different and we need to value those differences. That difference is a positive thing for many reasons as described earlier and it is more than simply tolerating differences.

"You manage things; you lead people." —Rear Admiral Grace Murray Hopper

---

To truly value differences we need to recognize that:

- There are many differences among people and see that as a valuable asset.

- Our differences bring with them a better understanding of the world around us and in the workplace, this relates to what our consumers/clients want and need.

- Valuing differences is about valuing ideas and input from your **entire** team.

- Valuing differences is more than knowing when to kiss, bow, or shake hands. It is about being culturally fluent and having intercultural agility skills. More on these skills later.

- By valuing differences, we can increase our openness and so solve problems much quicker.

In the last section of this book, I will discuss how you can develop intercultural agility skills to create a culture that values differences and diversity. This is at an individual and organizational level.

Understanding the Importance of Inclusion in Teams

The previous sections discussed the evidence and data that supports the theory that when we have a more inclusive workforce, we end up with more innovative and profitable organizations. The previous sections also looked at why inclusion is more important than simply tolerating differences in organizations. From this, comes the next challenge which is to incorporate inclusion into organizations at the team level.

"No man will make a great leader who wants to do it all himself, or to get all the credit for doing it." — *Andrew Carnegie*

The problem with building inclusive teams is although they are more productive, as can be expected when you have many different people with different ideas and different outlooks and backgrounds, managing the team dynamics can be very challenging.

For this reason, creating inclusive respectful teams have been described as a double-edged sword. This is because while they bring with them benefits that increase productivity, they also are not automatically a success. If leveraging differences among team members was left to their own devices, they would rarely create high productivity. They often fragment under the pressure of different demands, which is the result of the different perspectives that give them their advantage at the same time. They need to be controlled and they need someone to lead them. The idea of having an inclusive leader/coach as discussed in earlier sections, demonstrates how this can be achieved. In a sense, homogenous groups are like people teaching themselves how to play an instrument whereas divergent teams are like an orchestra; the latter needs a conductor to keep them together. Without a conductor they will lose their rhythm and play out of tune very quickly.

Just as teamwork doesn't happen automatically, inclusive teams do not just happen either. An inclusive mindset needs to be embedded into the team as a specific behavior. Without this effort, teams are just groups and do not function higher than any other group.

The trick is to use an inclusive leader/coach to create the culture of inclusion within the team. If this happens at the forming stage and becomes part of the rules and guidelines of the team, it is likely it will become a flourishing part of the team. As in earlier sections, there needs to be work on unconscious biases to develop self-awareness. This can be the first step in developing tools to address these biases. The team must be involved in the development of inclusive practices that addresses these biases as well as any other tools used to increase inclusion and maintain it for the lifetime of the team.

Inclusion needs to become embedded into the team. It needs to become as natural as any other part of the teamwork. It needs to be rewarded but it also needs to become part of everyday work life. Without this, teams will not be able to stay in the performing stage and will soon drift back towards stages that are not as effective. It is the role of the inclusive leader/coach to ensure that this does not happen, and this is an ongoing role as part of the journey of the team.

Encouraging Your Team Starts With Respecting Your Team

The NYSE was founded 200 years ago in 1817, and today there are over 2,700 companies listed on the exchange. Every day over $160 billion is traded against these companies. Their value falls and rises depending on two things: their profitability and their productivity.

While these are no doubt important measures of a company's success, they do not tell the full story of how well a company is doing. If a company exists solely to produce profit and that is their goal, there will be little cooperation among the workers of that organization. As cooperation is reduced, the organization will build a culture based on self-interest and distrust. When companies move towards a focus on values instead, then they will begin to build teamwork and respect. As a leader, if your focus is on profits as the end goal, then you will create an environment of competition. If you focus on values such as teamwork, then you will create a culture of trust and respect.

"We have to bring this world back to sanity and put the greater good ahead of self-interest." - Paul Polman

---

In order for there to be trust among your teams, you need to trust your teams. Teams develop when they are respected and that starts with the respect they receive from their leaders.

In a study conducted by the Harvard Business Review, 20,000 employees around the world were asked about what qualities they wanted in a leader.[58] Again and again, one quality was always the most requested quality. Employees

---

[58] Porath, Christine, 2015.

simply wanted to be respected by their leaders. But it was not just simple a measurement of how well someone led their teams. It was also an indication into how much commitment they gave to their organization and as above, how engaged they were; "....when it comes to garnering commitment and engagement from employees, there is one thing that leaders need to demonstrate: respect. No other leadership behavior had a bigger effect on employees across the outcomes we measured."[59]

In that survey, people said that when they were treated with respect by their leaders, they were 55% more likely to be engaged. With more respect, 56% had better health and wellbeing, and 89% had more job satisfaction. When people felt they were respected by their leaders, there was 92% more prioritization and focus.

WHEN LEADERS TREAT YOU WITH RESPECT, YOU'RE MORE ENGAGED
Based on a study of nearly 20,000 employees around the world.

What is your level of engagement at work?

How often does your leader treat you with respect?

SOURCE ANALYSIS OF "WHAT IS YOUR QUALITY OF LIFE AT WORK?" SURVEY DATA BY CHRISTINE PORATH   HBR.ORG

Respect Matters.

It matters to your bottom line but more importantly, it matters to the

---

59 Ibid, 2015.

success and reputation of your organization in the long term. While respect cannot be measured in a way that you could use on the NYSE, it is just as important as the records of productivity and profit.

What is Respect? Respect is about making choices about how we behave towards others to show them that we value them. Respect is about behaving in positive ways to show that you value someone or a team. We show respect in a variety of ways including treating other people how they want to be treated, communicating assertively but not aggressively, being inclusive, listening and changing our behavior as necessary. All of our communication and behaviors can be used to demonstrate our respect for others.

- *What can you do to respect your teams more?*
- *What can you do to improve respect in your organization?*
- *How can you move from groups to teams and make sure that respect becomes a value used by your teams?*

Leaders can respect their teams by:

- **Removing as much hierarchy as possible!** The less hierarchy there is, the more teamwork there is. By removing hierarchy, you empower your team members and motivate them to take on new challenges and to become leaders themselves!

- **Encouraging your team starts with respecting your team!** Before you can encourage your team, you need to respect them. Respecting your team shows that you value them and without this it would be impossible to encourage them.

- **Recognize hard work!** When you see good work, recognize it. It is a huge reason why people are motivated and more engaged. Want to people to feel respected? Tell them when they do good work.

- **Let them figure it out!** If you give out orders every day, you automatically are telling your employees you do not want them to make decisions. Respect them by letting them solve problems and make decision.

- **Delegate and then delegate more!** Trust your employees more by giving them more challenging tasks. Show them that you respect their capabilities and let them gain ownership of the work. Let go of micromanaging – it creates distrust and shows you do not respect your team.

- **Set goals!** Setting goals shows your team that you believe in their abilities. This was discussed in detail in earlier sections of this book. Setting challenging goals is a way to show your team you respect their abilities.

- **Empower your employees!** Highlight the strengths of everyone in your team. This shows how much you respect them, and it also motivates them as well.

- **Build a Strong Foundation.** This is perhaps the most important way to build respect. Let everyone know that you work for them as a leader, and not the other way around.[60] Your employees should be seen as **your first customers.** Earn their trust and respect and they will treat other people with trust and respect. They will also treat **your second customers**, your consumers, clients, customers, with trust and respect.

KEEPING IT REAL: I consulted in many locations around the world for an organization that had invested millions of dollars in something they called "The Total Employee Experience". Everyone who worked for the company was getting this drilled into their vernacular on a daily basis. The importance of keeping this at top-of-mind awareness was very obvious and several senior leaders were incredibly proud of this initiative. Their own data showed that customers didn't necessarily feel that they were receiving the level of attention and commitment commensurate with this effort. Sure, they heard the words, but

---

[60] Pozin, Ilya, 2013.

they sensed that it was just that, lip service and toleration.

Upon completion of several focus groups with employees, the problem became immediately evident. While this was truly an admirable effort to make sure everyone felt the service of the customers had to be at top-of-mind awareness, employees felt they could not take this commitment seriously. They said the right things, acted the right way, and towed the company line. At the end of the day, the problem was that the company had omitted one critical step from this massive global process.

There would never be a true commitment to **The Total Customer Experience**, if the organization didn't firstly implement a massive effort linked to **The Total Employee Experience.** In a focus group, one employee said it very well. "How can you expect me to super-serve a customer when the organization does not super-serve me or my team?" Employees were not feeling respected. They were not getting from their employer, what their employer wanted them to give to their customers. RESPECT! As was mentioned above, this meant:

- Removing as much hierarchy as possible.
- Encouraging your team starts with respecting your team.
- Recognize hard work.
- Let them figure it out.
- Delegate and then delegate more.
- Set goals!
- Empower your employees!
- Build a strong foundation.

"Your vision will become clear only when you look into your heart.
He who looks outside, dreams. He who looks inside awakens."

- Carl Jung

In a Harvard Business Review survey, over 54% of respondents stated that they don't regularly get respected by their leaders.[61] This means that in 54% of those cases, there were highly reduced levels of engagement. Those organizations were not as successful as they could be. We always need to get more out of less. By respecting employees, leaders can achieve this and also improve the value and success of the organizations.

Teamwork and Inclusion Takes Commitment, Effort and Courage

"As you move outside of your comfort zone, what was once the
unknown and frightening becomes your new normal." – Robin S.
Sharma

There are reasons why organizations struggle to introduce inclusion; it is difficult to achieve, it takes a long time, it is a process, and it is hard to measure.

In most organizations, metrics and numbers are king. If you want to discuss any part of the organization's performance, you will need to measure it. It would be difficult to describe performance without using some form of metrics. Most Offices of Diversity, Equity, and Inclusion have created techniques to measure metrics or statistics related to head count that really have

---

[61] Porath, Christine, 2014.

no indication of the level of inclusion or impact on organizational business metrics. Measures such as how many women, immigrants or people of color do you have in your organization today versus three years ago. These numbers have little bearing on how you have impacted the topline (revenue growth), the bottom line (cost reductions), or the pipeline (recruiting, retention and/or talent management) in fiscally quantifiable ways.

How many tables have you sponsored at the Hispanic, Asian, African American, or Diversity Council event has little significance to employees looking for ways to gain new skills, compete for the next promotion, improve their ranking on the high potential list, or much of anything that matters to many of your stakeholders including your diverse employees, customers, and investor specific stakeholders.

Most progressive organizations recognize how important teamwork is for their ability to fulfill their vision and mission. Measuring the level of teamwork within an organization is not as easy as the metrics linked to the changing demographics or awards and tables sponsored.

Say for example you want to work out how much teamwork your organization has, how would you do this? It is possible but it is not a simple process. It would require a large amount of analysis before some sort of quantifiable survey could be launched and data collected on that basis. However, the data would have to be **both quantitative and qualitative.** You would have to understand what people thought teamwork meant, you would have to look at what types of teams exist, you would also need to understand if people think teamwork is growing or decreasing. There would be many other areas that you need to think about. One of the more challenging aspects would be the ability to structure quantitative measures that validate the fiscal benefits or costs associated with your successfully implementing teamwork initiatives or not having reached those specific goals.

Measuring the level of inclusion would be equally difficult. How do you measure how valued employees feel? How would you measure if people feel accepted? How would you measure your team's ability to accept new ideas and input? It is definitely possible to measure these "softer" issues, but it is much harder than measuring simple metrics related to head count and awards received. Many organizations keep an inclusion scorecard, so they measure various inclusion factors over time and monitor the growth or decline of these. This will be discussed further in the organizational section of this book.

There is another reason why teamwork and inclusion are so hard; they require commitment, effort, fiscal commitment, and courage. This means that organizations have to make clear decisions to invest their time in changing the institutional culture. They have to ensure that these measures include dedicated teams working to ensure that an inclusive mindset remains a priority and process and that they persevere when the challenges emerge.

Engaging Your Team Starts With How They Show Up

In November 2016, Gallup conducted a poll that demonstrated that 70% of employees consider themselves to be disengaged at work.[62] That is 7 out of every 10 workers across America. That means that only 30% of employees are working to achieve organizational goals. In the last section, we showed how efficiency can be improved when employees become engaged team members. Imagine the transformation of any workforce if 70% of workers are transformed into engaged workers!

Gallup also identified that there is a correlation between engagement and the following nine performance metrics:

1. Quality and Defects
2. Safety incidences
3. Absenteeism
4. Shrinkages (theft)
5. Turnover

---

[62] REFERENCE

6. Productivity

7. Profitability

8. Customer Ratings[63]

If a manager does not have the skills or experience to lead inclusively, they will struggle. Introducing an inclusive leader/coach with the skills and experience to achieve this is one way to solve this problem.

The problem is that in order to introduce an inclusive leader/coach, an organization needs to know that **they need one.** They also need to be aware of the various stages of team development and how best to move their groups through these stages. The executives will in some way need to monitor the inclusive leader/coach to ensure that they do a great job!

It is rare for leaders or managers to get this type of training as it is very specific. This is unfortunate as a small amount of training can mean that groups moving towards becoming teams can avoid a lot of challenges by being led by managers and inclusive leader/coaches who can guide them through the harder stages. As a leader or a manager, having these skills demonstrates how you have decided to **show up.**

Take this example. You work in an organization as a senior manager. Your boss would like there to be more teamwork in the organization, so has decided that the senior managers will work as an inclusive productive team on a particular project with a specific two-year goal. Your boss sends out a memo and asks you to organize a meeting to set up the first team meeting. They ask you to lead the meeting and to tell everyone else about how the goal will be achieved. They do not provide any other instructions.

- *How would you achieve teamwork from these instructions?*

- *How would you react?*

- *More importantly, how has your boss showed up?*

---

[63] https://www.liquidplanner.com/blog/7-ways-to-get-your-team-members-more-engaged/

- *Do they really value this effort?*

- *Do they really want teamwork to be developed?*

- *Or are they just following an order?*

- *Do they know the best way to form an inclusive productive team?*

- *Do they know how to develop teams?*

This example has happened before – I have seen it in workplaces many times when leaders have decided to come to work but do not show up to work. What is the difference? A leader who comes to work, enters the workplace physically but they stop there. They do the minimal amount of work, they avoid conflict, they make sure everyone is doing their job, but they do not push anyone towards excelling, and they want teamwork but do not provide a success toolkit.

On the other hand, a leader who shows up to work, comes into the workplace both physically and mentally. They are there. They understand how to get the best out of the people in the organization and they understand the importance of developing teams.

A leader who comes to work might be able to create a team that is enabled but only a leader that shows up to work will be able to create a team that is engaged. In the last section, this distinction was made as follows:

"The norming stage is an enabled team while the performing

team is an engaged team."

This is described as the jump that moves teams from working together to teams that are working towards shared goals.

Engagement is not just about satisfied or happy employees. Engaged employees are continuously progressing, they are connected to the organization, make stronger contributions, and have defined roles in the organizations. They are a clear sign of a team in the "performing" stage.

Engaging teams starts with how organizational leaders decide to show up.

If you are an organizational leader, then how **you show up** will determine how successfully engaged your teams will become.

- Inclusive leaders who **show up**, want to move their organizations forward and they have a desire for employees and organizations to succeed and grow.

- Inclusive leaders who **show up**, communicate confidently and assertively; they listen, and they take on criticism.

- Inclusive leaders who **show up,** stand for something positive and those around them know what it is they stand for. They are expert decision makers.

- Inclusive leaders who **show up,** create positive change and lead that positive change.

- Inclusive leaders who **show up,** can quickly take in large amounts of information and quickly make objective purposive decisions that are the best way to further their organizations goals.

- Inclusive leaders who **show up,** bring out the positive capabilities in people. They don't criticize to bring people down; they point out mistakes to help people learn and grow. They value mistakes as a way to do better and as a way to learn.

- Inclusive leaders who **show up,** understand that a work/life balance increases the effectiveness of workers. They understand that getting the job done is not the only part of life and that people with full lives are better workers. They realize that "rushing around" can lead to burn out! They help people they work with to spot this and avoid it.

- Inclusive leaders who **show up,** innovate and they draw people in who come up with new ideas. They don't see 'Idea Makers' as 'Troublemakers'; they see ideas as a way to improve and learn. They see innovation as a success and that this stems from the ability to welcome new ideas.[64]

- Inclusive leaders who **show up,** define realistic goals to achieve engagement.

- Inclusive leaders who **show up,** connect to team members on an individual level.

- Inclusive leaders who **show up,** care about the lives and work of their team members.

- Inclusive leaders who **show up,** always focus on their team member's strengths and try to develop these.

- Inclusive leaders who **show up,** make sure new team members are engaged and actively make sure they successfully integrate into the team.

- Inclusive leaders who **show up,** successfully enhance the wellbeing of their employees.

As they say, there are no bad teams, just bad leaders. When inclusive leaders don't show up, things fall apart. As a leader, groups and teams look up to you and will emulate your behavior. If you simply come into work, so will your employees. If you decide to **show up**, so will they. As a leader you represent the values and goals of the organization and your actions will be mirrored. If you don't work towards your organization's goals, how can you expect anyone else to? If you don't work towards growing, how can you expect anyone else to? This is why teamwork depends so much on leaders; they set the behavior necessary for teams to succeed. Who we follow in life determines what path we take and so if you follow a leader who is not moving forward, then you will not move forward either! The better the leader you follow, the better you will become, and vice versa. The better the leader you are, and if you are a leader who shows up,

---

[64] https://www.forbes.com/sites/glennllopis/2015/02/02/6-things-wise-leaders-do-to-engage-their-employees/3/#3a98df1020dc

the more your team will be engaged.

Eliminating the R.O.A.D. Mentality

We all know of coworkers who are not engaged anymore and so quit and leave. But what about coworkers who quit and stay? People can become so disengaged with their work that they have already quit doing any more than they have to do. For the majority of people who are in this position, it normally relates back to the working relationship they have with their manager. In the military they had a phrase to describe people like this, R.O.A.D. – Retire On Active Duty! They basically had already checked out, before it was time to check out. In many organizations today there are people who are R.O.A.D. or as one organization I worked for as a consultant referred to their prematurely retired employees who simply stopped trying, they were 'vested and rested'.

Workers who are R.O.A.D. are extremely difficult to incentivize or motivate as they have completely disengaged. The military term is used within all branches of the service to describe people who are not doing their work, proactively, because they are ready to retire. They are supposed to be doing their job and are supposed to be committed to doing it, but they know there is little you can do about it if they simply coast by the time you initiate any remedial actions they are already out the door. Their outlook is, "I am going to be leaving soon so why should I bother?" It will no longer be their responsibility, so they do not care about the work and so apply as little effort as possible. Let me be clear, as a military veteran myself, I am not painting all soldiers with this brush, just those that are R.O.A.D.. (Retired on Active Duty)

There are many reasons why people chose to do this but there are two main reasons:

1. **Poor Accountability**

   This is the biggest contributing factor to the possibility of people quitting and staying or being on R.O.A.D. If there are clear goals set for every worker that are measured, then it is hard for them to avoid giving their best effort at work. Managers who have strong accountability of their workers rarely have staff who quit and leave. Managers who don't follow up on goal completion, target setting, and ensure that work is being done will end up with a lot of "R.O.A.D.ies" on their hands.

2. **Unclear goals.** Similar to accountability, having unclear goals also means that workers will struggle to perform consistently. Performance plans should reflect very clear goals that allow all team members to fulfil their obligations with clarity of purpose. The goals need to be clear and measurable or else less motivated workers will have an additional reason to not work towards them.

Is it possible to eliminate the R.O.A.D. mentality? The answer is no, it will always exist to some degree. There are some steps that you can take to reduce the behavior.

One key is coaching the specific employee. This is only possible when you are aware of the person and their reasons for quitting and staying. The coaching needs to be caring and firm to help the worker deal with their lack of motivation and help them to get back to working towards their goals. If they are truly about to retire, perhaps they can be given a new short-term project to work on that is more exciting than their normal work.

They can also be asked to mentor a younger coworker and hand-off their knowledge. This could give them pride in their work and also increase the diversity of their tasks. They could be given a goal of working with more than one coworker or developing a toolkit from what they have learned in their role as a way of setting them a specific task.

"The best way to predict the future is to create it." - Alan Kay

---

Team Members in the Right Roles

When teams first start, during the forming stage, the manager normally starts off by choosing the members of the team. The decisions that go into selecting the team members are very difficult decisions, but they also determine the success of the team, the way the team works, and the project or goal they are going to be working on.

"Rowing harder doesn't help if the boat is headed in the wrong direction." - Kenichi Ohmae

---

The goal is to create just the right mix of different skills that are necessary for the project. If you have too many people of one skill, then you will waste resources and it may mean that some team members do not have enough to do. This can lead to the R.O.A.D. mentality or Turn-Under™ developing as discussed above. This is something that you want to avoid! If too few workers are selected, and some skills are missing then you could stall the project and you might not be able to reach your goals.

There may also be situations when team members are able to cover different roles at once and this needs to be considered when selecting team members. It is also not adequate to simply choose a particular person just because they have a desired job title, they must also have specific skills. You may also need a combination of skills, so you may have to decide among a group of people with specific skills to find the right combination.

There are two additional things to consider **before** recruiting team members:

1. **What is your goal?** This might be obvious as it was probably the deciding factor in setting up the project and needing a team. But the only way to make sure that the right team members are recruited is if the goal of the project is very clear. The goal needs to be challenging and what it will achieve must be specific. Using this goal, you can then list what skills you need to achieve it.

2. **What skills do you need to achieve your goal?** Without realizing this, recruitment of team members is impossible. As above, this needs to take into account that some skills may come from one team member and you may need more than one person to achieve one particular part of the skill.

   Each person then needs to be given a very specific responsibility with clear targets. This is all within the forming stage and occurs while targets, rules and guidelines are set.

Supportive Environments.

Recruiting the right team members for the right roles is impossible without supportive, inclusive environments. In order to create effective teams, as established in previous sections, there needs to be an inclusive organizational culture to achieve this. The leaders of an organization play a big role in the setting of the culture and moving towards any inclusiveness in the organization. Equally, they play a role in setting an environment where team members can be selected with the right skills for the team. The key to this is open, effective communication that includes the way in which feedback is incorporated.

Supportive environments are where people have the resources, they need to meet their goals. This is not just the financial resources that immediately come to mind. This includes support in the form of collaborative encouragement from leaders and coworkers, information, equipment, and other tools. This also includes having an environment without barriers to growth or performance. Workers need to be able to get things done without being stopped by organizational bureaucracy.

Performance Barriers Eliminated

The process of selecting the right team members must also focus on eliminating performance barriers. These include unconscious biases and attributes that individuals or groups may perceive to be preventing them from meeting their goals. Inclusive leader/coaches should look out specifically for certain attributes, to try to eliminate performance barriers.

- **Poor communication**. This can have a very negative effect on teamwork. If team members are poor communicators or do not follow specific communication standards, then they can break down communication for the whole team and in effect prevent the team from reaching their goals.

- **Poor planning skills.** Teamwork relies on everyone being able to achieve the specific role in an interdependent way. This requires a lot of planning and you end up relying on other people in the team for their planning skills. If someone in the team has poor planning skills, they can prevent the team from progressing.

- **Poor goal setting**. This is one of the most common things that stops teams from <u>meeting</u> their goals. This can be from just one individual and can lead to the goal of the whole team not being met. The lack of this skill is a big thing to avoid when selecting team members for their roles.

Ideally, the best way to prevent problems from selecting team members is to pick strong team members with diverse and inclusive competencies. The best way to do this is to focus on the skills that you need and find people who have those skills. You can also look for people with combinations of skills that you need. Either way, the idea is to look for people who are already strong in the areas that your project requires. The idea is to look for the positive rather than avoid the negative. This will be discussed in specific detail and another tool to add to your success toolkit will be provided.

Gallup Strength Finders

To create effective teams, we need to know the particular strengths of the different team members. Additionally, once the team is up and running, we then need to be able to measure the skills of the team members and see if these change at all. One of the most important aspects of teams are the particular skills of individual members. The overall effectiveness relies on different skills coming together to work on a particular problem.

The question is then, how you discover and then measure the talents of the group. In a book called "Now, Discover Your Strengths", Gallup released an online assessment tool called Strength Finders.[65] Since then it has been released as Strength Finders 2.0 as a new and improved version of the very popular assessment tool. The key to this book is not only does it help you to find your talent, but you can also use the book to then apply your strengths to different situations.

The book stems from the idea that rather than looking at how we can fix our problems in the workplace, we should focus on what we are good at. We should focus on our talents instead of looking to remove or repair our flaws. The book argues that fixing our flaws and problems is the path of most resistance, while boosting our talents is the path of least resistance.

The Strength Finders assessment looks at 34 specific traits that are then used to determine where a person's skills reside. None of these traits are negative ones, instead when you take the test you key in on all of your virtues. The range

---

[65] REFERENCE Gallup Strength Finders.

of skills included is wide enough for anyone to find something that they are very good at; and that is the point.

The analysis then produces your top five traits and then provides you with the skills to use them! You can also get an assessment of how you did for each of the 34 traits and see a detailed analysis of this. This helps you find out which skills you were weakest but also it gives you more than just your five strongest ones. The test can also be administered at different ages so you can determine before you go to college, for example, what your strengths are, and you can work towards a career in those. You can also get specific tests done to test your leadership skills, your teamwork skills, and so on.

If you visit the offices of Gallup, the inventors of the test, you will find next to every desk a score card listing their five skills. Employees at Gallup say it is a great way to break the ice with colleagues, but it is also effective in forming new teams.

The entire test is based on an idea called positive psychology. This is the study of how we function in an optimal way. It focuses on our greatest satisfactions, personal potential, our strengths, and our happiness. This is somewhat unusual in our culture that seems to always focus on fixing or working on our weaknesses. Instead, the StrengthsFinder looks to help to build strong teams, strong people and so strong organizations. The idea is to find strong skills, focus on those and build strong organizational cultures that embrace the skills of all members.

This links very well with teams that are trying to grow workplace equity and inclusion. If you are focused on trying to form teams that are respectful of everyone on the team, then you will need to know what the skills are of your team. The StrengthsFinder helps you to do this so that each individual can be valued and respected and so included. Subsequently, it also helps to then build your team as you know what skills you have available and you can build your team based on those skills. The tool helps to bring strong teams and it helps to build inclusion. The reason why the tool was developed was to reduce turnover and improve employee morale by allowing organizations to discover the skills available to them in their organizations and then use those to advance the organization. As a tool to develop inclusive teams, it is perfectly aligned with this and is an extremely valuable tool for anyone's success toolkit.

"It's not what the vision is, it's what the vision does." - Peter Senge

---

The Link Between Courage & Enablement

First of all, we need to look at the relationship between enablement and effectiveness.[66] It is generally accepted that Enablement + Engagement = Effectiveness.

Without enablement, even the most engaged workers will fail to meet their goals. The previous sections looked at engagement and keeping workers and leaders engaged to achieve their goals. But what about enablement? What role does it play?

If workers have pay, benefits, developmental opportunities, respect, recognition, quality focus, confidence in leaders, and a clear direction then they will be engaged.

What about enablement?

To achieve this there is a slightly different list of ingredients. Workers need work structures, processes, collaboration, training, resources, authority, empowerment, and performance management. This results in the supportive environment described in the last section and optimized roles which leads to enablement.

The combination of these two turns into employee effectiveness. By

---

[66] This will be discussed in more detail in Section 3.3.

increasing these two you can do more with less and by doing so, enablement allows organizations to tap into the true value of human capital. The key with this is that the people need to be selected to join the right teams and be given the right roles. And the right environment is needed to support them in this position. This was discussed in the last section in more detail.

Enabling employees involves giving them access to resources. Enabled workers are put in optimized positions and roles on teams that are based on their best skills and abilities. This means acknowledging these and working on these. Enabling workers also means giving them the information, technology, tools and supportive environment they need to achieve their goals. As a leader, to enable your employees, you will also need to give them the space to do their job – **you have to get out of their way**. This takes courage as it means giving up a certain amount of your authority. By letting workers take on further responsibilities, the leader is giving the employees the signal that they are capable of effectively working. Like the move beyond tolerance to inclusion, this takes courage to implement organizational changes that will have a large impact.

"Creativity Takes Courage." – Henri Matisse

Teams With Purpose

Every section of this part of the book – the team journey – has had one thing in common. In order for teams to perform at the highest stage, they need to have a goal. They need to work interdependently towards achieving something as a team.

At the start of this section, sports teams were used as an example of what teamwork looks like. They also make a good analogy when thinking about how purpose and goals can play a part in the success of a team. If you think of any sport that relies on teams, there is always a goal that the team is trying to reach.

Whether it is the championship or the league or best team of the year, the team is always working towards a goal. When members of the team are interviewed after a game, they are asked about how things went, and in most cases, they relate this back to that goal. They talk about how that game helped them towards the championship, or how they will use that game to get to the next game so they can move towards their goal. It is a focus that keeps the team together and provides the team with one thing – purpose.

If a team has no answer to the question "why" they will easily fragment. It is important that all team members not only understand the purpose but are also supportive of the purpose. All team members should be working towards this one goal and they should be able to explain to anyone why the goal is important.

A team without a purpose is a team that will have no passion. They will lose drive, motivation, they will easily become disengaged, and there will be no real reason to become enabled.

While it is the leader's responsibility to set this purpose and to motivate the team as they go along, keeping them focused on this purpose, it is also the responsibility of each team member to do the same.

Every member of a sports team knows that part of their role is to encourage their teammates; they offer them support and try to boost them when things are bad. They celebrate together when things are going well. All of these actions are a way to keep the team focused on the goal. The coach/ leader has a large role in achieving this and keeping the focus on the purpose. A good coach will make sure that every single thing the team does is somehow related to their purpose. In a sports setting, they will train and the coach/leader reminds the team constantly that they are working towards their ultimate goal.

The same is true of teams in the workplace; there needs to be a continuous focus on purpose. Every action needs to be justified by how it helps the team to achieve its goal.

One of my clients for several years was MD Anderson Cancer Center, ranked the #1 Cancer Care Center in the World, located in Houston, Texas.

They have a singular clarity of purpose that everyone who works at any of their facilities can tell without hesitation. If you ask the person sweeping the floors in the hall what is their purpose, they have the same answer as the head of oncology. If you ask a pediatric care nurse or the cook in the kitchen preparing meals, the answer is the same. If you ask the nurse's aide who is changing soiled bedsheets or the phlebotomist who is drawing blood from a patient, if you ask the x-ray technician or the person operating the ultrasound lab, without hesitating, their answer will perfectly match what everyone else will tell you. Their purpose is…

To Make Cancer History….

- *What would your employees, coworkers, managers, supervisors or others say if the same question were asked of them?*
- *What is our organizational purpose?*
- *Is it inclusive?*
- *How does what you do connect to that inclusive purpose?*

How is an inclusive purpose different than a goal? A goal can be to increase profit by 10%. This is not something that will inspire people to do their best as part of the team. An inclusive purpose instead gives team members a reason to be excited about getting up and coming into work every day. Instead of a focus on profits, an inclusive purpose is a value statement. An effective inclusive purpose is one that is about improving something in a way that improves people's lives.

The inclusive purpose of the Disney company is not to increase sales by 50%, but to "Make Dreams Come True" (For Everyone!) An inclusive purpose is something that provides excitement to people beyond the team. It is about the difference the team is making.

Developing teams with an inclusive purpose is a part of the team development process and starts with the formation stage. This is when the inclusive leader/coach can work with the team to achieve this. The team must step back and look at the bigger picture. They need to look at what their goal will achieve for people in the wider world outside of the team. They should look at what is the positive impact of the project that they are working on. The inclusive purpose will come out of this. The team should ask themselves, where they are going (goals) and what they are going to do when they get there (plans). They then must think about how they will contribute (roles) and what they get from participating (rewards/recognition). Once these have been answered, they can then ask why they are doing this (inclusive purpose.)

"I think if the people who work for a business are proud of the business they work for, they'll work that much harder, and therefore, I think turning your business into a real force for good is good business sense as well." - Richard Branson

---

From Group To Team Discussions / Questions

1. Is our team dedicated to a common vision or purpose?

2. Do we have shared written goals?

3. Can our team members express that unified purpose if asked?

4. Is there a plan, understood by all, to achieve that purpose?

5. Are their short-term, mid-term, and long-term goals?

6. If a coworker doesn't come to work, are they missed as a person and not just their work? (Sense of Belonging)

7. Is everyone on our teams clear about what is expected of them?

8. Are there regular meetings, methods, and discussions keeping everyone appraised?

9. Do we ensure there are ground-rules for respectful behaviors when communicating as well as in meetings? What can we do better?

Examples / Samples

Micro-Aggressions Include:

- *He's very religious, but he's open minded.*
- *No one could call you a shrinking violet huh!*
- *You are so articulate! (To a person of color.)*
- *You don't sound black.*
- *You are so energetic for a baby-boomer.*
- *I thought the same way when I was your age.*

Workplace Bullying/Abusive Conduct (Examples)

Examples of abusive conduct, may include:

- Persistent insulting or offensive language.
- Spreading misinformation or malicious rumors.
- Behavior or language that frightens, humiliates, belittles, or degrades, including unwarranted criticism.
- Feedback that is includes yelling, screaming, threats, or insults.
- Making repeated inappropriate comments about a person's appearance, lifestyle, family, or
- culture.
- Regularly making someone the brunt of practical jokes or pranks.
- Distributing embarrassing photos or videos via social media.
- Excluding, isolating, or marginalizing a person from normal work, intentionally.

Chapter 4

The Leadership Journey

opefully we have all had **THAT** leader. You know the type. They make you feel like your work is important. They make you want to come into work in the morning. They encourage you; they make you feel proud of being part of a team. They are a unifier but at the same time they challenge you to do your best. If you have not had this kind of boss, then at least I hope you have heard of this kind of boss. They are out there!

These kinds of leaders understand that leadership is not a position, it is not a title – it is more than this. As Senator Cory Booker said: "Leadership is not a position or a title, it's an action or example." You can put the sign on the door saying "The Boss" or a sign on your desk saying "Director" but without the action that follows, you are not a leader.

If You Are Out in Front... And There is Nobody Following,
You Are Not Leading; You're Taking a Walk!

- *So how do people become leaders?*
- *And how do you become the type of leader you would want in a boss?*
- *What is the leadership journey?*
- *And how does leadership fit in with inclusion?*
- *What kind of leader do you need to be to make leadership work?*
- *Can inclusion work without leadership?*
- *Then what makes an inclusive leader?*

As the previous sections have shown, inclusion is an effort. It takes courage, work and cannot be achieved by assembling an increasing number of differences among co-workers. As workplaces become more diverse, if you want to leverage successful outcomes in your organization, these differences must be backed up by a matching level of effort and a matching level of courage. But is that all it takes? If you put in a little elbow grease into your leadership practices, can you magically turn differences into an inclusive team?

If it was that simple, I would not need to write this book! If it was that simple, every organization would have already solved this problem and every organization would be inclusive.

What is important to recognize is that most people believe that differences can turn into inclusion **on its own**. In a research study of Future of Work consortium members, only 18% understood that inclusion requires "a different kind of conductor to get the whole symphony to play together."[67]

This recognizes that **inclusion is not a destination, but a journey.** This was demonstrated in the last sections. Moving beyond tolerance towards inclusion is a process that needs continuous management. Whether it is about individuals recognizing that they need to understand their unconscious biases or inclusive leader/coaches guiding a team's inclusion strategy throughout their existence, the process is continuous.

To move beyond tolerance and translate differences into inclusion, the organizational culture needs to reflect inclusivity but there also needs to be appropriate inclusive management and leadership. The latter creates and sustains the former. It is an interesting aspect of the problem; having differences in ages, religions, nationalities, thinking styles, races, and more in the workplace, will become relatively easy; that will happen without any real effort due to the demographic changes. Becoming inclusive will become the real leadership

---

[67] Deloitte, *The Radical Transformation of Diversity and Inclusion: The Millennial Influence,* *2015*

challenge; accepting, valuing, and embracing the inevitable differences is a choice. It is much easier to simply avoid or tolerate differences. Any coward can do that. It takes courage to go beyond the minimalist approaches of tolerance to do the hard work of respecting and valuing differences. As we saw earlier in previous sections, even Google, with all of their financial resources, struggles with developing the types of leadership that can manage and sustain an inclusive culture.

Why do leaders find inclusion so hard? Why is it such a difficult state to embed into our organizations? Why is it so hard for our coworkers to move beyond tolerance?

Unfortunately, it is a natural barrier. We are all homo-sapiens and there was a time in our history when we were all hunter gatherers. We had to find and hunt for everything we needed; we roamed around our specific area to survive. If we met with a "different" group, they automatically were a threat to our ability to hunt and gather. They were a threat to our group; we were wired to see the world as our group vs the other group who could try to stop us from hunting or gathering in our own area. We were dealing with survival and that created the "us" versus "them" nature of our shared behavior. Think about politics today and you will see this trait. Think about your favorite sports team and you will see this trait. Think about being proud of our great country and you will find this trait still embedded from when we didn't even have an understanding of the concept of a country. It is a long-established behavior that dictates much of what we do today. Because it is so deeply embedded it becomes hard to find ways to create workplaces and social structures that do not emulate the trait of us versus them.

Does this mean it is an unsolvable problem? Again, if it was, I wouldn't be writing this book! Not only is it possible to create organizations that are inclusive; it is possible to do this and sustain this behavior.

In an earlier section, I looked at the personal journey we all need to take in order to understand that we need to move beyond tolerance and the steps we need to take to start creating inclusive environments. In a subsequent section, I talked about the teams that we need to create to continue this journey. When individuals and teams have an aligned purpose, it can propel an organization towards success while developing intercultural skills that create inclusive workgroups.

In this section, the focus is on what skills leaders need to guide the organization on an inclusive journey. It will look at intercultural agility in more detail and look at how leaders are built and embraced. It will also look at the role of both creativity and compassion in creating leaders capable of managing inclusion. This will be vital to maintaining an inclusive mindset so that it becomes embedded in the organizations culture.

"I must follow the people. Am I not their leader?"

—*Benjamin Disraeli*

The aim of any leader should be to create a respectful inclusive organizational culture that **remains** inclusive once they've left.

The main skills that define inclusive leaders are the following:

1. Inclusive leaders are those with the skill to see all attributes of difference as both inevitable and a strength.

2. Inclusive leaders are those who actively create and then develop and nourish the differences that exist in the workforce, workplace, and marketplace.

3. Inclusive leaders are those who can build inclusion and avert institutional hierarchy from preventing the success of this journey.

4. Inclusive leaders are those who understand that creating an inclusive culture is about embracing and leveraging organizational change.

5. Inclusive leaders are those who understand that building an inclusive culture is about embedding it at every level of the organization.

6. Inclusive leaders are those who understand that inclusion needs legitimate buy in from all organizational levels.

7. Inclusive leaders are those that appreciate how an inclusive culture is an ongoing journey of change and not a destination.

8. Inclusive leaders are those that understand that there are many attributes of difference that cannot be seen, but still need to be embraced, even those attributes of difference that are not visibly evident.

9. Inclusive leaders are those who value their staff no matter where they are on the maturation continuum. Simply because someone may have blind spots doesn't mean they cannot learn to appreciate and value all attributes of difference.

10. Inclusive leaders are those who create an environment where people are treated **the way that each person wants to be treated**. (i.e. The Platinum Rule)[68]

Becoming diverse is an organizational and societal inevitability. The goal is to be inclusive when the ever-changing levels of difference manifest. The skill that allows you to be inclusive is cultural competence. When talking about differences that exist in the workplace, here is an analogy:

Diversity is being invited to the dance, but inclusion is being asked to dance. Cultural competency is knowing whether to do the twist or the tango when you get to the dance floor!

[68] https://www.linkedin.com/pulse/20141209114733-78681328-inclusive-leadership-diversity-is-just-the-tip-of-the-iceberg

Being Culturally Competent Drives Inclusive Leadership

Inclusive leadership is required of leaders who want to make workers feel valued for their unique and individual talents. An inclusive leader achieves this without alienating people based on their differences. They are able to use the differences in a positive way and avoid negative implications. This creates better teams and a more effective organization.

Inclusive leaders demonstrate confidence in their team members; they hold them accountable for performance factors within their control. They stand up for what is right even though it can mean risk taking. An inclusive leader learns from criticism. They admit when they make mistakes and try to move beyond their own limitations by getting contributions from others. They also grow their teams by enabling them and encouraging them to create new skills, new ideas, and solve problems.

In homogenous environments, leaders only need to understand one specific group of people, mindset, or approach. They learn to understand the motivations of one specific group of people, and tailor their management style to them. The learning curve for managing in a monolithic environment makes it easier to understand and adapt to. In today's changing workplace, leaders need a more nuanced form of management that understands, leverages, and relates to the differences on their team.

Juliet Bourke and Bernadette Dillon at Deloitte looked at the traits that were necessary for inclusive leadership to determine exactly how to create an inclusive mindset. They came up with six "signature traits of inclusive leadership"[69] that they argue are essential for any type of inclusive process to develop within an organization. They argue that leadership must drive the movement from tolerance to respect to inclusion and that in order for this to be successful, leaders need to embrace six traits – Commitment, Courage,

---

[69] https://dupress.deloitte.com/dup-us-en/topics/talent/six-signature-traits-of-inclusive-leadership.html#endnote-sup-42

Cognizance of Bias, Curiosity, Collaboration and Cultural Intelligence.

These are discussed below, however, their model misses a crucial point. All six of these traits are necessary but none of them effectively translate into inclusion without Socio-Cultural Intelligence^tm or SCi^tm. More on this topic is presented later in this book.

Trait One: Commitment. The first trait requires leaders to be committed to the issue of inclusion, which comes when the values of inclusion match a leader's personal values. As we have pointed out, moving beyond tolerance towards respect and inclusion is not an easy task. It takes time and it takes a lot of effort. Leaders will have to be motivated to make this investment. Leaders cannot escape that best-in-class organizations will lead in the move towards an inclusive culture. Those organizations that embrace it will lead, and those who don't embrace it will fall behind. But is the commercial motivation enough? If leaders are simply being inclusive to improve the bottom line, is this enough? The more motivated a leader is to embrace inclusion the more likely they are to understand the cultural values behind it and the more likely it is to succeed. I will use health and safety as an example.

Many organizations have health and safety regulations that they must follow by law. Those that don't follow these will be fined and this will affect their bottom line. Those that follow these laws will not be fined. There is a third group of organizations. Those that follow these laws **and** actively train their staff to embrace a culture of safety to improve the culture in the workplace as well as **reduce** the number of safety related incidents.

Not only is this last group not fined, but they also have fewer safety problems and safer staffs. This in turn leads to staff who feel more valued and become more productive. Although safety and inclusion are markedly different, it is easy to see how being committed to the values of inclusion will allow for an easier, stronger, and more sustained implementation of this organizational change.

Trait Two: Courage. To implement inclusive organizational change, leaders also need to embrace the second trait, courage. You must have the courage to undertake an institutional change initiative in the first place. Inclusive leaders will need courage to implement organizational change. They will need courage to be able to challenge and confront the organizational status quo. They will also need to face their own personal status quo. We are good at becoming comfortable with where we are and this needs to be addressed to develop inclusion. Inclusive leaders also need to challenge both the system and others around them to create inclusion. The current system is enrichened by our individual and organizational willingness to be tolerant. For this status quo to change, leaders will need the courage to stand up and be the change, then be willing to call for change.

The reason I keep referring to the word courage is the risks that are required in order to move beyond tolerance. I've had multiple occasions to have to make a choice. Many of the decisions associated with moving an organization from the status quo to becoming best in class will require you to make a stand of consciousness.

EXAMPLE:

As a consultant for global organization, I was engaged to assist them in making a significant cultural shift to raise the level of dignity and respect within their operational units, specifically their plants.

Upon completion of the cultural assessment, a new global HR leader was brought in. It was immediately obvious that because of her sexual orientation, with no experience in doing diversity work at all, she deemed herself to be an expert in everything diversity.

Once she took a look at the contract that had been negotiated with their CEO, she immediately said there was no need for my services since she already had the insight to help the organization based on her gut level, not on her skillset.

Upon discussing the delivery of a pilot workshop, the new head of HR questioned why the organization should pay for training materials. She stated

198

that she had gone through a diversity workshop with another consulting organization 10 years ago and she still had a copy of all of their materials. Her statement to me was "Why should I pay you, when all I have to do is just photocopy their materials and use them at no cost!"

On hearing her statement, I knew there was no way that I would deliver the pilot workshop without her taking my material, photocopying it, and using it without paying me as she was suggesting she would do with the previous consulting organizations material.

I knew that this was not an organization that I could continue to work, with such an unethical executive now playing a key role. I walked away from close to $500,000 worth of business, one of the largest hits to my revenue stream in 20 years. Walking away took courage... I have never regretted walking away. I have regretted never letting the CEO know the other side of the conversation.

Disrupting the Status Quo With Purpose.... Takes Courage!

AUNT SUZIE: God Takes care of fools & babies.

Inclusive leaders will also need courage to be able to recognize limitations in themselves, in their organization, and in others in a way that inspires others in the organization. They need to be able to find value in others and build upon that. The attribute of humility must be seen as one of the main characteristics of an inclusive leader, but it is rare to associate this trait with many leaders today.

These factors in turn create a third area where courage is needed. Challenging the status quo and recognizing limitations brings about the natural vulnerability of change. In order to overcome change, courage is essential. Sometimes it is hard enough to have the courage to face our own limitations and biases.

Trait Three: Cognizance of Bias. Returning to the first section of this book, inclusive leaders need to be extremely aware and mindful of not only personal but also organizational blind spots. This is necessary to create an equitable organizational culture. Without being aware of unconscious bias, you cannot act on it. As discussed in earlier sections, the action to take to reduce unconscious bias means ensuring that structures, processes, and policies are put in place to try to lessen the impact of these biases. In order to do that, inclusive leaders will need to have a very good understanding of how these unconscious biases manifest.

"The first responsibility of a leader is to define reality. The last is to say thank you. In between, the leader is a servant." —Max DePree

---

Trait Four: Curiosity. Learning is based on curiosity and all leaders need to be able to learn in order for their organizations to grow. Curiosity is more than learning; it is a motivation to ***continually*** learn. This creates leaders who can then take in a broad range of ideas and perspectives. This then fuels other values such as empathy, inquiry, and open mindedness. To be truly curious, leaders also need to be **effective** listeners. They need to have a level of curiosity that drives them to be active listeners to the opinions and ideas of others and then learn how to use those inputs to create change. This also means holding back on judgement until you have heard all ideas. Often people will prejudge a suggestion even as it is being presented. This tends to thwart the understanding of the current thought as well as the emergence of any other ideas. In a circular way, curiosity creates learning, which promotes open minds, which promotes ideas, which promotes curiosity!

Trait Five: Collaboration. To develop teams, as described in section 2, there needs to be a managing coach. Leaders will also need to achieve collaboration among teams that are becoming increasingly more diverse. This is often where many challenges arise. It is easier to develop teamwork and collaboration when the group is homogeneous. Collaboration is all about working together and when this is done successfully, individuals feel valued and work together towards solving problems. This is where the sense of belonging starts! Effectively collaborating involves empowering individuals to not be afraid of sharing ideas and participating in the work. This can only be spurred on by a leader who is both collaborative and who understands the value of collaboration.

Inclusive leaders understand the need to be courageous and committed to move beyond tolerance. Courageous leaders know that lasting inclusive change comes from moving beyond tolerance to embrace an inclusive mindset. Without a collaborative mindset, leaders can exclude certain team members from feeling their input or contribution is wanted. When this occurs, people shut down. No one likes to feel ignored. In today's competitive environment, with an eye on margin enhancement, organizations can't afford to underutilize people. When people feel marginalized, they tend to withdraw, not lean in.

In order for the trait of collaboration to translate into inclusion, leaders need to be **culturally agile.** This is more than just a trait but a disciplined approach to the ways in which inclusivity can have a positive effect. It includes social, emotional, and cultural intelligence. We will address this in much more detail later in this book.

Without being culturally agile, leaders will struggle to be truly inclusive. This is a value that leaders need to commit to in order for there to be an effective transition into having an inclusive mindset. As said earlier, cultural agility is more than just knowing whether to kiss, bow, or shake hands. It is also more than just understanding the various cultural frameworks such as Hofstede's cultural theories inclusive of the cultural dimensions of power, distance, individualism, collectivism, masculinity, and femininity. Inclusive leaders understand that cultural agility encompasses much more.

Cultural and anthropological studies are frequently re-evaluating the way in which culture is interpreted and understood. It is understood very differently today than 50 years ago, for example. Learning from these changes is essential for leaders to have an inclusive mindset as they will need to continuously deepen their understanding of working in diverse environments. Only through embracing the importance of understanding all aspect of cultural differences can an organization build stronger connections among all staff members.

This **cultural intelligence or CQ** is different to IQ, EQ, or SQ. It is made up of four different parts that are similar to the ideas above of what an inclusive leader looks like:[70]

Motivated - Leaders that **WANT** to learn about and engage in different cultural experiences.	**Cognitive** - Leaders have **KNOWLEDGE** on and **WANT** to learn the different cultural practices.
Behavioral – Leaders **UNDERSTAND** that cultural interactions must be include appropriate nonverbal and verbal actions.	**Metacognitive** – Leaders must **UNDERSTAND** conscious cultural awareness throughout all of their interactions.

This way of understanding cultural intelligence (CQ) can be applied to having an inclusive mindset from a leadership or management perspective. There have been a number of studies that have shown that there is a positive relationship between many different aspects of organizational growth and cultural intelligence.

"Leadership is the capacity to translate vision into reality."

—*Warren Bennis*

The Importance of Intercultural Agility (IA) in Leadership

Looking back at the last section on cultural thinking and inclusion, it was clear that inclusive leaders needed to have intercultural awareness, or an ability to manage interactions with someone who does not share the same cultural background as themselves. The aim of being **interculturally agile** (IA) is to reduce the negative effects of differences between people to improve collaboration between teams and individuals. It is about how we not only recognize cultural differences in religious variances, social codes, languages, dress, movement, nonverbal actions, and verbal actions; but how we also adapt to these in our surroundings. This agility refers to an ability to adapt our thinking and understanding quickly and adapt to new situations.

Intercultural agility (IA) is a high level of System 2 thinking – thinking slow. We need to spend time thinking about who we are in order to be able to understand the cultural actions we make. We cannot see cultural differences around us without understanding our own culture. It is about being self-aware which requires slow, thoughtful analysis. It is impossible to achieve this without using the energy draining System 2 thinking. Intercultural agility takes time and can give rise to strong emotions. Importantly, this leads to acculturation; we don't lose our own culture entirely but instead we adapt and modify our behavior slightly in different situations. This molding and adaptation is the basis of intercultural agility. This provides leaders with an ability to communicate and operate in diverse situations and in different cultures. Without this, leaders would be unsuccessful in diverse situations. Success in today's global marketplace is based on a leader's ability to communicate and operate across and within cultures.

IA creates leaders who have the skills to be better decision makers. By being able to consider problems and issues from different perspectives, leaders can then make strategic decisions within diverse environments. Leaders also gain communication skills that are appropriate and based on cultural awareness. Leaders with intercultural agility are also more thoughtful and so more successful in operating in uncertain contexts. This agility provides leaders with an ability to navigate the many cultural differences that affect how workplaces work with the increased levels of differences in the workplace. Differences in how we influence others, motivate others, earn trust, and communicate with others all vary according to our cultural values and intercultural agility (IA) provides us with the tools to understand these changes.

Inclusive leaders know that IA has three main components. They know when to integrate, override, or adapt culturally diverse practices. They understand that these three can be used when appropriate and can be applied at different times as necessary. In a way this is a balancing act that inclusive leaders must be able to apply and it is only with intercultural agility can they use these comfortably, quickly and effectively with different situations.

"Before you are a leader, success is all about growing yourself. When you become a leader, success is all about growing others."

—Jack Welch

Like developing inclusion in an organization, developing intercultural agility requires effort and courage. It is more complex than most people assume and involves more than simply getting a passport stamp or visiting a new country. In fact, many leaders who have diverse experience often do not develop these skills because they assume that their presence in another culture alone will create these proficiencies.

Developing intercultural agility requires an active committed decision to learn new skills. Personal reflection and developing self-awareness to understand your own culture is part of this process, but it also involves actively engaging in experiential learning and knowledge acquisition[71].

As in previous sections, the first step in developing intercultural agility is questioning your assumptions about your own culture. Have you taken the time to proactively stretch your cultural comfort zone??

CELL PHONE CHALLENGE

- *When was the last time you did this?*
- *When was the last time you reflected on how your culture effects how you do everyday things?*
- *Think about your colleagues at work. When was the last time you thought about what you have in common and what differences you have in the way you do things?*
- *How were these similarities and differences affected by culture?*
- *Is this something we think about during our day to day?*
- *Although there will be many similarities shared with people we work with, what differences are there?*

We become socialized through our commonalities such as the colleges we go to and the organizational culture we align with, but we are also shaped by our cultural differences that form the basis of who we are. When developing intercultural agility, the first step is understanding your own culture including your own stereotypes and unconscious biases. This allows you to recognize the differences.

---

[71] https://www.td.org/Publications/Magazines/TD/TD-Archive/2013/03/Develop-Your-Cultural-Agility

The next logical step is to understand specific cultural differences. Many leaders and organizations that may have a domestic or regional focus to their business, can sometimes be dismissive of whether this topic applies to their organization or their leadership skills.

EXAMPLE: I lived in the greater Houston, Texas area for twenty years, working at the University of Houston (UH) in the College of Business as a contractor. The UH is the second most diverse four-year public university in America! The students speak over 150 languages! Rutgers University's students speak about 160 languages!

MY POINT: You don't have to be a global organization to have a need to understand the importance of 'culture' on the people you hire, organizations you do business with, your customer, clients, patients, and more.

For intercultural agility to grow and be maintained, these skills need to be continuously developed and encouraged in your teams that you work with. Not only are they necessary as a leader but they are also necessary for team members. We all will need high quality developmental opportunities to ensure intercultural agility is maintained over time.

"A leader is one who knows the way, goes the way, and shows the way." —*John Maxwell*

Inclusive Leaders Drive Engagement, Empowerment & Enablement

Before we discuss how inclusive leaders effect enablement, some definitions are necessary. This topic was discussed briefly in Section 2.13: The Link Between Courage & Enablement. In that section, I looked at the difficulty in creating teams and the importance of enabled team members.

The term enablement often sits alongside engagement and empowerment and these three terms are often used interchangeably when in fact they have specific criteria:

Engagement	This is basically how much an employee values their relationship with their organization. This includes their relationship with their line manager and if they are proud of their organization. Engagement is also when employees have a voice and believe in senior management. When engagement is high, employees have higher levels of productivity, there are higher amounts of continuous improvement, and there is more discretionary effort given.
Empowerment	This is when employees feel valued, so they step up and take more responsibility and ownership. They are given the power to think **for** themselves and so they do more <u>by</u> themselves and <u>for</u> themselves. This can only happen when there is an environment that people feel trusted. They must also trust that there are no negative consequences for them to speak out or make decisions. The organization needs to focus on problem solving rather on assessing blame. When this happens, if an employee makes a mistake after being empowered, there will be no negative consequences. Their mistake is seen as a learning opportunity.

Enablement	With engagement and empowerment, the relationship is with the organization. **Enablement is an employee's relationship with their own talent.** When workers are enabled, they have more talent, more capability, and more potential and are applying them to their role. This is achieved through training and coaching and is one of the most important ways to increase productivity in an organization. However, if workers are enabled but they are not empowered and they are not engaged, there are two outcomes. They will quit and leave, or they will quit and stay. They will lose motivation to work for your organization and look to find an organization that values their work and their participation.

When employees feel that they are empowered, engaged and enabled, they feel[72]:

- That they are more innovative in their jobs and can be more creative with ideas.

- That they are team players and go beyond their own individual duties to help the team.

- They are willing to wear the t-shirt of the organization and so strive to do well for their organization.

- That their values align with the organizations values and so are more committed to the organization's goals.

- **That they belong to the organization and belong to their teams.**

- That they understand that there are differences among team members of the organization but that these differences can be positive.

---

[72] http://www.catalyst.org/knowledge/inclusive-leadership-view-six-countries-0

- That they understand that there are similarities among team members of the organization and that these can be used to meet the organizations goals.

In the sections above, the characteristics of an inclusive leader were the "6 C's": commitment, courage, cognizant of bias, curiosity, collaboration, and cultural intelligence (CQ). These skills are related and are outcomes of achieving a workforce that is engaged, empowered and enabled.

Engaging employees involves collaborating with them and developing collaborative teams. It also involves leaders who are curious about ways in which employees can become engaged, how to maintain that engagement and on how to assist other managers in engaging their teams. Without curiosity, new techniques and tools could be missed.

Leaders will also need to be cognizant of their biases when engaging employees to ensure that all employees feel the belonginess that comes from being intentionally inclusive.

If biases are not mitigated or eliminated, leaders may inadvertently engage only a small section of their organization. When this is visible by other employees, this can be devastating for morale throughout an organization. Engagement is a process of commitment; it is not a one-off quick event. It involves a long-term strategy to keep the engagement going.

"I start with the premise that the function of leadership is to produce more leaders, not more followers." —Ralph Nader

Empowering employees involves providing them with a voice. This requires all of the "6 C's". If leaders are not committed to empowerment, it will be temporary, employees will lose trust and they will become disempowered again. To give employees power requires letting go of some levels of authority.

This takes courage.

To empower ALL employees, leaders need to be cognizant of their own biases that may interrupt this process. They will also have to be cognizant of the biases of other team members.

- Without curiosity, leaders will not develop the pathways necessary to introduce empowerment. They will not feel brave enough to embark on developing the power of employees around them.
- Without collaboration, leaders cannot create an environment of trust necessary for empowerment. Collaboration is essential for creating problem solving environments that focus on learning and developing solutions.
- Without collaboration, organizations focus on assessing blame which is a clear pathway to disempowerment.
- Lastly, cultural intelligence allows leaders to be able to introduce empowerment measures in an inclusive way.
- Without understanding the cultures of the organization, leaders will not be able to deliver empowerment for all.
- Without CQ, leaders would empower only a homogenous section of their organization; this disempowers others and defeats the purpose of the mission.

Enabling employees to have and embrace an inclusive mindset, requires them to have a combination of all the leadership skills needed for inclusion as well as the tools to embrace engagement and empowerment.

- It requires leaders who put aside their own personal interests to work towards meeting the organizational goals.

- It requires leaders who act on their own principles and convictions to ensure that they are aligned with the organization's goals of creating an inclusive culture.

- It requires leaders prepared to take risks.

- It requires leaders with the humility to admit that their teams need training and coaching to excel.

- It requires leaders who also look at the need for improvement rather than looking to assess blame.

Inclusive leaders drive enablement because they want to go beyond the status quo and the limitations that prevent their organizational growth. Inclusive leaders drive enablement because they allow direct reports to thrive and do not see this as competition. They see this as the basis of organizational growth and strong teams, which make strong organizations.

Inclusive leaders drive enablement, and they realize that it must come with engagement and empowerment to realize true gains.

Understanding (Inclusive) Situational Leadership

The more diverse our communities become, the more diverse our organizations will be. This entire book is dedicated to how to achieve positive organizational growth by harnessing the benefits of an inclusive culture based on the changing dynamics in the workforce and workplace.

In terms of leadership, this involves developing the skills necessary to manage teams with an inclusive mindset as described in previous chapters. This poses an interesting dilemma.

- *If organizations are becoming more diverse, should the leadership approach be just as diverse depending on the organization?*

- *Can the same organizational approach be used with every organization that is moving beyond tolerance?*

- *Can the same tools be applied in each situation?*

With all forms of leadership approaches these questions arise. Developing an inclusive mindset requires specific tools and approaches that are foundational no matter what the organization. Two key variables are where the organization is on the inclusion continuum and the type of organization or industry.

In the 1970s, the "Situational Leadership® Model" was introduced by Paul Hersey and Ken Blanchard. It has been one of the most effective, utilized, and recognized tools in the behavioral sciences. Its application to leadership and organizational development has been vital in changing leadership style to become more flexible and has allowed leaders to succeed in the face of institutional change.

This model was designed specifically to look at the problem of how to apply leadership models to different situations. The fundamental part of this theory is that the style of leadership applied in organizations cannot be summed up as one best type. They argue that effective leadership is based on looking at relevant tasks and that leaders who are willing to adapt their specific leadership style are the most successful. This adaptation depends on the individuals and the groups or teams that they are leading. This adaptation also depends on the function, job, or task that is being undertaken.

If we look at engagement, empowerment, and enablement, the stage of the team or individual in achieving these would depend on the type of leadership used. Teams that are not empowered would not benefit as much from a leader that focuses on team decision making. Before team decision making can occur, the teams would need to feel that their voice is valued and that their contributions would be acceptable. That level of inclusion and respect is key. If individuals did not feel empowered, they would not participate in activities requiring them to speak out and leadership that did not understand this would falter. An inclusive mindset on the part of people and organizational leaders is a critical enabler in order to be effective in driving participation by all employees being impacted by ensuring that dignity and respect are core cultural and leadership drivers.

"A leader takes people where they want to go. A great leader takes people where they don't necessarily want to go, but ought to be."

—Rosalynn Carter

The Situational Leadership® Model was developed to address challenges in leadership in changing environments. Creating an inclusive culture involves undertaking vast amounts of organizational change and so this model is very applicable to the inclusive leadership model. It focuses on leaders who are flexible in their execution of solutions to organizational growth and also requires them to navigate through increasing changes in the workforce, workplace and marketplace.

This produces leaders who look at the challenges of leadership and specifically of inclusive leadership by focusing on tasks and looking at the employee's level of motivation and ability. In this way it is similar to the inclusion models described so far and represents a dynamic, specific and targeted type of coaching that creates a specific type of behavior change among employees.

Building and Embracing Intrusive Leaders

Intrusive leadership sounds like an oxymoron – it sounds like something that doesn't make any sense. Someone who is intrusive is someone or something that is unwelcomed. The true definition is something or someone that causes disruption or annoyance because they are unwelcome or uninvited. If you are holding a party and someone comes uninvited, they are intrusive. Leadership on the other hand, is meant to be inspirational, motivational and guiding. Marrying the two words together seems to be a mistake or at least it seems it describes a negative idea of leadership.

However, intrusive leadership is an important concept, and it is often something that is neglected even by the most inclusive managers. Intrusive leadership is about not waiting for your employees to let you in. Instead, it is about actively, and professionally, understanding what is going on in their lives and understanding that their wellbeing will have an impact on their performance.

In this way Intrusive Leadership is actually a positive concept.

Working as a young executive in a broadcasting company, I worked with an intrusive leader and I learned the value of using this style of management. I also noticed it when I served in the US Air Force. Let me describe an example.

While working in broadcasting, I went through some professional challenges and had to make some decisions to either live courageously or be a coward. One coworker I worked with did not know much about my struggle as they were heads down, results focused and had little time for emotional, social, or cultural intelligence. More on each of these later.

When I was going through my professional crisis, my performance remained the same and I met and or exceeded my targets. But I was less engaged in my work as my focus was on the decisions and challenges, I was facing in my career. My coworker who was clearly an intrusive leader, spotted this and called me into his office. We sat down and talked about the challenges I was facing and the decisions I knew were inevitable. As an intrusive leader with a high degree of emotional intelligence, he knew there was something happening that was impacting my engagement. We discussed what support I needed in the workplace and I explained the problem-solving techniques I was using in confronting the career changing decision I was facing. After several discussion, I had clarity about the choices I was facing and the outcome of each possible decision. Without that intrusive leader and that specific moment in my life, I would have made decisions that I would have regretted for the rest of my life.

Intrusive leaders take time to check in, to care, to be empathetic. Intrusive leaders get down in the weeds with their employees; they try to understand them on many levels by getting to know them beyond the office.

- They talk about challenges, obstacles, and concerns in a professional way and support employees in the professional environment with whatever is going on outside of the day-to-day tasks of their job.

- They understand that when we come to work, we don't leave our lives at the door and that what is happening beyond the office affects how we deal with the office.

- They also understand that the politics of the office can be a career enabler or a career delimiter. Not everyone understands, desires, or is equipped to deal with the office politics.

- It's hard to play the games when you don't know the rules.

"Great leaders are almost always great simplifiers, who can cut through argument, debate, and doubt to offer a solution everybody can understand." – Colin Powell

---

An intrusive leader understands that there is a level of intrusion that is professional and that this can only be achieved by gaining trust from employees. Specific communication is needed for leaders to become intrusive leaders. They will need to be able to adapt their communication style to deal with potentially sensitive situations and to deal with problem solving personal and professional solutions in a professional way.

Intrusive leaders also know that they need to be active listeners and that this needs to be a continuous conversation.

- If you "intrude" into someone's life in January and then are uninterested for the rest of the year, you will lose the trust of employees who will doubt your sincerity.

Likewise, if you intrude into someone's life, find out if they want your input, or simply want you to hear and see them. Some want your input and your perspective.

DON'T ASSUME: ASK! A simple question can go a long way to demonstrating empathy as well as establishing mutual expectations. After hearing someone out, without interrupting them, while providing verbal and non-verbal acknowledgement that you are listening, ask the following:

"Would you like my thoughts or would you just like me to listen."

Intrusive leadership is more than just asking "how are you" or "how was your weekend." It is about asking if your employees' son did well at the flute recital. It is about then, asking continuously about any future recitals and how things are going with their son. For it to be effective, leaders must be genuinely interested in their employees. This is a skill that can be learned over time and developed with practice.

Intrusive leadership has been adopted by the US Military for obvious reasons. When teams need to be tight knit and rely on each other, the wellbeing of each individual member is important and vital to the success of that team. Military units are also based on trust and confidence, and intrusive leadership is a way to develop both of these.

Intrusive leadership allows leaders to be able to get involved in the wellbeing of individuals on a professional level. The leadership style is based on the idea that the leader and the employee are both responsible for the success or failure of the employee. It is about valuing employees and making sure they are aware that they matter. It demonstrates that leaders are aware of the effect of wellbeing on an individual's performance and so any successful inclusive leader will need to be an intrusive leader.

To be an intrusive leader, leaders need to be proactive and responsible. They also need to be available for future discussions about the topics in an employee's life or career progression.

One of the main benefits of intrusive leadership is the ability for the leader to motivate individuals and teams. By getting to know the team, leaders are then able to understand what motivates them, what problems may arise with motivation and also helps to better understand the goals of each member of the team. For teams to succeed, each individual has to have the organizational goals as their own goals. These will sit alongside the individual's personal goals. If you are unaware of what the personal goals of your team members are, it will be difficult to convince them to take on the organization's goals.

Intrusive leadership requires rapport and trust. This requires patience as this needs to be built over time. Understanding your employees or team members is not a form of analysis and it is a mistake if anyone uses it in this way. It is not about trying to "read" your employees so that you can form conclusions about who they are. It is about getting to know them in the same way that you would get to know a friend; it is really about trust. Once employees and team members trust that you are genuinely interested in their wellbeing and are willing to support where possible, they will begin to confide in you, and they will also encourage others to do the same. The most important part of intrusive leadership is that it can sit as part of situational leadership. It is not a one solution fits all approach. It needs to be adapted to each individual situation.

Given that intrusive leadership can reveal sensitive information, the style used needs to be based on having an inclusive mindset (more on this concept later), emotional intelligence, and active listening. Intrusive leadership is about taking care of team members and employees. Getting it right is just as important as implementing it to begin with. It will also involve changing mindsets among your organization so that people have enough trust to come to you for help and support. Using leadership skills illustrated in previous sections is vital in achieving this.

Understanding the Power of Influence

"If your actions inspire others to dream more, learn more, do more and become more, you are a leader." – John Quincy Adams

---

Moving beyond tolerance towards inclusion requires a certain kind of leadership that is capable of changing the status quo, with purpose. This is a complex exercise that will require a number of success toolkits. None of this can be achieved without leadership that has the power of influence.

Influence is an interesting aspect of leadership. It is normally assumed that influence comes with a position and that it is a natural part of taking on a leadership role. This is not the case. It is something that exists not because of a label but because of the characteristics and attributes of a leader.

Here is an example. We have all been in this situation. You are in a meeting and everyone is talking except one person. The discussion goes on for a long time, but the group cannot decide on what action to take. Finally, after a long-time discussion, the group turns to the one person who has been silent the entire time. That person simply nods their head in agreement, or they say a few words backing one decision and then the decision is made. Influence is more than **just** talking; it is about being a leader and it is about taking charge. It is more than just this though – it is more than just a label.

Influence involves understanding the roles that nonverbal signals, expertise, emotions, and positions play.

Without an understanding of the complexity of influence and these four factors, it is difficult to be an influential leader.

Influential leaders don't DEMAND respect based on job titles.

They COMMAND respect based on how they treat people.

We will look these in more detail. Positional power as mentioned, is often thought of as the main way in which leaders obtain the power of influence. In some ways, this is true and certain positions do create the power of influence. CEOs will automatically have a level of influence just because of their position.

Due to this, they are more likely to talk more, guide conversations more, choose what topics are discussed and also interrupt what is going on more.

Many people in positions of power use these tools to demonstrate that they are in a position of power. In this way it becomes a chicken and egg situation.

Are positions of power influential because they are positions of

power or are they positions of power because they are

influential?

In the military this is manifest in many ways. When an officer enters a room, those that are junior officers and enlisted stand at attention. The conversations stop. They wait for the officer, with positional power, to tell them they can resume business as usual. **This happens regardless of the capability of the officer.**

It doesn't matter if the individual has demonstrated their capabilities, concern, or empathy. It is predicated on their rank and title alone.

The problem with many who have positional authority or power is that many of them are actually not respected by their subordinates because they misuse that title and authority. They not only expect that they are the sharpest tool in the shed, they demand that you treat them as such.

In a consulting engagement, I was working with an organization that had just undergone a merger. The board required the CEO to keep the CFO of the acquired company and release his own CFO. During a discussion about human capital strategies, the CFO expressed a thought that was met with this response from the CEO.

"If must be tough, being a 30-watt bulb working on a team full of 100-watt bulbs!"

That level of disrespect was not challenged by anyone on his team. When I spoke up, the rest of the team looked at me as though I had lost my mind. My first comment was; ***"Ouch!"*** The CEO looked at me and said, "What is the ouch for?" I chose to address his comment with the following steps:

1. Explain How It Landed / Felt
   - *"John, I was a little uncomfortable with how that might have landed in the room.*

2. Assume Good Intentions
   - *"I'm not sure if you meant that the way it came across for me."*
     i. Even though I was fairly sure he meant it the way it sounded.

3. Ask For Insight
   - *"You seemed to be disappointed in something Bill said. What was it about Bill's comment that didn't meet your expectations?"*

4. Engage The Group, If Possible, In The Conversation
   - In order to keep everyone engaged in the conversation.
   - *"How else can we look at the issue that Bill brought up?"*

This approach can deescalate, illuminate, and allow everyone to communicate.

Another form of influence is emotional influence. This involves using passion and emotions to affect power and influence. One example of this is seen in passionate speeches by politicians or lawyers who are arguing to people in positions of power. They are using emotion to create influence. This happens in organizations, but the emotion is often subdued due to the professional culture of organizations.

In certain situations, the person with the most influence is the person with the most expertise. This is true especially in technical situations. The epitome of this would be a meeting at NASA where the technical engineers would have more knowledge about specific topics than people in positions of power. In some organizations the positions of power are held by experts and so the position has additional influence.

The last form of influence is nonverbal signals. This is used subtlety and if used effectively can be more powerful than other forms of influence. This is why face to face meetings are more effective than phone conversations; so much is missed when we do not read the nonverbal signals and it is why cross talk (talking over one another) is more common on the phone than in face-to-face meetings. It is hard, however, to use this form of influence alone, and it is often used in combination with one of the other forms of influence.

Influence is highly impacted by the 7-38-55 rule ᵗᵐ. This concept identifies how important non-verbal aspects of communication are. The rule states that:

- 55% - Fifty-Five % of meaning is communicated through body language.
- 38% - Thirty-Eight % of meaning is communicated through tone of voice.
- 7% - Only seven percent of meaning is communicated by the <u>words</u> we use.

As a leader, you need to understand the types of influence and ways to integrate them into your leadership style. Using these in combination is normally the most effective method but they can be used separately as well, as described.

Influence is about convincing others that your decision, your request, your ideas are the right thing to do. Steve Jobs has often been described by some as one the most influential CEO's of all time. Why is this? And what does this say about the power of influence?

Steve Jobs used a combination of all four of the forms of influence in all aspects of his leadership and this was why he was effective. As a founder of Apple, and the CEO, he had **positional power**. Additionally, his position had been questioned and he had been removed. The company then failed and had to recall him to the position. The company then thrived again once more when he was in control again. His influence from his position of power was verified. He was also an expert in his field and beyond, which increased his influence. He was passionate about his work and often demonstrated this in the many talks and speeches he made about what his vision was. The success of his ideas spread and created passion in his field. Lastly, in his speeches he used significant nonverbal signals and was renowned as being able to control many situations with nonverbal signals. There are countless essays written about Steve Jobs' nonverbal communication and how influential it was.

Steve Jobs is a good example of the power of influence, but most leaders have influence to some degree, depending on how they use the four forms of influence. We all use varying forms of influence, but inclusive leaders need to be competent in all four if they are to wield influence effectively. The more tools you have to influence others, the more likely it is that you will achieve your goals.

In 1936, Dale Carnegie wrote his now very famous book "How to Win Friends and Influence People". In this book he stated that there were six ways to get others to like you and, in that way, be able to influence them:

1. Be genuinely interested in other people.
2. Smile.
3. Remember how much value we place on our own names.
4. Listen and encourage others to talk about themselves.
5. Talk to the other person about their interests.

6. Sincerely try to make the other person feel important.

These tools are still used today as keyways in which the power of influence is achieved in many different situations. Interestingly, how many of those can you recognize as attributes that inclusive leaders need to have?

Leading with Compassion (Emotional Intelligence)

"Become the kind of leader that people would follow voluntarily, even if you had no title or position." —Brian Tracy

Linking leadership with compassion is not a new exercise; it is just not used as often as it should be. This is unfortunate as it has been demonstrated that being a compassionate leader has a significant correlation with productivity and profitability. Compassion in this sense, is defined as understanding people's motivations, difficulties, hopes, and the ability to create the right type of support that can help people to achieve their goals and become the best that they can be. The best performing organizations have leaders who understand this and spend the time to develop and value their staff.

Leading with compassion is a specific leadership tool that is on the opposite side of the ledger from workplace bullying, leading with empathy and concern has emerged from the psychological field of mindfulness. As leadership studies have moved towards inclusive leadership, compassion has gained more and more prominence. It can be seen as a way to bridge intrusive leadership with organizational purpose. In true terms, intrusive leadership is a form of compassionate leadership as it focuses on valuing individuals and team members.

Compassionate leadership is not about allowing employees to get away with not doing their job, nor is it about ignoring poor behavior or excusing low productivity. Like intrusive leadership, the focus is on valuing employees.

Compassion is about treating other people the way they want to be treated. If a situation arises where an employee is behaving poorly, then a compassionate leader will talk to them about this in an understanding way, to comprehend what the problem is. The focus will be on continuous improvement and how they can solve any problems they are facing.

A leader in advocating compassionate leadership, is the Search Inside Yourself Leadership Institute (SIYLI), started within Google as a mindfulness center. It has since grown to become an international center of compassionate leadership. The center specifically defines compassion into three main areas that can be used by leaders as the basis for compassionate leadership:[73]

1. **Empathy** – Feeling what someone else is feeling in a particular situation.

2. **Cognitive** – Understanding why someone is feeling and thinking the way that they are, including understanding why they hold certain opinions.

3. **Motivation** – Wanting to take care of others and reduce their suffering.

Compassionate leaders start off trying to feel what others are feeling and then trying to understand why they see things in certain ways. They try to treat others the way other people want to be treated. The main motivation of the SIYLI is to try to understand how compassionate leadership, using the above three factors, can improve organizations by reducing stress. The focus on feeling and thinking aims to get employees and leaders to think more in the moment and by doing so practice more mindful techniques.

As with all aspects of Google's work, this is based on data, which has backed up the positive correlation between mindfulness and productivity. By providing employees with the skills to manage their feelings and thoughts, they

---

[73] https://www.forbes.com/sites/margiewarrell/2017/05/20/compassionate-leadership/#3db7f3925df9

are working towards reducing our natural responses to conflict, anger and fear. By reducing these we can better manage different situations that are often taken over by irrational behavior.

Being mindful through compassionate leadership can provide situations where we can quickly understand our fear and anger and control it allowing rational thoughts to control the situation instead. Additionally, research has shown that "dedicated mindfulness practices don't just change the neural circuitry in the brain over time, they expand an individual's capacity to remain focused, diffuse conflict, build collaboration, perform under pressure and positively influence the behavior and wellbeing of others."[74] There is an obvious impact on the bottom line.

But it goes further. Mindfulness among leaders increases memory and creativeness of leaders and can have positive health effects on leaders as well as those who are led. More specifically, when leaders are asked to be compassionate, they become more courageous; just the skill necessary for implementing an inclusive organizational culture.

Asking your teams to make large changes such as introducing and embracing an inclusive mindset is hard work, takes effort, and requires courage. When change is introduced, fear and anger are often the first emotions that are evoked; this comes from our System 1 way of thinking. It is a natural reaction to change, something that is physiologically wired into our brains. Through using compassionate, disruptive leadership; with a purpose, we can overcome this and use instead, System 2 thinking to create positive change.

---

[74] Ibid.

"Leadership is a matter of having people look at you and gain confidence, seeing how you react. If you're in control, they're in control." – Tom Landry

---

When leaders act with compassion, they use System 2 thinking. This means that in situations where there may be conflict, they will use rational thinking and will appear calm and in control. They will confidently assess and understand particular situations and when this happens team members and employees will see them in control and will have increased confidence in them.

Marie-Claire Ross, the CEO of Trustologie, wrote that there are 8 ways to build compassionate leadership[75]:

1. **Listen**. This skill was also a key aspect of intrusive leadership. Compassionate leaders listen more than they talk, and they listen effectively. Ross writes that the best way to determine the resilience of a leader is to observe them when they receive bad news. If they are compassionate and resilient, rather than jumping to conclusions they will listen and want to understand the situation. They will ask for more information and listen effectively to what they are being told. **In this way, to become a compassionate leader, talk less, listen more.**

2. **Assume The Best**. This is true of employees and team members. Assume that everyone is trying the best that they can and that if they do something that is not up to your standards, assume they have tried to do the best thing that they can at the time. Ask and see how you can help. Being optimistic of others allows you to have high expectations of them and this in turn leads to increased performance as discussed before. Avoid labelling people and instead focus on **why** people do

---

[75] http://www.digicast.com.au/blog/bid/93259/8-Steps-to-Leading-with-Compassion

things and work on **how** to help them improve.

3. **Check Your Emotions**. When we return to our base emotions of fear and anger, we are evoking System 1 thinking. It is our immediate fast brain thinking on display. This type of thinking is controlled by our emotions. Rather than "feed" these emotions, we need to be able to understand why we feel certain ways and by understanding the 'way' we can begin to think rationally instead and use System 2's slower thinking.

    - Ross gives a great example of how we react to reading a newspaper. If you read a newspaper article and it makes you angry, how you then act demonstrates how well you understand your emotions.

    - Compassionate leaders in this situation will try to understand why they think the way they do and will then move on.

    - Leaders who don't understand their emotions instead will remain angry and write an angry letter to the author of the article.

Which type of behavior leads to a more productive organization?

1. **Be Interested in Others**. Ross best describes this as stop talking about yourself! Intrusive leaders with an inclusive mindset, are examples of this. They get to know the people around them and try to understand who they are and what their background is. This is not because they want to judge them or to come to a conclusion about them, but rather it is to try to develop a strong professional relationship with them.

2. **Accept Responsibility**. Instead of searching for ways to blame others, compassionate leaders accept responsibility for their actions including their mistakes. They accept that they are not perfect and will never be

perfect. They examine themselves and take responsibility for their behavior.

3. **Be Open To Feedback**. This will be discussed in the next section in more detail, but it is the main way in which anyone can improve. Think of someone you have worked with or someone you know personally who does not accept feedback. Think about what problems this causes. Think about how different the situation would be if they did accept the feedback. The main problem with not accepting feedback is that the problem is not acknowledged and without acknowledging the problem, there is no way in which improvements can be made. Compassionate leaders understand this and try to improve this ability among staff they work with.

4. **Support Others**. Compassion is about reducing suffering and by supporting others around you can achieve this. Compassionate leaders will go beyond their job to help others and have a generous spirit. This support needs to be applied uniformly and not specifically towards any particular person or group of people you may feel more comfortable with or feel you relate to better. If others are to accept and trust your support it must not be seen as biased.

5. **Avoiding Personal Criticism**. This seems like an obvious statement to make but it is very common for leaders at all levels to forget about the negative effect that this can have. If personal criticism is used by leaders, it is extremely hard to build any of the positive relationships mentioned in this book. As soon as personal criticism is used it is seen as an insult, trust is lost, and it will take a long time for it to be restored, if at all. If you receive personal criticism, as a compassionate leader, you must check your emotions. You need to try to understand why they are doing

this and look at how it is making you feel. You can then react without using emotions and implement a rational action. If criticism needs to be conveyed compassionate leaders will use constructive criticism that is matched with positive feedback to increase empathy and reduce stress[76].

Ultimately, leading with compassion is about trying to become more mindful of how we treat others and also how we treat ourselves.

Seeking Feedback

Organizational growth requires leaders who are willing to learn. Curiosity to find out about new tools and methods to grow the organization is one way in which leaders grow themselves and their organizations.

Another method that is central to learning is feedback. This is beyond just the quarterly or annual feedback reports. While they are undoubtedly vital to an organization's success, they do not paint the full picture of an individual's position and they need to be accompanied by other forms of feedback.

Annual reports do demonstrate the importance of feedback for learning and their longevity is evidence of this. Annual feedback reports provide an overview of an individual's performance over the last 12 months. It would be hard to imagine an organizational leader trying to improve growth and productivity without knowing the capabilities and performance of their team from the past.

Feedback in the day-to-day management of the organization, can be a difficult thing to manage for a number of reasons:

1. It is often difficult to receive feedback as it often focuses on the negative attributes of performance.
2. It is often not timely. As it is a difficult thing to manage, feedback is

---

76 http://www.digicast.com.au/blog/bid/93259/8-Steps-to-Leading-with-Compassion

often not prioritized. This can lead to problems with providing enough
feedback and feedback that is relevant.

3. Feedback is often vague and general. Nonspecific feedback is difficult
to use for learning purposes as it does not identify specific problems.

Receiving feedback can be perceived as negative and due to this it is rare
for people, especially leaders to ask for feedback. Imagine your boss sees you on
the elevator this morning and says, "Stop by my office at the end of the day
tomorrow. I have some feedback I need to share with you." Few people would
assume that the conversation is constructive or positive. The first thought most
people would have is; "***What have I done wrong***?" It would be a long day
waiting on that conversation. There would likely be some sleepless hours
replaying the events of the past week or month as to what this feedback could
be about.

When feedback conversations are held more frequently, they become less
stressful and the easier it becomes to ask for feedback. Feedback meetings are
normally held during performance reviews. More progressive organizations hold
these once a quarter. Some will wait and have them once a year. I consulted for
a global oil and gas company that the average length of time since the last
performance evaluation for its leaders was over four years! That's a long time to
go with no awareness of your performance.

Many employees see feedback as a very stressful exercise that is often
linked to promotions, compensation, and job retention. If informal feedback
conversations occur outside the performance review structure and without
correlation to job retention, then they can be used to improve and learn. Imagine
if you held a '***check in and chat***' meeting once a month to learn about where
you can improve. When it came to a formal feedback meeting once a quarter,
the meeting would be less of a challenge and less stressful.

When we ask for feedback that is both negative and positive, we can
increase our job satisfaction. We are able to adapt quicker to new situations as

we evaluate our performance in a timely way. It also means that we can be prepared for other feedback systems.

As a leader it is important to get feedback in order to learn. In order for this to be effective, you will need to understand the purpose of the feedback and what it is you are looking for with the feedback. The feedback should focus not only on ways in which you are succeeding but also on areas where you can improve. Additionally, by asking for feedback from team members and employees, your humility and desire to improve helps to build working relationships.

Asking for feedback in real time is a successful way of receiving insight into a specific project or task that has been completed. It is better to get the feedback sooner rather than later. In this way, it becomes more relevant. Timely feedback discussions also reduce the vagueness of the information provided. Receiving feedback immediately after a task or project allows you to receive specific actionable feedback.

Another key to successfully getting feedback is asking the right questions. Rather than asking for general feedback, ask for specific areas where improvements can be made. Ask for one specific area of improvement, or one specific area related to that specific project. The idea is to view the feedback as a form of coaching. If the questions are posed correctly then this can be achieved. Likewise, if you are looking to provide feedback to other team members and employees then this can be directed around very specific questions that drive the conversation towards coaching topics.

In many cases, feedback is far too general and cannot be used for improvement. General feedback can include large statements like, "you are not a team player" or "you are too aggressive". This can be too vague for any coaching or learning to occur. It also means that people can become labelled and this is detrimental to coaching. Rather than vague general statements, feedback needs to be about specific ways in which you can improve. So rather than giving feedback that "you are not a team player", provide specific ways in which actions helped the team and ways in which it didn't help the team. You can also identify or ask for ways in which things could improve.

Given that most feedback is given via performance reviews and in formal settings, it is often presumed that feedback is only given by leaders. This is not the case and feedback can be received from any direction in the organization. As a leader, getting feedback from people you manage is a very useful way of learning about your leadership style and its effectiveness. It is a good way to learn about your weaknesses as a leader and ways in which you can improve. It can also help to build relationships with your team members and help to understand what types of support they need.[77]

Team members can also do the same in searching for feedback. By doing this you can establish regular feedback that comes from different areas of your work. In return for asking for feedback, you can also offer to give feedback to others in your team. This encourages learning across the team and helps to ensure that the feedback is objective and based on a desired goal of learning and continuous improvement. Feedback settings don't need to be formally scheduled meetings. They can be informal and brief. This flexibility creates trust that can translate into positive experiences with feedback processes. It also allows for feedback to be given in the moment and as the need arises.

Seeking feedback should become a natural part of leadership and a natural part of any inclusive management process. It should become an objective tool for learning that allows organizations to grow and become more inclusive. Demonstrating an inclusive mindset and being an inclusive leader means it is important to recognize whether or not inclusive goals are met and whether or not employees feel valued and respected. Without feedback mechanisms there can be no room for creativity and innovation in any organization. Leaders that promote and enhance feedback, enhance creativity and innovation, but while this is one way of doing this, this can be achieved through other means. The next

---

[77] https://hbr.org/2015/05/how-to-get-the-feedback-you-need

section looks at this in more depth.

Enhancing the Opportunity for Creativity and Innovation

"The best executive is the one who has sense enough to pick good people to do what must be done, and self-restraint enough to keep from meddling with them while they do it." —Theodore Roosevelt

Creativity and innovation are primary ingredients for organization growth and organizational performance; they are a primary indicator of whether or not an organization will survive in the long term. They improve engagement, empowerment and enablement and help move towards inclusion.

Creating workplaces that develop innovation and creativity can be a difficult enterprise. Like other aspects of creating inclusive workplace cultures, innovation and creativity also need effort and courage. They need leaders who are committed to creating environments where creativity and innovation can thrive. This can appear daunting as it is often assumed that driving and enhancing innovation and creativity is expensive and complex.

Most organizations already have innovative and creative individuals, and this translates into creative and innovative teams if this is valued by leaders. This is the first step. Leaders needs to value employees so that they feel that their contributions are seen as important and so that they become willing to contribute. Previous sections detail how this can be achieved with inclusive leadership.

It is also important for organizations to recognize that innovation and creativity are different processes. Creativity is about generating new ideas, whereas innovation is the application of these ideas; innovation can be seen as the application of creativity. Both of these terms have cultural implications. If the organizational culture is inclusive, then creativity will rise because people will know that their ideas are welcomed. The challenge of becoming innovative is also a cultural issue. Innovation is the application of creativity. Applying new ideas can also be risky. In a risk averse culture, innovation will be much more constrained that a culture that sees failure as a learning opportunity.

There are four main types of tools that can enhance innovation and creativity:
1. The design of the workplace.
2. Encouraging collaboration.
3. Connecting teams.
4. Harnessing the virtual workplace.[78]

Enhancing the workplace.

Normally in workplaces, innovation and creativity are standardized processes. A brain storming session is conducted and workers gather at a specific time to develop new ideas.

And yet in our workplaces, most workspaces are not developed for idea generation; rather they are focused on productivity. They reinforce hierarchy and often ignore the sharing of ideas.

Many organizations are waking up to this and ensuring that their workspaces have areas that are prepared for creativity and innovation. You may have seen the office spaces of innovative companies such as Google and Apple who have not only understood this idea but have also used it effectively to encourage idea generation. It is no surprise that these companies lead when it comes to innovation.

---

[78] http://www.innovationmanagement.se/2015/06/02/four-tools-to-support-creativity-and-innovation/

Encouraging Collaboration.

Innovation in organizations without collaboration is a difficult exercise. Exploring new ideas involves communicating new concepts, projects and insights that relies specifically on collaboration between team members. Working together for innovation requires learning in the face of external changes. Organizations that can achieve this develop the most innovation and creativity. This is a cycle: the more people learn, the more innovative they can become and the more innovative they become, the more they learn. The more people your organizations gets involved in this cycle of improvement through innovation, the better the process. The more collaboration there is the more people from different areas of expertise are involved, the more effective the innovation is.

In our personal lives when we need to generate ideas, the process is normally a collaborative one. We ask a range of people for input; we get as much information as possible and share our own ideas with many people. In this way, we can then try to come up with the best idea or solution to the problem we face. This is often forgotten in the workplace especially those with strict hierarchies. Often the ideas for innovation can come from the most unlikely places. I used to work with a young man who had not gone to college and he would sit silently in meetings while the leaders discussed the problem. Towards the end of the meeting, he would calmly raise his hand and offer an insight to the problem that none of the college graduate leaders had seen. After this happened a few times, he was always invited to provide insight during the meetings. An inclusive mindset and inclusive leadership means understanding that everyone has contributions that are of value. Sometimes the term thinking outside the box has to be changed. A truly inclusive mindset means kicking down the walls of the box completely.

Connecting Teams

In Steve Wozniak's autobiography, he tells an anecdote about a change in the office that changed the way in which teams at HP connected:

"Every day at 10:00 am and 2:00 pm they wheeled in donuts and coffee. That was so nice. And smart, because the reason they did it was so everyone would gather in a common place and be able to talk, socialize and exchange ideas."[79]

He goes on to say that when small coffee pots were introduced, the shared coffee time disappeared and along with it went this twice a day social time. In a similar way to the design of the workplace, designing spaces to encourage social connections is just as important. Social connections are often left to the "annual picnic" or to holiday parties. These one-off events become forced exercises and often can become awkward situations that are not seen as genuine exercises in generating social connections.

Developing social connections is about developing regular initiatives that can help build professional relationships that enhance innovation and creativity.

Post Covid Environment: Harnessing the Virtual Workplace

If you used your smart phone today, it is likely that you used an application. The development of applications is an example of how virtual workplaces enhanced creativity and innovation. They were first designed as part of the first iPhones. Steve Job and his team realized that if the apps for iPhones were designed in house by Apple teams, it would limit their innovation and creativity and they would soon run out of human and financial resources to develop the potential number of different applications needed.

Instead, they developed an online innovation ecosystem where developers could design apps within the iPhone system and then sell their product. This increased the number of potential apps that could be designed. It would have

---

[79] INSERT REFERENCE

been impossible for Apple to develop all of the apps that are available today, not simply because of resources. They would have limited the creativity and innovation behind the design of applications.

In a similar way, organizations can benefit from online innovative ecosystems to provide innovative and creative ideas. Getting feedback from customers, partners, suppliers, experts, and so on, opens up the processes behind innovation and creativity. As part of this, all organizations can also use software tools to develop new models and ideas. This system is called **Open Innovation** and there are many ways in which this can be used by organizations to enhance their internal idea generation.

THOUGHT PROVOKING QUESTION:

In what areas can open innovation be applied in your organization? Human capital systems, recruiting methodologies, retention strategies and more!

Creating an 'Ownership' Mentality

> *"As we look ahead into the next century, leaders will be those who empower others." – Bill Gates*

Another aspect of developing inclusive organizations is leaders developing an environment where people want to work. In a recent Gallup poll, 52% of Americans said that they were disengaged at work. It is clear that the attempts to improve wellbeing at work and improve engagement are not working.

- So how do organizations change this?
- How do they develop teams that have an 'All-In' mentality?

Part of developing an inclusive organization aims at addressing this problem. When employees understand the organizational purpose, it is easier to align with that and bring a proprietary mindset to their tasks.

WHAT IS AN OWNERSHIP MINDSET?

- When you get your employees to move beyond seeing the company/organization as a source of a paycheck and instead see it as **their company.** everything changes!

Different tools can be used with different teams to address this problem. The tools used need to be adaptable that can be applied to different situations. The first step is for the CEO to think of themselves as the Chief Engagement Officer. The CEO must lead the engagement and they must lead in promoting an 'Ownership Mentality'.

The Chief Engagement Officer must develop tools that can help employees to measure, first of all, their current levels of engagement. This needs to be an innovative tool based on trust; it must show that all employees are valued.

This also starts with having a CEO that has an inclusive mindset. The next step is to then set goals with high expectations; these are the hard goals discussed in section one of this book. These are very effective tools as they communicate to employees that they are capable of achieving at a high level.

There has to be an organizational purpose that goes beyond the bottom line and shareholders. Of course, there must be a focus on being profitable and a good steward of the institutional resources. To move the needle, for most progressive organizations, they have to realize that the real value of an organization is not reflected on its balance sheet.

The real value of an organizations lies between the ears of its employees.

In order for that value to be realized and leveraged, their also has to be a connection to the heart and passion of employees in order for them to have an ownership mentality.

In a study, conducted by the Equitable Workplace Institute, people were asked what percentage of their best efforts they gave at work on a regular basis.

1. Only you can answer that question, because only you know what your best efforts are.

2. People were not asked if they give 100% of their effort, 100% of the time. That is not fair to expect of anyone.

The results were pretty surprising. Fifty-seven (57%) percent of employees self-stated that they give less than 100% of their best efforts on a regular basis.

When asked what would incentivize them to give more of their best efforts, the number one answer was not pay, perks, or benefits. It was '***having a boss that treats me with dignity and respect***'.

When people are interviewed for a job, often the person hired has skills and capabilities that exceed the job requirements. This competency that exceeds the job requirements is called *discretionary effort*. As long as the employee does what is required, there is little an employer or organization can do. When people feel they are not treated with dignity and respect and when they do not feel connected to the organizational purpose, they revert back to doing only what the job requires.

If you want people to have an ownership mentality, it starts with having an inclusive mindset. It means having leaders with high levels of emotional and cultural intelligence. It means connecting people with the organizational purpose that exceeds the top line (revenue growth), the bottom-line (cost reductions), and the pipeline (recruiting, retention and talent management.). It also includes having a heart-line!

Ultimately this is an inclusive leadership issue; when leaders are engaged and have an ownership mentality it is usually connect at a head, hands, and heart level (affective, behavioral and cognitive!). When that occurs, employees are all in!

Moving Towards Inclusive Situational Leadership

"People buy into the leader before they buy into the vision." —John Maxwell

---

Given that so many people are disengaged from work, it is not surprising that more and more people are now looking for ways to validate their work. We want to be heard, for our contributions to matter and for our voices to be heard. We want our work to be important, so we are not taken for granted. We want to be relevant and we want our skills to be respected. We want to be useful and we want to be part of an organization that is making a difference. We want to be part of achieving a goal and part of an organization's success.

In short from the moment, we show up at work, we want to be inspired. This is not always possible; it is impossible to be inspired all of the time.

Many leaders are creating environments where no one is inspired at any time; as a result, employees are expired – R.O.A.D.

Having an inclusive mindset means rather than create a single model to earn the trust and respect of all employees, inclusive leaders must recognize that they need to create adaptable plans to help improve performance and build loyalty. There are no magic ingredients that can create plans to engage employees. There is no perfect list. The idea is for leaders to be ***Inclusive Situational Leaders*** who have a basket of tools that they can apply in different situations.

If leaders want to move from having an increasing number of employees who have quit, but just haven't told you yet, to having teams that are inspired, they must demonstrate to employees that their contributions can help to solve the organizations problems and work towards the organization's goals.

In one organization, over 40% of their employees were capable of retiring at a moment notice. The time it took to train and certify their replacements was twenty-four months. The reality of this crisis meant that if these union represented employees were dissatisfied with something, they could walk out the door, start collecting their retirement checks and the company would be in jeopardy of not being able to sustain itself while training, qualifying and certifying their replacements.

When I refer to vested and rested employees, I am referring to those whose retirement plans were already vested and they could walk out at the end of their shift, if they chose to. Many of these employees continued to work in order to pay for something that they considered to be optional - that new truck, the boat, that hunting camp, the condo on the beach.

During a corporate culture assessment with a group of 'vested & rested' employees, an engineer who was completely disengaged, said he viewed his employment contract to be renewed every two weeks. He said, *"When you hand me my paycheck, my employment contract ends. It starts again the next day for two more weeks, until you hand me my next check…. assuming I show up!"*

This is a further example of someone who falls into the category of 'turn-under'. Not someone who has quit and left, but someone who has quit and stayed.

Inclusive leaders with a disruptive inclusive mindset need to work towards creating a purpose people can believe in and not just focused exclusively on institutional profits. Working towards a purpose allows employees to feel like they are making a difference with what they are doing that is more than just profit. Leaders that are compassionate also get to know who their employees are and understand their personal goals and aspirations. These can then be matched to the organizational goals to create more inspired employees.

Moving Towards Inclusive Situational Leadership is about using a combination of all the tools described in this book. The trick is to use different ones depending on the needs of your organization **and** on how inclusive your organization is.

Different levels of inclusive culture require different tools at different times and the success toolkit that your organization develops should reflect this. Instituting an organizational culture of inclusion and having an individual inclusive mindset has one goal – to make employees feel valued; to let the know you see them; to make sure they know they belong. From this they can become inspired.

"When you're surrounded by people who share a passionate commitment around a common purpose, anything is possible."

– Howard Schultz

What Do You Focus On?

In this way, one of the most important characteristics a leader can have is focus. Leaders need this to be able to meet goals but also to be able to stay on track and not be deterred by distractions, and other demands.

In this way, leadership styles are made up of two distinct parts:

1. The focus on relationships and people.
2. The focus on tasks, processes and results.

These two things can be seen as either being high and low, and it is a mixture of these that create an individual's leadership style. Leaders with high levels of focus on processes and tasks tend to be focused on getting the job done. They are often direct, and goal focused. On the other hand, leaders who are focused on people tend to focus more on how their team is doing. They are more compassionate (EQ) and more intrusive (in a positive sense).

To create inclusive organizations, leaders need to adopt a mix of these two styles. They need to be focused on their people, but they also need to be focused on purpose and organizational goals. They need to be able to apply different levels of each as necessary; they need to be situational.

Change Your Focus from the Rearview Mirror to the Windshield

"Create your future from your future, not your past."

— Werner Erhard

When organizations produce their annual reports, the focus is on what the past years earnings were. The document illustrates where the organization has been successful and in what ways. In a way, the document is like looking in the rearview mirror to see where you have been. It shows stakeholders how the organization has performed, and it demonstrates where they have been on their roadmap. Most of these reports do indeed project a forward-looking view, but that is often predicated on the past performance being emphasized in the annual report.

When we focus on the past, we can find out where we went, how we did, what choices we made, and use this to determine where we want to go. The rearview mirror helps us to see how the past has created our present. The annual report is an example of this.

It can be to our detriment to place too much focus on the past - the rearview mirror. When you are sitting in the driving seat of the car, you have more than one mirror. You have the rearview mirror that helps you to see where you have gone. You have the two sideview mirrors that help you to see who is travelling alongside you. These are your competitors and your sideview mirrors provide you with information about what they are doing and where they are going.

However, your car also has one other more significant viewpoint and that is your windshield. Through your windshield you can see where it is you are going. It is the biggest view you have while in the driver's seat. The view ahead is changing drastically for organizations. One of the most important roles for a leader is having a vision and understanding the landscape ahead.

One of the top three expenses for any organization is people or people related costs. The clear differentiator between a market leader and their competition is the effective deployment and utilization of all resources, especially its human capital.

The human capital landscape is changing in critical ways. As said earlier, in the United States over seventy-five (75%) percent of people entering the workforce are women, immigrants, or people of color. In some organizations there are as many as five generations in the workforce. These changes are not just US centric. These changes are occurring on a global basis with immigration being a major topic around the world.

The significance of having inclusive leaders and an inclusive mindset is a windshield issue that cannot be overstated or overlooked! It is not an optional competency. Therefore, the look through the windshield requires organizations to understand not just the importance of having an inclusive mindset, it also means understanding the importance of Emotional Intelligence, Social Intelligence, and Cultural Intelligence. The windshield is becoming increasingly more important.

For example, if there is a problem in your organization, there is a benefit to look to the past to find out how this was solved in the past. There is also a benefit to use the sideview mirrors to see where the competition is and where they might be heading to trouble shoot the cause of the current state or challenge your organization is facing.

There is also a benefit to take stock of the current state understand the existing problem and then look to the future. You can try to imagine what it is you want your organization to look like once the problem has been solved and work towards that ultimate goal. By doing this, you become more innovative.

EXAMPLE: If your organization is having trouble finding, hiring, and retaining the increasingly diverse employees found in the marketplace today. Understanding how you got there is important. Understanding what to do moving forward is mission critical.

The windshield offers more ideas and more pathways to choose from and in this way, it is the more creative and sustainable option to choose. We cannot change the past, nor can we influence it. But we can change and influence the future. We can choose whether we want to focus on the small rearview mirror or on the large windshield. We can appreciate the sideview mirrors to gain an understanding of the competitive landscape. Yet we must also remember that no two organizational cultures, visions, or purpose are identical. Our focus has to be on our own windshield with an appreciation for the rearview and side view mirrors. We have the option to choose if we dwell on the past or focus on the future.

You have probably heard it many times before. Someone will blame their past for their problems today and say that this prevents them from being successful today (Fixed Mindset). They dwell on things that happened a long time ago and say that these are the determining factors to their current successes **and** their future successes. Imagine trying to drive a car by focusing solely on the rearview mirror. This is what focusing on the past is doing. It is ineffective and dangerous. It will not create the most successful future you can have.

Using annual reports to analyze how your organization is doing is important as it shows the current state of the organizational financial status and strategy and it can highlight crucial mistakes as well as provide some insights about the desired state. But it should be used only as a **partial** tool in determining where your company should go next. Investors are interested in how your organization got here. They are most interested in where you are going next!

"Just as people cannot live without eating, so a business cannot live without profits. But most people don't live to eat, and neither must businesses live just to make profits." – John Mackey

---

Developing inclusive organizations requires leaders who can see that the past has gone, and the focus now is on building something new. In order to achieve that successfully, we need to look forward with an inclusive mindset and use our future goals to develop the organizations we want to work for. Rather than saying we are an organization of tolerance and we want to move beyond that, you must start by saying we are going to build an inclusive organization and then define what this looks like for you. Once you have done that you have created your road map. You then have the windshield, with a purpose, in front of you that lays out where you need to go to achieve this success toolkit. What are you waiting for?

Asking the Right Questions

Throughout the discussions on leadership in this book, the focus has been on generating leadership with courage. Part of this is being able to understand situations by being curious about what is going on. This requires the courage to investigate what is really happening. It means spending time to go beyond the minimum and really figure out what is happening in situations. The skills needed to do this include asking the right questions.

It is rare for people to discuss this skill or to see it as an important leadership skill. It is definitely not something that comes up in job interviews or in job descriptions. No one ever asked me, "How well do you ask questions?" and it is not taught at schools or as part of most work-related training programs.

But it is such an important part of any leader's role that it should be seen as an integral part of any leader's role. Think of any of the skills I have discussed in this book. Without asking the right question, it would be extremely hard to develop these skills. Without asking the right questions to determine where you already sit with any particular skill, it is impossible to know what learning is needed.

"Make meaning not money." – Brian Scudamore

Think of this scenario. You are a leader of a large project team and you are working towards a tight deadline. Your team frequently seems to be slowing down their work as you approach the deadline, and you cannot seem to motivate them to meet the deadline. In desperation, you call a team meeting to try to understand what is going on. You start by asking the team some questions to try to get them talking about the problem. You ask them why they cannot meet the project goals. You ask them why they are failing with the project. They do not answer, and they remain silent. You decide to give them a pep talk and you talk to them about how important it is to meet deadlines. The meeting ends and you continue your work.

One month before the deadline, you notice that the team is still not working to the required efficiency to meet the deadline. Frustrated you call in a team leader to talk to them about what is happening. You ask them the same questions you asked in the team meeting. This time, they respond. They tell you that they think that the team does not have the right resources to complete the project on time and that they have been trying to fix this. They have not spoken up about this as they were concerned that they would be seen as having a negative outlook. You get angry at this and ask the team leader why they didn't tell you this before. The team leader responds: **"*You didn't ask this.*"**

- What questions could you have asked in this situation that would have allowed you to understand what is going on?

- How could you have better tried to understand the situation?
- What other factors impacted on your ability to understand the problem?
- Could it be more than the wording of the question?
- Could there be cultural implications associated with the disconnect?
- Do you have the needed social and emotional intelligence?

While teams need to be empowered to communicate effectively in all situations, including communicating problems in this scenario, the manager focused too much emphasis on the **blame** rather than the problem. The manager's questions created a situation where the team members were unlikely to discuss the real problem as they would fear that their performance, outlook, or commitment would have been questioned. In this case, better questions to ask include:

- On a scale of 1 – 10, do you have enough resources to complete your tasks?
- What parts of the project can be delivered on time?
- What have been the main successes of the project?
- In what ways do you need support to complete the project?
- How can the project plan be adjusted to meet your project goals?
- What can we learn from this project?

These questions are based on the tasks and not on the individual's performance and so create a scenario where the team members are more likely to discuss what is going on. With the right questions, the true situation can be discovered.

In the scenario above, it is also easy to see how asking the right questions can actually increase the effectiveness of the manager. The manager asking questions about the deadline doesn't demonstrate empathy. *It is not disruptive*

thinking. It does not demonstrate cultural or social intelligence. It ignores the true issue that is going on and has directed the discussion to be about blame.

The second set of questions creates a compassionate and effective manager that is interested in finding out what the problem is. It is focused on solutions and not guilt. The second set of questions also helps team members to understand that their input is valued, and they are respected members of the team. This would also help the team members to build on their relationships and develop together as a team. Asking the right questions is also important when looking to build self-awareness among leaders.

Asking the right questions about yourself can help you to analyze your unproductive habits and unconscious biases. Asking the right questions about yourself can help you to find out what you are good at and what you can do better. The idea is to base the questions on constructive frameworks as opposed to destructive blaming frameworks.

The best questioners are those whose inquiries allow team members to arrive at their own conclusions about how to fix a problem. This creates empowerment and engagement in very effective ways. Asking the right question is also a helpful way for teams to constructively demonstrate what is important. It also allows you as a leader to share what you are thinking about.

Inclusive leaders who ask the right questions also know what questions to ask about the organization itself. They know what questions will help the organization become more effective and will focus their questions on structures, processes, and practices.[80] They will always be asking whether or not there is a better way to do things. They will be able to ask questions without employees becoming defensive and they will always investigate in a constructive way.

One of the reasons why asking questions is such a difficult task is that it is humbling. Asking the right questions means that leaders need to admit that they

---

[80] https://www.forbes.com/sites/ronashkenas/2015/06/19/how-great-leaders-ask-great-questions/#52861aa9c49f

do not have all the information. They are admitting that they need to learn more about a particular situation. Perhaps this is why it is such a rare skill. Ironically, the strongest leaders are those that can admit that they do not have all the answers and so need to ask the right questions. They are confident enough to admit that they don't know everything. When leaders presume that they have all the knowledge, the egotism creates an automatic barrier to forming inclusion in the culture of the organization.

Keep in mind there are cultural dynamics at play when asking questions. In some global cultures, leaders are expected to have all the answers. Implementing a collaborative approach to problem solving and process development can be perceived as the leader not knowing what they are doing.

I was working with a client on a global project team. They assigned a leader from the USA to head their operations based in Singapore. The new leader, interested in formulating a collaborative approach, held a meeting with supervisors, managers, and directors from the ASIAN region. He asked the group for their input about ways to improve the manufacturing processes and streamline production, performance, safety, and improve profitability.

After being met with silence, he then began to individually ask the participants for their input and found virtually no response or input being provided. He became a bit annoyed that no one seemed interested in suggesting the improvements and modifications the organizations should consider. He adjourned the meeting.

Over the course of the next two weeks, over 65% of those in that meeting abruptly resigned. The exit interviews were all the same, they found a better job. The CEO asked if I would head to Singapore and conduct one-on-one interviews and focus groups to try to prevent the remaining leaders from leaving. Everyone, including the new leader was extremely interested in getting to the bottom of what was happening.

The issue was a cultural difference in how collaborative leadership is viewed through a US Centric lens versus the way it is seen in other parts of the world.

From the US cultural perspective, it is acceptable even encouraged to get people at various levels in the organization, to share their thoughts and input. Their cultural lens expected those in leadership to have the answers. Leaders instruct what is to be done and the workers carry out their assigned tasks. This specific company was in the oil and gas production business. The refining process can be very incendiary and thus lives are at risk every day. These employees perceived the collaborative questions to be an indicator that their new boss didn't know what he was doing and that their lives were potentially in jeopardy. Therefore, they resigned as fast as they could.

Asking the right questions should be seen as an opportunity, but there are also cultural implications in today's increasingly diverse workforce to keep in mind. It is normally a way to find out how to improve relationships and processes. Asking the right questions can also be used to develop better relationships with stakeholders such as customers. These questions can help to find out challenges and problems in your organization, and they help to create more opportunities thorough strategic planning. Lastly, and perhaps the most important part of asking the right questions, is a basic tool for creative thinking. By asking questions starting with "How" or "I wish I could" you are offering up the challenge of solving problems to your team[81]. You are saying to them that you trust them with the problem and have confidence in their ability to solve the problem. This is an extremely empowering tool and allows innovation and creativity to thrive.

It's Critical to Find Activation Points

Just as knowing what the right questions are, it is also critical to be aware of when the right time to act is. When these are aligned, this is called an activation point:

---

[81] https://www.inc.com/rhett-power/great-leaders-ask-the-right-questions.html

"An activation point occurs when the right people at the right time are persuaded to take action that leads to measurable... change."[82] As I discussed in earlier sections of this book, in order for people to act they need to be engaged. They need to think that the problem they are working on is aligned with their own values and it is relevant to their lives. They must also believe that the change that comes from their actions is first of all possible, but also that it will result in a positive impact. The definition of positive impact/change varies from person to person and for many organizations, positive change can simply mean a profit is made. For the activation point to give rise to a positive result for the organization, the positive change must align with both the organizations goals and the person's goals.

In order to discover when an activation point has arrived, leaders will need to ask certain questions about the situation. As was mentioned earlier, the skill of asking the right question is essential, especially in this case.

Questions that can be asked include:

- Why is this project important?
- What will this project achieve for the organization?
- How does the project link to your organization's goals?
- Who needs to be involved?
- Who is on board?
- Who needs to do what?
- What needs to be done to test the project?
- What is the strategy of the project?
- What barriers will the project face?
- Who is aware of the project?
- Who understands the situation of the project?

---

[82] https://faunalytics.org/feature-article/discovering-the-activation-point/

- Is the project valued?

- Is the project understood?

- Do people care about the project?

- Has there been an interest in the project?

- What are the rewards for implementing the project?

- What is the timeline for the project?

- How is the project relevant to other existing projects?

- Do leaders understand the project?

- Are leaders committed to the project?

This leads to three stages of activation points:

1. Asking the above questions will lead to the first stage where team members know about the project and they know enough to value the project. They build an understanding and through this they create ownership and commitment on the project. Leaders need compassion to develop this.

2. The second stage is when team members have enough will to act and begin the project. They will only do this if they own the project and know the benefits of the project.

3. The third stage is the activation of the project itself. They must be given a reward at this stage in order to validate the first two steps and to further cement the commitment and ownership.[83]

As a tool for engaging team members, activation points are a very critical way of developing ownership and motivation. As demonstrated, without asking the right questions, it is difficult to achieve effective activation points.

"Whatever you can do or dream you can, begin it. Boldness has

---

[83] https://faunalytics.org/feature-article/discovering-the-activation-point/

genius, and magic and power in it. Begin it now." - Goethe

Empowering: Focusing People on What They Can Give, Not What They Can Get

When talking about empowering individuals, the focus is normally on what leaders must provide in order to build up employees. The idea is often that if employees are given the freedom to make their own decisions then they will become empowered. They will then feel valued enough to step up and take responsibility for the work that they do. This needs an environment of trust and creates employees who make decisions.

But is this enough? Can this be expanded? Is there a way to get more out of team members through empowerment?

"A leader is best when people barely know he exists, when his work is done, his aim fulfilled, they will say, we did it ourselves."

–Lao Tzu

Yes, there is. What if empowerment not only gave people the confidence to make their own decisions but it also gave people the confidence to solve problems on their own and to take on challenges on their own? In this way, empowerment would focus not so much on what employees get, but what they can give.

If this is achieved, then employees will have become engaged in their activities. They will be focused on the goals of the organization and will be actively looking to solve problems within the organization. That is, they will want to remove the barriers to an organization's success, and they will drive this process. This will be autonomous and independent processes driven by employees and team members.

So how can you develop teams that take on challenges and solve problems by their own initiative? How can you create teams that are empowered and focus on what they can give?

The Forbes Coaches Council was asked this precise question. From their answers, the following steps can be followed as part of your success toolkit[84]:

1. **Stop micromanaging.** Let go; let your team members run things and delegate properly. This will build trust. To do this, you will need to assess their capacity, assess their capability, develop commitment, and generate "buy in" from everyone involved. You will need them to believe that you think that they will succeed, so spend less time monitoring and encourage teamwork, taking on responsibility, and encourage the team to implement their own strategies.

2. **Place the ball in their court**. To do this, you need to take yourself out of the picture and give responsibility for developing outcomes to the team. The outcomes need to be related to the goals of the organization and as a managing coach, you just need to show them that their actions will help to develop the organization. You need to encourage them to understand that their actions create value for the whole organization.

3. **Align your organizational goals**. For team members to become engaged they will need to feel as though the goals of the project are aligned to their own. They need to connect to the project's goals. They need to align with the organization's goals. To do this, find out what the goals are of the team members and find those that align with the organization. Use these to then engage the team member.

4. **Ask questions and ask the right questions**. As above, finding out

---

[84] https://www.forbes.com/sites/forbescoachescouncil/2017/09/22/10-ways-you-can-start-empowering-your-employees/#716b7ce07af0

what is going on indicates that you have confidence in your team. Rather than dictating solutions, asking questions gives the team a chance to solve the problems by themselves.

5. **Stretch your team's abilities**. Set hard goals that show them that you believe they are capable.

6. **Focus on the goals and the end result**. Focus on the purpose of the organization and relate this to how individuals feed into this goal.

7. **Value ideas and contributions**. Create an environment where team members are encouraged to add ideas.

8. **Stay positive**. It is always easy to spot the problems and spot what is going wrong. It is what we normally do. Instead, include a focus on the positive parts of the project as well and look to always find out what was done well. If team members have not been empowered before, they will be reluctant to come forward if the focus is always on the negative. Prove that they can become empowered by focusing on the positive and by looking for ways to learn from mistakes instead of allocating blame.

9. **Trust your teams**. Trust that the decisions made, and actions taken are the team trying to do the best that they can. They may not be what you would decide to do but trust the team that they are focusing their efforts on achieving their goals. If they are empowered, engaged, and enabled it is extremely likely that they will be focused already.

Focusing empowerment in this way, does not just create more effective employees. It also allows you to get more out of less. By working with your employees to develop their abilities to become more effective, you can increase their productivity, in a very effective and efficient way.

Disturbing the Thinking of Stakeholders

"Anyone can hold the helm when the sea is calm."

— Publilius Syrus

Engaging stakeholders is a key role of any leader and is a key part of most organizations' goals. Anyone who takes on a leadership role will perform some sort of stakeholder mapping task to understand where to put energy in developing relationships with stakeholders.

The aim of this task is to get all stakeholders engaged in the process of developing an inclusive mindset focused on respect. Organizational change is only successful, and it is only long lasting when all stakeholders involved are committed to the change and are empowered to be part of the change. Many stakeholders often do not understand their role in being part of the goal because many organizations do not have a purpose statement.

Understanding Your Purpose as an Inclusive Leader

"Leadership requires the courage to make decisions that will benefit the next generation."

– Alan Autry

Throughout this book we have been referring to the idea of purpose and relating it to the importance of teams, leaders, and organizations. It is often assumed that purpose exists in these places because they have a mission, a set of goals, a vision, plans and objectives. It is often assumed that developing a combination of these will automatically provide the team, leader, and organization with purpose.

When we talk about goals, plans, and objectives and so on, we often do not expand to consider what the purpose of all of these are. Say for example the mission of your organization is: "To spread product x throughout the world", this does not indicate the purpose. You can still ask why. Why does this product need to be spread around the world? If you do manage to spread it around the world, what do you achieve? What is it for?

This is purpose and this is where effective leaders come in. Additionally, leaders also will have a purpose statement relative to their role. Purpose within organizations does not have to be based on social mores but can be linked to shared values of team members within the organization. The way in which purpose is decided among leaders, teams, and organizations is a subjective exercise and very much depends on the situation. There is no one size fits all. In non-profit organizations, the purpose is the drive behind every activity. It is the reason why the organization was developed in the first place. Many businesses can benefit from taking on this approach by focusing on what their product achieves and looking at what purpose this fulfills.

"Being the richest man in the cemetery doesn't matter to me. Going to bed at night saying we've done something wonderful, that's what matters to me."

— Steve Jobs.

Positive psychology has researched the effect of working with purpose. It sustains creativity, productivity, and wellbeing. Harnessing purpose develops this by giving team members meaning to their work. This is more than just reaching goals. Say for example you are a sales manager at an oil company. Your goal is to reach a certain target in a month. If you get that goal, then you get a bonus. You meet the target, and you get a bonus. Then the following month you have a new sales target. You then reach that target and get that bonus. This goes on every month. The overall mission of the organization is to transform from an oil producing company to a renewable energy company. This is backed up with a purpose developed by the leaders to work towards developing solutions to climate change. How are your monthly goals linked to this purpose, if at all? And how would you feel that what you are doing was important to the organization working towards its purpose?

To develop inclusive organizations; purpose is even more important and leaders with purpose drive this process. Leaders with purpose are defined not by who they are leading but by what they follow. They develop meaning behind the goals and objectives of the organization so that everyone in the organization feels as if they are working towards something important.

- What is the purpose of inclusive leaders?
- What is their role and how does it relate to purpose?

Without inclusive leaders the effort to move beyond tolerance is extremely unlikely. An inclusive mindset starts with an individual and becomes a widespread organizational cultural change. In order to achieve any cultural change, it starts with the leaders themselves. Inclusive change can only occur when leaders themselves are inclusive. Becoming inclusive starts with an inclusive mindset.

As with any type of change, the leaders need to model the behaviors and values that they wish to achieve. In the example of the sales manager at an oil company, if the purpose of the organization was to move towards different energy sources, the leaders of that organization would need to believe in this and be committed to this value. If the leaders for example, were promoting another value such as increase in oil production, then it would be hard for employees to take their commitment to the organizational purpose seriously.[85]

The purpose of inclusive leaders is to drive the inclusion process and to move the organization from tolerance through to respect and inclusion. Inclusive leaders must be aware that without purpose driving their actions, they will not be able to develop effective inclusion that is long lasting.

---

[85] http://www.transformleaders.tv/why-connecting-to-purpose-makes-us-better-leaders/

Chapter 5

The Organizational Journey

"The future belongs to those who see possibilities before they become obvious." John Scully

Throughout this book, the idea has been to present a selection of tools that you can use to start your own journey towards becoming an inclusive organization that has purpose. By doing so, you can generate courageous leaders that will take your organization to the next level.

In this last section, lets looked at the role of leaders with courage in developing long-lasting inclusive organizations. The main point of this section is that without leaders with purpose, that is, leaders who are committed to inclusion, motivated by becoming an inclusive organization, and leaders who lead by example, inclusive initiatives are likely to fail.

When we embark on an organizational journey to develop an inclusive mindset and culture, we will make mistakes. We will falter, we will make statements using the wrong choice of words. We will miscommunicate ideas. We will stumble, and we may need to change our plans and reinvigorate our teams along the way. Leaders will need to have the courage to start this journey but will also need courage throughout the entire process. Leaders will have to understand that this is an organizational journey. Organizations will need to incorporate inclusive values that ensure that this journey of change, respect, and innovation is long-lasting so that these achievements are maintained. Even if inclusive values are developed, leaders still need to work to ensure that these become incorporated in every part of the organizational culture. This effort must be ongoing and not a one-off exercise. It also has to be part of every process within the organization, or the value will be weakened.

This book began by discussing the personal journey we all have to take to start on the road towards an inclusive organization. Disrupting the status quo begins with a personal journey. Teams and leaders must also be part of the trip. Ultimately though, the process is a holistic one; it is an organizational journey.

At the organizational level, a journey requires purpose. Inclusion without purpose is merely checking a box. An inclusive mission needs to align with organizational goals, increased competitive advantage, and sustained growth. It also needs to be based on core values and the core purpose of the organization.

The inclusive journey needs to be linked to a business strategy that is right for your organization. The process must be flexible and reflect the needs of your institution. It needs to be aligned with the values of your organization, and the strategy should include the success toolkits such as those mentioned in this book.

"Vision animates, inspires, and transforms purpose into action."

- Warren Bennis

Inclusion needs to become embedded in your organizational DNA, and leaders need to guide and direct this process. Leaders committed to inclusion creates organizations committed to inclusion. Inclusion is not a journey of compliance, but it is about changing your organizational DNA or your organizations' purpose.

CASE STUDY EXAMPLE: After years of experience working with oil, gas, and energy companies, one consistency exists. Regardless of whether they produce natural gas, refine oil, provide electricity, manage production stations, injection facilities, operate floaters, or storage facilities, there is a uniform cultural approach to working safely.

Over the last twenty years, there has been a boom in health and safety professionals, departments, procedures, regulations, training, and shifts to develop a cultural mindset to work safely.

This change didn't happen instantly. It was also non-negotiable. There was not an option of compliance when it came to working and operating safely. These facilities have in place what is called a 'lockout – tagout" approach.

They have policies and procedures in place that empower every employee with the ability to lockout and tagout a piece of equipment that is deemed to be unsafe. This approach applies to all members of the organization. A janitor is empowered to shut down a piece of equipment in the production process if they perceive there to be a potential safety issue. There is no retribution or remedial action taken against the employee who stops a process or piece of equipment based on their perception that there was a safety issue. This mindset of operating safely is a core organizational tenet that everyone lives by. It's in their DNA. Having an inclusive mindset and an organizational culture that values respect has to be seen as a critical business enabler, just like safety, for it to become part of the cultural DNA of an institution. This approach requires disruptive thinking with a purpose!

Disruptive thinking is at the core of developing an inclusive culture. Leaders with purpose will be able to utilize this valuable skill as part of a tool kit aimed at changing not just their own thinking, but also that of their teams, other leaders, and the organizational culture.

One description of organizational culture is it is how things work in your workplace. Included in this definition are shared values, shared understandings, structure, language, and behaviors.[86] It helps us to understand what our workplace rules are and the shared meaning we apply to our workplace. Culture is not static, it is deeply entrenched in how we interact with the world, but it is not inert. It changes slowly, subtly, and in ways, we often don't realize. Culture allows us to move forward in the same direction, and it helps organizations to be able to function in stable ways.

If we do not change the culture, then organizations remain static, they lack innovation and creativity, and the organization will fail to reap the benefits from inclusion. If organizations ignore the importance of an inclusive mindset in their business strategies, they will not achieve the levels of creativity and innovation needed to excel. If they continue to recruit from the same places, they will miss out on the benefits of hiring leaders from the changing communities that represent their consumers and business partners. They will also lose motivation and retention of increasingly diverse employees who may begin to question the truth behind the organizations' core values.

The last section of this book will be focusing on how to build organizations that reflect a culture of inclusion. The focus is on transformation. It will look at how enabled organizations create the possibility of becoming transformational organizations. It will also look at how increasing efficiency and leveraging your talent strategy are related to having a culture that embraces inclusive thinking.

The focus is to build a culture of respect that then leads to organizations with purpose; the purpose that changes cultures, causing them to be intentionally inclusive, equitable, and respectful.

---

[86] Edgar Schein's 2004 book, Culture and Leadership.

Transforming Organizational Culture

One of the most difficult challenges for any leader is transforming organizational culture. On a personal level, our culture is so ingrained in who we are that trying to change it is akin to changing who we are.

> *"A leader's role is to raise people's aspirations for what they can become and to release their energies so they will try to get there."* - David Gergen

For anthropologists, culture is something that is governed by our interactions with others and is often aligned with repetitive behavior. The more you practice a particular custom, idea, or behavior, the stronger it becomes and the more significant part it plays in our culture. It is also something that creates an identity among individuals, groups, communities, and society. Anthropologists define culture as "the complete whole, including knowledge, belief, art, morals, law, customs, and any other capabilities and habits acquired by a person as a member of society."[87]

When this is applied to an organization, technically, it becomes a sub-culture. Sub-cultures are based on the culture of the broader community that the organization exists in. Culture helps us to belong to a specific community, and this is true for organizations. We understand the rules and customs of our organization, and by following this behavior, we are signaling to ourselves and to others that we belong there.

To gain an idea of what your organizational culture looks like, you and your teams can ask yourself the following questions in a team meeting:

- How does your organization care for the well-being of team members?

---

[87] https://blogs.scientificamerican.com/anthropology-in-practice/what-do-companies-mean-by-culture1/

- How do people in your organization interact during times of stress?

- Is it acceptable to ask questions in your organization? Why or why not?

- How receptive is your organization to suggestions for improvement?

- Are team members allowed to admit to making mistakes?

- How are team members rewarded? What recognition programs are there?

- What is the quality of the professional relationships?

- Are team members honest with each other?

- Do team members trust each other?

- How does the team deal with emotions?

- Is there openness to feedback and learning?

- How is power dealt with?

- What style of leadership is there? Are leaders compassionate?

- Do the leaders set the example?

- Do leaders collaborate?

- How much delegation occurs in the organization?

- How do leaders and team members deal with rumors?

- When mistakes are made, does your team solve the problem or solve the blame?[88]

This is not an exhaustive list and any online search will provide you with many ideas on how you can determine what your organizational culture looks like in more detail. By asking questions like this and discussing all of this within your team, you will soon establish an overview of what your organizational culture looks like and you will find out what is important to your team. By establishing what your organization looks like, you will also be able to identify

---

[88] http://blog.beingfirst.com/transforming-organizational-culture-to-ensure-successful-transformational-change

strengths and areas where improvements can be made.

What makes culture so powerful? Why is it so hard to change? Why is successful change so difficult?

Why Is Organizational Change So Hard?

It can be boiled down into a number of reasons:

1. Culture determines how we act and so defines part of who we are. Changing culture means asking people to change how they do certain things, and this can sometimes feel like we are being asked to change who we are.

2. For behaviors to become part of our cultures, they are repeated until they become part of the rules of the way things are done. In order for something to become part of our culture, it cannot be temporary, easy to change, or limited.

3. Culture is such a strong force because it provides us with psychological security. Cultural rules and norms provide us with stability and change can threaten this security.

4. Often people see cultural change as a threat to their position in that culture. They may fear that may they lose their position of power or that they may lose a level of influence. When people feel this way, change is resisted at all costs.

5. Emotional attachment is a strong reason to resisting change. We place value in culture and the practices of culture. If these are threatened, then we fear the loss of things that we are emotionally connected to.

6. Culture is made of many different elements that fit together to form a larger whole. When change is initiated often it is focused on one specific area and the connections between this area and the rest of the organization are ignored. This is why 'single fix changes' often fail; they target one particular area of the organization through the introduction

of a new process or new knowledge management technique. For this to work, the change management processes need to include how this will affect other areas and this is often ignored leading to a failure in the entire process.[89]

This is why unconscious bias training and similar types of workshops have not yielded the result that organizations were hoping for. Creating training content in a vacuum only increases the likelihood that the training will not work. Without looking at the entire talent management and human capital life cycle it is impossible to understand the interdependencies that are all connected to the specific behavior or change that a workshop is designed to address.

If a leader is undertaking a large task such as changing organizational culture, this requires many different tools to impact the thinking and behaviors of everyone in the organization. There is a significant reason why leaders need courageous thinking to decide to begin this task and to see it through until the journey of inclusion becomes part of the organization's culture. When instituting a large-scale change process such as developing an inclusive mindset, the process and journey will be long and arduous!

The most successful organizational transformations have come when the leaders involved base the change on an organizational purpose. The goals are set. The purpose of the journey is understood by all. This is accompanied by a clear success toolkit; management tools, roles, control systems, monitoring systems, recognition programs, leadership systems, and team development processes are all in place and are core parts of the process.

Leaders who recognize that transformational organization change will be a bumpy ride are also the most likely to succeed. While we must set hard goals (as mentioned in section one) we must also have realistic expectations. We must understand that organizational change is hard and accept the fact that we will

---

[89] http://futureofcio.blogspot.de/2013/05/why-is-successful-change-so-difficult.html?m=1

face problems along the journey.

Leaders will need to also make sure that the behavior changes that are a natural part of organizational modifications, become permanent for the change to succeed. If this is not a primary goal of the transformation, then it is unlikely for the change to become long lasting.

When describing what successful transformational change looks like, I have used the word "need" many times. While some of these tools are essential, the way in which you transform your organization will be unique and will differ from the way other organizations develop their customized approach. It is also important to recognize that when implementing change, employees should see the process as a collaborative activity that is being led by the organization's leaders. If it is perceived to be a forced process or that they are being coerced into doing, then it becomes less likely for ownership to develop. This approach is perceived to be compliance and the result is that it is very difficult for the change to be adopted by and embraced by employees.[90]

Earlier in this book, an example was given about a leader who sends out a memo to announce that 'being inclusive' is now part of the organizations culture. There is no follow up and nothing else is done to explain or implement this institutional value. The likelihood of this one action, a memo, resulting in organizational transformation is very unlikely.

Likewise, imagine the last time you made a change in your life.

- What did it feel like?

- Who told you to make the change?

- When you were told to do this, were you involved in the decision?

- Were you involved in the development of the processes of change?

- Did the change work?

Now imagine the last time you were involved in a needed change that was

---

[90] https://www.forbes.com/sites/stevedenning/2011/07/23/how-do-you-change-an-organizational-culture/#1020155339dc

part of a collaborative process. Ask yourself the same questions.

In most cases, successful change comes from motivated, participative, committed, and inclusive leadership. When Steve Jobs rejoined Apple in the early 90's the company was on the brink of bankruptcy. It is now one of the first trillion-dollar companies in history. What happened? What change processes were used? One key lesson to learn from this success story is that before any changes were made, Steve Jobs went back to the heart of the business. He went back to the drawing board and looked to redefine the purpose of the company. The company began as a personal computer company and its products had been unsuccessful for many years. Steve Jobs famously started the company in his garage and metaphorically when he rejoined the company in the 90s, he took the company back to the garage.

To understand why they were failing, Jobs reviewed what the company was good at and from that designed a vision. Apple computers have always been more aesthetic than other personal computers, simpler, more innovative, and more intuitive. The core values were redeveloped to reflect this, and this was what drove the transformation.

Once this was achieved, and only once this was done, Jobs then looked at what transformation tools they could use to change their organization. He used two tools predominantly – design and marketing. He worked with the best designers to create innovative products that reflected the vision and he then added $85 million to the marketing department's budget to fund a marketing strategy that established the brand of the vision and innovative products.

Alongside this, inclusive values were introduced to the organizations culture as demonstrated above. The process was considered a journey that could always be improved on and owing up to mistakes was a key part of this. Apple realized that they need to be flexible while initiating change and able to recognize when things worked and when things failed.

The key lesson from this is how important it is to develop purpose and vision **before** launching a change initiative. People need to know why they are doing something and what it will achieve. Without this, ownership is difficult. If people are behind your idea and agree with the process, they are going to be motivated to achieve the goals and work towards making the transformation a success.

For the process to be efficient, leaders will have to identify who are the main stakeholders who will drive the change. They then need to be supported continuously throughout the process. Leaders should respect the skills and capabilities of those driving the change and if they have been engaged, empowered, and enabled they will successfully be able to take on the responsibility. Communication should be through these leaders and they should develop and drive the change communication processes. This process normally happens after the vision has been developed. The success toolkit needed to start the change can then be discussed and decided through collaborative processes. This must involve deciding what behaviors will need to change.

To find out what needs to change, you can ask the following questions:

- What is the difference between the vision of change and what the organization looks like now?
- What behaviors are needed to achieve this change?
- What behaviors does the organization already have that create the new vision?
- What expertise does the organization already have with this vision?
- What can leaders do to act as role models for these behaviors?
- How can these changes be communicated?
- What tools can be used to reinforce these new behaviors?[91]

Finally, the process needs to be implemented and behaviors need to

---

[91] http://blog.beingfirst.com/transforming-organizational-culture-to-ensure-successful-transformational-change

change. The latter is the hardest part of the transformation process.[92]

The next parts of this section will elaborate on how this can be achieved, by looking at behavior change in more detail.

Improving the Organizational Efficiency Ratio

Before covering this topic, I think it would be useful to describe the difference between efficiency and effectiveness. Being effective is being able to accomplish a task. Effectiveness implies that the expected result will be achieved. An effective tool is one that fulfils its purpose. Efficiency is when a task is completed with the least waste of effort or time. It is when we perform in the best possible manner to reduce waste and maximize our resources.

"Being effective is about doing the right things, while being efficient is about doing things right." – Gareth Goh

So, what is an efficiency ratio? Traditionally, this ratio has been used as an accounting tool – expenses/revenue – to work out how much it costs for an organization to be profitable. It is used to analyze an organizations ability to turn liabilities and assets into sales. Efficient organizations will have less invested into assets and so they need less capital to generate sales and they will also need less to make more. They will, in effect, make more out of less. Originally this ratio was applied as an accounting tool to understand the performance of large financial institutions, but it is now being used as a more general way of understanding organizational efficiency. It is an easy way to demonstrate, in a quantifiable way, how much an organization needs to meet its goals. It provides a percentage figure that can be used to compare organizations quite easily. The lower the percentage, the lower the ratio, the less it costs the organization to

---

[92] https://www.thebalance.com/how-to-change-your-culture-1918810

generate profit.

If an organization has a revenue of $1,000,000 but expenses of $100,000 then the efficiency ratio is 10%. If the following year, revenue remains the same, but expenses go up to $200,000 the efficiency ratio is now 20%. The cost of creating revenue in effect doubled, with obvious negative impacts on profitability.

The efficiency ratio can also be measured by looking at liabilities and revenue to assess how much in assets it takes for an organization to create revenue.

There are two ways to improve the efficiency ratio. Increase revenue or decrease expenses. Most organizational leaders agree the best way to improve the efficiency ratio is to decrease expenses. Getting more out of less. Easier said than done right?

Luckily there are some tools that can be used to do this as part of developing inclusive organizations and courageous leaders.

Teri Beckman of Skillful Means, has developed "Instant Efficiency Builders" that can be used by organizations to improve this ratio. These are simple effective tools that can improve productivity so your organization will get more out of less. Throughout this book, moving beyond tolerance towards respect and inclusion has been with the goal of increasing productivity. There is also a correlation between respectful inclusive workplaces and improved profitability, performance, and reduced costs. So, it is no coincidence that some of the "Instant Efficiency Builders" have similar traits as the characteristics of inclusive leadership[93]:

1. **Let Critical Information Flow Freely**. This was discussed in previous sections of leadership qualities. Information is a vital resource and managing it effectively can be a good way to improve the way resources are used. If employees do not have critical information when they need

---

[93] http://skillfulmeanstraining.com/five-way-to-instantly-improve-organizational-efficiency/

it, production processes can be slowed down. If efficiency ratios are high, an assessment of the way in which critical information is used can be a useful way to discover if it is the cause of the efficiency ratio. This can include communications across the organization to assess how improvements can be made. Improving the flow of critical information can also help leaders to monitor progress towards goals and effectiveness of teams.

2. **Kill The Deadly Boring Meeting**

We have all sat through boring meetings that seem to go on forever. They are a killing machine for efficiency and they also decrease the effectiveness of teams. List all of the meetings that you regularly have and list their purpose. Do they help your organization meet its goals? Do they match the organizations purpose? Are they engaging your employees? Are they empowering your teams? How do they enable your teams? If the answer to any of these questions is no, then the meetings might not be the best use of your organizations time. Changing the way your teams meet and fine tuning them to make them more efficient can have a big effect on your efficiency ratio.

3. **Find Out Where You Are And Share It**. Sharing progress towards goals, what leaders are doing, and strategic plans can make a big impact on your efficiency. If you do not share this information then your employees will have to spend a lot of time trying to find it or worse yet, they will make guesses on what it is. One of the key attributes of inclusive leaders is that they involve their team members in all parts of the organizational change. Sharing information is a crucial part of both improving inclusion and improving efficiency.

4. **Dissolve The Silos**. The more connected your teams are, the higher they will perform. This was discussed in detail earlier in this book. Connecting team members improves productivity and it can also increase efficiency. Silos are debilitating structures and make it very hard

for team members to connect. We need structure in our organizations, and it is a useful tool to drive effectiveness, but we need to make sure that these structures help team members connect and share information. Leaders can analyze working patterns across teams and within them to see if the silo effect is impacting efficiency.

5. **<u>Avoid The Mass Firing Urge</u>**. I have seen this happen in many organizations. Things go bad and the leaders think that the solution is to reduce staff, to fire the problem away. In many cases, the problems could have been solved internally by changing the dynamics or by introducing a more inclusive organizational culture. Rather than address the toxic culture, the leaders engage in mass firings, and then mass hiring. It took nearly six months for the entire process to conclude. At the end, the new staff entered an organization with a toxic culture and so the problems continued, and efficiency did not change. In some cases, it is necessary to remove people who are not working towards the organizations goals but removing entire teams can often create more problems than it solves. If the leaders had addressed the toxic culture, they could have spent less time and less money to solve their productivity problem.

These are ways to start to improve your efficiency ratio. There are many other tools that can be used, and it is important to find the right balance for your organization.

Leveraging Your Talent Strategy

Moving beyond tolerance requires disrupting your status quo as it relates to organizational development. Leveraging your talent strategies helps to define what processes and structures are needed to help develop inclusive, courageous leadership thinking to improve efficiency and productivity.

- How do inclusive leaders leverage their talent strategies as part of this process?

- How can inclusive talent management be used to improve on organizational development?

- What parts of your inclusive talent strategies are important in implementing organizational development?

"You've got to think about big things while you're doing small things, so that all the small things go in the right direction." - Alvin Toffler

---

LEVERAGING YOUR TALENT STRATEGY

<u>Start with finding out where are you.</u> Review your existing talent strategy. Review the goals and plans that exist within your current strategy. Define what the goals are of the strategy moving forward. Are they aligned with the purpose of your organization? Find out if the existing strategy is equitable and if it is that inclusive tools are included or needed in the strategy.

<u>Assess engagement, empowerment, and enablement.</u> Survey employees to find out what your baseline is for these categories. Focus on how inclusive talent management will lead in the process to develop targeted programs that will increase all of these.

<u>Assess your leaders.</u> In order to change your leadership thinking, you need to know what your current leadership style is. Find out the values of your leaders. Assess how aligned they are with your organizational goals. Measure how empowered they are in developing and leading change. Assess what tools they need to become courageous inclusive leaders. Develop recognition plans and continuous plans for enablement. Allow them to help develop and lead the change processes.

Develop clear action plans. Your talent strategy should be part of an overall organizational change plan that is focused on continuous action. It must be about preparing for the inevitable changes that are coming and include contingency plans.

Install systems to get qualified people. The right people at the right time need to be recruited for the right jobs. They need to be passionate as well as qualified. Talent strategies need to be inclusive and bias needs to be purged from the systems. You must include a plan to ensure that all new hires are aligned with the organization's culture.[94] Earlier in this book, details were provided on how your talent strategy can be used to develop a culture of inclusion. Developing an inclusive mindset can be seen as a key resource as it will determine how you leverage your people as resources for change.

People are your most important resource and your most important stakeholder. They provide the energy for every part of your organization's growth. Leveraging your talent strategy in an inclusive way, is making sure that you are using this resource both effectively and efficiently. Doing so also ensures that your organizations growth and any change associated with it, is inclusive, sustainable, and positive.

Below are several of the best practiced components of an inclusive talent management strategy. Has your organization examined these through an inclusive filter? Have you discussed and identified potential areas where cognitive bias might enter the process? Have you developed a process to mitigate the areas where employees and the organization might be impacted? Included are things such as equitable and inclusive:

- Employee Planning: This refers to the process of analyzing your

---

[94] http://www.executiveevolution.com/TalentBullets.htm

organizational needs in terms of the type of employees' skills, experience versus education, numbers and associated values of those individuals you source and develop.

- <u>Performance Management</u>: As you develop processes that allow you to measure employee performance, develop specific metrics, and create mechanisms for feedback; have you examined areas where an inclusive filter makes a difference?

- <u>Learning & Development</u>: Many people who do not have learning and development responsibilities, see the L&D function as a part of the organization that is responsible for training. Best practices also include the role of L&D in career planning, mentoring, coaching, on-the-job training, succession planning, as well as high-potential development.

- <u>Talent Acquisition Planning</u>: Does your talent management strategy take into consideration:
  - o How your brand is perceived by different constituent groups?
  - o The way you measure the capability of potential talent?
  - o Placing an early emphasis on developing a comprehensive retention strategy? This should precede your work on an inclusive recruiting strategy.
  - o What the implications are of finding the 'right' fit or 'cultural' fit?

The 'Right Fit' Conundrum / Bias

When looking for ways to leverage your talent management strategy, many in Management, HR, Talent and Leadership refer to candidates as either having or missing the ability to feel like they are a 'good fit'. This term can become a default justification for eliminating candidates from consideration. This term has an underlying potential for the decision about a candidate or prospect's capability or potential to be based on intuition. There is an abundance of metrics, models, and processes available that provide an analytical assessment of an individual's match with a role, team, or organization that rely on data and not perceptions.

Leveraging your inclusive talent strategy requires you to incorporate it into your overall organizational strategy. This means that it will become a key part of your plan to implement organizational change and effectiveness.

The inclusive talent strategy should align to your institutional strategy and be featured as a prominent part of your goals, processes, tactics, and roadmap. One keyway to use this strategy is to assess how your organizations current structure supports your plans for change.

Conducting an organizational culture assessment will provide the quantitative and qualitative data needed to ensure that you have an accurate snapshot of the current state, areas of opportunity, centers of success, competencies needed, and more.

Too often the process of changing organizational culture is left entirely to the talent management department and they are given instructions on what to do. Too often this leads to disconnect. Why? Organizational change needs to start with the leadership team. It needs to be driven by leaders who are motivated and committed. Without the process being driven by leaders the change will be transient. Yes, talent management will play a key role, but the process must be delegated from leaders.[95]

Inclusive coaching strategies within your talent strategy are excellent tools for introducing change and developing the team skills necessary for inclusive organizations. Talent strategies are just one part of your tool kit and these should include coaching. This can help to:

- Challenge employees to work outside of their comfort zone.

- Help to support employee enablement.

- Support further training and learning opportunities.

---

95 http://businessmagazinegainesville.com/leveraging-talent-management-strategies/

- Reduce the risk of taking on large organizational change processes.

- Help to identify talent gaps and then fill them.

- Allow for talent to be further developed.

- Provide an easy way to improve your efficiency ratio.

- Allow for individual development plans to be created.

- Improve team strategic plans.

Coaching can take on many different shapes and forms. The best leaders are always aware that talent management accounts for 29% of the difference between low and high performing organizations.[96] Organizations that successfully leverage talent strategies that are linked to business strategies and are aligned with the organizations purpose, can directly improve their bottom line. Sections that follow will look at how data and analytics can be leveraged alongside this process to get a real understanding of your talent and its role in organizational growth.

Embracing Creative Abrasion

Working with others brings so many benefits. Every part of our society has been created by people working together. Along with this creativity and productivity, working together brings conflict and abrasion. It is an inevitable part of working with others. Even if teams are homogenous, team members will bring to the table different cultures, different expectations, and different ways of dealing with conflict. When teams are diverse, team members will also add different norms, and behaviors. Many assume the immediate recourse when confronting these differences will require conflict resolution skills. That should not be the first thought when these differences manifest.

---

[96] http://www.russellreynolds.com/newsroom/human-capital-leveraging-your-company%E2%80%99s-greatest-asset

Conflict resolution implies that there is one solution to conflict and once that solution has been implemented the conflict goes away. As we all know, conflict is a constant in our lives. We will always have it. The only thing we can change is how we manage conflict – how we deal with it.

The goal of conflict management should not just be reducing the negative impact of conflict. Rather, we can look at it as a way to learn from a particular situation marred with differences. Conflict, when managed well, can help to develop into new ways of looking at the same problem. When this is achieved, we have embraced our creative abrasions. Amplifying differences that naturally arise allows us to take advantage of abrasions and manage conflict in a positive way.

If you think about any innovative product, the process to develop that product and to move it from an idea to a successful product would have been littered with creative abrasions. So many decisions need to be made when innovating and those decisions often create challenges, debates, and discourse. Without these rough spots often, an idea never becomes successful. It is through the creative abrasion that accompanies differences that a unifying solution and approach are often found.

Embracing creative abrasion is an understanding of this process it is the ability to create ideas by debating and discussing differences. It is understanding that addressing conflict is a process and not a resolution. Conflict management should be a part of any organizations management's strategy and within that, embracing creative abrasion is one tool.

Linda Hill, professor of business administration at the Harvard Business School, has argued that a core part of embracing creative abrasion is bringing in naïve points of view. She argues that people with limited experience in a particular area are valuable for the innovation process as they can see things that others might miss. They may "see the trees for the forest"; they may be able to see small things that get lost in the larger idea by people with more experience. I call this the "Amen Approach™."

I worked with a very innovative leader about 20 years ago who told me a story that created this approach to my own conflict management style and to how I embrace creative abrasion. This leader worked with a team of project managers who were developing software processes for a large company. Within that team, they also had a number of interns and a number of junior team members. One of those team members was called Amen. He was the most junior member of the team. This leader explained that when Amen joined the company, he was shy and would not contribute very much. As time went on, his confidence grew and he began to contribute more. During team meetings, Amen began to add many ideas that other more experienced team members had not seen. He would add creative suggestions and comments that none of the more experienced team members would have seen before. He was barely out of college but was coming up with ideas that people with 20 years in the business had not seen. Luckily for Amen, he worked with an inclusive leader who encouraged everyone to speak out, to learn from mistakes, and to be enabled. The leader was an expert at bring out the best in her team and so Amen felt comfortable in bringing up his ideas in front of people with more experience than he had. He knew there was a risk that he would make a mistake with his comments, but he understood that the team was supportive of him and would help him learn if he did a mistake rather than make him feel bad for being naïve. This was the "Amen Approach™."

As he was new to the team and to the project, he saw things with a fresher outlook, and this benefited the entire team.

How we structure our teams and how leaders manage conflict is essential to innovation and to being able to embrace creative abrasion. Innovation does not arise simply because of one person's idea or from one leader's visions. It is a collective product and in order for teams to innovate effectively they have to be inclusively managed.

In order to implement creative abrasion strategies such as the Amen Approach™, an inclusive mindset as well as inclusive leadership is necessary.

Team members need to feel valued and they need to be confident that their point of view is respected. Without this respect and inclusion, innovation is limited.

To really embrace creative abrasion, leaders will need to find a balance of developing new connections among team members while at the same time challenge ideas and processes of the team. Inclusive leaders must pull and push their teams at the same time. How is this possible?

This is creative abrasion. As Jerry Hirshberg described it, creative abrasion is creating "ideas that really rub against each other productively as opposed to destructively."[97] This is achieved by bringing in a diversity of cultural differences, viewpoints, and talents so that your innovation processes, product development processes, or the project processes are abrasive yet collaborative. Without bringing in a diversity of ideas, organizations risk falling behind their competition because they are not exposing them to as much innovation as possible.

"It comes down to trying to expose yourself to the best things humans have done and then trying to bring those things into what you have been trying to do." – Steve Jobs

Leaders need to understand that this is not about developing consensus. Consensus is very damaging to generating ideas. Big ideas that are game changers are those that normally sit outside of consensus and they are the ones that normally cause conflict. Consensus is stable and it can create mediocrity. Innovation on the other hand, is necessary for inclusive organizations, courageous thinkers, and leading with purpose. Innovation is often disruptive, unpredictable, and messy. This is a good thing. This is what leads to new ideas that change the way we do things for the better. This is what creates long lasting organizational growth.

Ryan Tomlinson sums this up very well: "Personally, some of the best working relationships I've experienced are with people who I've had heated debates with; those that couldn't care less about hierarchy, job titles, or roles but

---

[97] https://www.scientificamerican.com/article/how-to-manage-a-creative-organization/

who care more about doing the right thing. They don't argue or make conflict for the wrong reasons or for personal gain but believe passionately about what they're proposing and who aren't afraid to let it be known."[98]

As you can imagine an inclusive coaching-leader is necessary to be able to manage this delicate interaction. Not only do team members need to feel confident enough to speak out and offer their opinion, there also needs to be inclusive leadership to guide the team through the process and develop a solution that is an outcome of successful conflict management.

Being Intentionally Inclusive

"If I am not intentionally inclusive then I am unintentionally exclusive." – Michelle Ewing Nuff

---

Organizations that are inclusive normally have one thing in common; they are intentionally inclusive. They have adopted inclusion as part of their core values, and it is matched by an inclusive purpose. Inclusive organizations spend time thinking about why their organizations are not inclusive and then try to spot the barriers that exist in their organization preventing them from becoming inclusive. They also spend effort and energy on removing these barriers. They look for ways to make sure that employees feel valued and part of the team and respected. They spend time and divert resources to completing this goal.

When diversity was first introduced as a management technique, it was common for organizations to set up the "Office of Diversity". This was the focal point for improving the diversity performance of the organization and was responsible for ensuring that diversity became part of the organization's values. You probably have a diversity office in your organization. How effective have these offices been? Have they been intentionally diverse?

---

[98] http://www.ryantomlinson.com/creative-abrasion-why-conflict-is-key-to-team-cohesion/

Being intentionally diverse means incorporating inclusion into every part of your organization. For example, many organizational leaders argue that specific inclusive recruitment practices are not necessary as the inclusive practices of the organization on the whole are sufficient.

Consider this example. A large PR organization holds its annual management retreat every year. It normally lasts a week and only senior managers attend the meeting. Ten years ago, the organization decided to begin a process of becoming an intentionally inclusive organization by developing and supporting an inclusive culture. They changed their diversity department to the Diversity and Inclusion Department. They conducted training for all staff on inclusion and developed a process that would allow for employees to become enabled with these inclusion skills in a continuous way. The processes ran smoothly and there were some indications, through employee feedback and quantifiable data, that inclusion as a business process, was improving in the organization. This continued for some years.

Eventually the D&I suggested that the annual management retreat could also benefit from some inclusion processes as it was a very closed off event. Traditionally, no information about what was discussed at this meeting was shared with other employees. The D&I team suggested that each department could send someone as a representative to this meeting as a way for the retreat to become more inclusive. They also suggested that what was discussed at the retreat become open knowledge and suggested live events from the retreat be made available to staff. They also suggested that some sort of communication document be released before, during, and after the retreat.

THOUGHTFUL QUESTIONS

- How do you think the senior management should respond?
- Do you think the suggestions are reasonable?
- Do you think that they could do more?
- Or do you think they are unnecessary?

- What else could they do to improve inclusion?

This example was based on a real PR organization that I have worked with. To begin with the senior managers were reluctant to move forward with any processes to change their retreat and the way it was done. They kept it an exclusive event for a few years. They struggled to improve their levels of inclusion; engagement in the organization fell, so the D&I team brought me in as an external consultant to try to address this. We began by running a large assessment with all employees to find out the levels of engagement, empowerment, enablement, diversity, equity, and inclusion. We then discussed with employees, ways in which this could change, and they then presented suggestions to the D&I department and senior management.

It should come as no surprise that the exclusive retreat was seen by most employees as evidence that the senior management team were not committed to inclusive measures. Employees felt that this demonstrated that the D&I department work was not meaningful and there were still extreme hierarchical divisions in the organization. Many felt as though by refusing to be more transparent with the retreat, the senior management were hiding an alternative agenda.

In other words, the senior management were not being intentionally inclusive and by doing so, they were being intentionally exclusive.

One successful way of being intentionally inclusive is to establish a set of guiding principles for your process of changing your organizations culture. This is **alongside** your organizational purpose and visions and is an additional part of your process. This is not in lieu of organizational strategies, project plans, or other success toolkits described in this book.

To be intentionally inclusive, your "Guiding Inclusion Principles" can include:

- Increasing inclusion as a link to the success of the organization.

- Increasing inclusion is an integral and intrinsic part of the organizations purpose.

- Inclusion initiatives will intentionally create an environment that is mindful of every team member.

- Intentional inclusion will be implemented at the organizational, group, and individual level.

- The inclusion journey will focus on changing behaviors.

- Intentional inclusion will require behavior change from every member of the organization.

- Intercultural agility is a core pillar of the inclusion strategy.

- Listening to learn will drive the inclusive journey.

- Cultivating reflection is the responsibility of ever team member as part of the inclusive journey.

- Continuous improvement and responsive action will be used to turn inclusive values and cultures into practices and organizational culture.

- Intentional inclusion means that all members will be represented at every level of the organization.

- The purpose of the intentional inclusion measures will be so that every team member reaches their true potential.

- The inclusion measures recognize that underrepresented groups have historically been excluded and marginalized both intentionally and unintentionally.

- Marginalized members excluded systemically because of identity is wrong and does not maximize the potential of all members.

- Intentional inclusive practices are to increase the potential of all members and to address social inequalities.

- Intentional inclusion means valuing all contributions and the voice of every member.

- The organization will value both domestic diversity and international diversity.

- Intentional inclusion assumes that the entire organization becomes a positive space.

- The organization will value intersectional inclusion.

  o **Intersectionality** recognizes that identity markers (e.g. "female" and "black") do not exist independently of each other, and that each informs the others, often creating a complex convergence of oppression. [99]

- The organization will disrupt groups and transform them into inclusive teams.

- Intentional inclusive practices are necessary for competitive advantage and competence; they will drive organizational growth.

- Intentional inclusive will address unconscious bias, tolerance, and will harness creative abrasion.

- The success of the inclusion measures will affect the reputation of the organization.

As with all the toolkits in this book, these are not exhaustive, and your team will need to develop their own guiding principles to shape your inclusive journey.

That latter point is something to reiterate. The guiding principles **themselves** need to be inclusive. They need to be developed by all team members and not just senior management. To be intentionally inclusive, the methods for developing inclusion also need to be inclusive and the opinion of all members should be included. The Amen Approach™ is a great technique to ensure that this is taken seriously and will help to demonstrate to all team

[99] https://www.ywboston.org/2017/03/what-is-intersectionality-and-what-does-it-have-to-do-with-me/

members that the inclusive journey is being taken seriously by the organizational leaders.

> *"Even small changes in behavior, if they are picked up by more than one individual, can ripple through an organization as others see their value and begin to act accordingly."*
>
> *— Jon Katzenbach and Ashley Harshak*

Instituting a Culture of Metrics and Analytics

I don't need to tell you how important data is for your organization's growth. Data, metrics, and analytics have become a by word for an innovative way to get more out of less. Using data in this way is one way that organizations can use metrics and analysis to develop insights into your organizations position.

> *"The best vision is insight."* - Malcolm Forbes

As the volume of data available to organizations has grown, so have the tools to analyze and use this data. The potential of this information is also growing as organizations realize that data, metrics, and analytics can be used to be able to reduce uncertainty and understand processes important for inclusion.

Benefits of using metrics and analytics include:

- The root causes of mistakes and failures can be identified in real time.
- Data lets you challenge your assumptions.
- Data allows for continuous improvement, which in turn leads to smarter decisions.
- Marketing in your organization can be driven by data and so it can be more reflective of your operational silos.

- Employees can be empowered by better understanding the organization and their performance.

- Purchasing habits can be used to determine pricing strategies.

- Understanding your customers becomes easier; customer loyalty and customer engagement become more effective as the approaches used are more objective.

- Equally, with enough data on your customer's preferences, their experience with your organization can be tailored to become personalized.

- Efficiency ratio can be improved as resource allocation can have a narrowed focus.

- Data can be used to quickly assess the risk potential of any decision.

- Metrics can be divided into macro and micro metrics.
  - Macro metrics can help to provide a big picture view of your organization.
  - Micro metrics can provide information at every level and so can be used at all levels to make decisions.[100]

- Metrics and analytics are used to add value to the interactions you have with your customers.[101]

Instituting a culture of metrics and analytics can also be applied to your talent management practices. This can have a remarkable effect on your ability to recruit team members who align with your organizations values and who are capable of using courageous thinking to develop inclusive cultures throughout the organization. Metrics can also provide insights about where anomalies in your talent practices are manifesting. This allows progressive-minded organizations to mitigate the discrepancies and leverage that data analytics for

[100] https://www.eystudios.com/2017/04/data-driven-culture-important/
[101] https://www.ngdata.com/what-is-big-data/

long term success.

Measuring all aspect of your human capital practices and strategies has become a large part of how you manage this asset. Most Fortune 500 companies now have HR analytics teams to understand risks, potential, culture, D&I, and behaviors of their workforces. The assumption is that if you don't know where you are, you cannot plan how to start your journey. If you want to move your organization from A to B, you need to have a good understand of where A is in order to plan this cultural change.

As data has increased, the technology costs of analyzing this data have fallen. Statistical modeling products in particular, have drastically fallen in price and should be harnessed to measure complex parts of your organization such as talent management practices, workforce and workplace behavior and inclusive culture.

Since 2012, a Mercer survey indicated that 90% of companies now use some form of metrics and analytics ranging from internal benchmarking, to predictive modeling, to cause and effect analysis. All of these tools in some way allow organizations to forecast outcomes from implemented organizational policies. With some forms of analytics, there is also the possibility of using these to calculate the return on investment.

An example is using analytics to measure the effects of attrition. Measuring turnover in relation to trained or untrained staff can then demonstrate the ROI for a particular intervention strategy. Using metrics and analytics is, in many cases, borrowing from the measurement techniques used in clinical drug trials. You can in effect observe interventions both pre and post-trial settings. When working on changing behaviors to bring about organizational change and inclusive cultures, this is especially relevant. And like clinical trials, these techniques can show not only the effect of the intervention but also how to get the most out of your interventions. There is that theory again, getting more out of less. Metrics and analytics allow you to improve your efficiency ratio by adjusting interventions after analyzing data.

"The workforce is the primary way to drive revenues." – Scott Pollak

---

Metrics are especially effective in making sure you have the right people at the right time in the right place. This will give you a competitive advantage that is sustainable over the long time. As data comes in, you will be able to use it to change over time. These tools allow your team to reflect your changing situation and your changing goals.[102] Think about how instead of measuring the time it takes to recruit a new team member and instead focus on how long each new team member stays. Equitable workplace data can be used to analyze succession planning. Measuring the access and effectiveness of learning and development of team members will help you to better understand how enabled your teams are, instead of just focusing on how long they have stayed.

If the goal is to measure the impact behaviors are having in your organization begin by establishing a baseline of what your organizations current culture is and go from there. All of these tools can be used to understand the cost and return on investment of the measurement and can also be focused to be more specific. Additionally, the above examples can be used to measure the impact on reputational capital, empowerment, engagement, curiosity, and enablement. All key factors in the success of an inclusion journey.

All of these tools allow your organization to move towards a culture of metrics and analytics, giving you a more scientific objective way of assessing your performance.

Even if the political world is becoming more and more based on 'alternative facts', using analytics to measure the right things, in the right way, we can create valuable tools to add to your inclusive journey. One key to analytics is that it is continuous – we adjust it to measure how we did in the past, where we are now, and what is the best path moving forwards.

---

[102] http://www.russellreynolds.com/newsroom/human-capital-leveraging-your-company%E2%80%99s-greatest-asset

Periodically, we can return to analytically measure our journey and confirm if we are still moving in the right direction. Once these processes have been set up, they are extremely efficient and offer a very good return on investment in the long term. They allow decisions to be made based on evidence and allow scientific method to shape some of our processes. It does come with challenges:

- The amount of data available can seem overwhelming.

- Moving towards metrics and analytics requires a change in organizational culture as some employees may still want to make decisions based on subjective analysis. This is the "feel it in my gut" approach and for many it is hard to move away from this.

- Collecting and analyzing data, especially big data, is time consuming and can lead to employees believing that more time will be spent on metrics and analytics than decision making.

- Data can be unorganized and messy and needs to be organized sufficiently to be useful.

None of these challenges are insurmountable. With coaching, training, and enablement, they can be overcome. As with all tools within the inclusion journey, leaders need to pay attention to purpose. Given how much data is flowing around, we could become stuck, overwhelmed by how much data there is, or overworked trying to analyze every piece of data. Analytics and metrics need to be tied to purpose and to the inclusive journey. Develop a few KPIs/KPAs/OKRs that can be used as the basis of your metrics and analytics and then go from there. To become best-in-class organizations in metrics and analytics, focus on:

- Asking the right questions.
- Find your macro and micro focus.
- Using the Amen Approach™.
- Get quality data by enabling your teams.

- Build teams with many skills.

- Focus on action points derived from data.

- Use loops and not lines – observe, orient, decide, and act, then observe, orient, decide, and act, then observe…[103]

- Communicate and exhibit your results and action.

- Talk about your data and then talk about it some more.

- Talk about your actions and then talk about them some more.

- Present your data. Make it user friendly.

- Use the data and use it continuously.[104]

When necessary and as resources allow, you can dig deeper into the data to find out more. The KPIs should be linked specifically to your purpose and to your organization's goals and vision.

The journey is unique with every organization, and how your organization implements a culture of metrics and analytics can also be tailored to allow you to understand more about your organization.

CASE STUDY

McDonalds has over 1.9 million employees[105] and has often used metrics and analytics to understand its organizational strategies. For a long time, they used staffing numbers and employee turnover to understand their reputation and to help shape innovation and new business opportunities.

But there was a problem. The data was not telling them very much about

---

[103] This is the OODA loop adapted from the US army but now commonly used throughout organizations.

[104] https://www.mckinsey.com/business-functions/digital-mckinsey/our-insights/making-data-analytics-work-for-you-instead-of-the-other-way-around

[105] This makes up a remarkable 0.05% of the global workforce and after the US Department of Defence, the People's Liberation Army of China, and Walmart, makes it the 4th largest employer in the world.

their reputation. Yes, it told them a lot about what employees thought of McDonalds, but it didn't say very much about what customers thought. The data that was coming in helped McDonalds to understand how they compared to their competition, but it was lacking two crucial pieces of information. Firstly, it was not in real time and so they could not tell how specific events affected their reputation or revenue. Secondly, it was also limited as it did not show what affected their reputation. When recruitment dropped, they could guess that this may be due to lowered reputation but there was no certainty with this. Correlation does not mean causation. How could they know that a specific event that had increased their reputation then caused an increase in recruitment? There was no cause and effect.

Meanwhile, with the advent of social media, they discovered that in any one year there are over 1 million discussions about McDonalds and its staff on social media. Analyzing these conversations is not only effective, but with the right statistical tools it is very efficient. While McDonalds still uses surveys of turnover and external employer surveys, they can now add real time consumer opinions based on metrics collected on social media. This data provides McDonalds with really clear insights into how people feel about the brand.[106]

Remembering Your 1st Day at Work, Every Day

Staying engaged in your workplace is an important way of implementing the success toolkits in this book. One of the best ways to stay engaged is to stay enthused about the job you are doing, the values of the organization, the organizations purpose, and your role in creating that purpose.

Our first day of work is normally the time when we have the highest levels of engagement and enthusiasm. How do we maintain this? Remembering our first day and how we felt can be a great way to motivate yourself every day. By treating every day as if it is our first day on the job, we continue to have fresh

---

[106] https://www.eystudios.com/2017/04/data-driven-culture-important/

eyes, fresh legs, and fresh minds.

"People want to do well and do good. They want to understand how they're making a difference in the world. Things change all the time, but your organization's purpose transcends any individual product or service." - Mark Weinberger

---

- How do we do this?

- Try to remember what your first day was like. How did you feel?

- How did you feel about the role?

- How did you feel about the organization?

- How did you prepare for the position?

- What made you start the job?

On our first day at work:

- We ask questions we are prepared to learn.

- We are curious about everything.

- We are friendly and introduce ourselves.

- We are open and value every team member we meet.

- We show up early.

- We are inspired.

- We have focus.

- We are ready to learn to be courageous.

- We are prepared for the unknown.

- We are excited about the unknown.

- We look forward to challenges.

- We want to work in teams.

- We are curious about the way things work.

- We are curious about the structures of the organization.

- We need to find out who does what, who leads, and who is led.

- We are strategic.

- We smile. We are open.

- We look and play the part.

- We listen and observe.

- We pay attention to how decisions are made.

- We talk to peers to find out how things work.

- We project high energy.

- We learn and abide by the professional rules.

- We are curious about the organizational culture.

- We adopt the organizational culture but challenge parts of it that are not effective and efficient.

- We take on the Amen Approach™.

- We put our cell phones on silent.

- We are interested.

- We are open to new ideas.

What do all of these things have in common? They are all characteristics of inclusive cultures.

Building a Culture of Respect

Considering that the most important factor in determining job satisfaction was respect, your inclusion strategy should be built on this principle. The Range of Respect illustrated earlier in this book demonstrated the importance of including a culture of respect into your organizational strategies. Ultimately, in any organization, what is important is how we treat each other.

Respectful Workplace Policies

Building a culture of respect is a continuous exercise. Focusing on building respect is superfluous if this is not matched with ongoing systems of respect. Start by developing respect on a personal level, change your own behavior. Use this as a basis to then change the behavior of your team, leaders, and finally your organization. Part of your inclusion guidelines should include guidelines on how to maintain a culture of respect. Start with these steps:

1. **Develop communication guidelines that are based on active listening.** Establish standard protocols for formal communication and expectations for informal communication. Develop these through an open dialogue with all employees. If these exist already, periodically review your existing tools. Develop ways to measure inclusion and respect perceptions. Regularly collect data on how well employees adhere to guidelines and request suggestions for improvement.

2. **Add respect to your inclusion guidelines as a core value.** Communicate this regularly and not just when establishing the guidelines. Repeating the core value and demonstrating it with matching respectful behavior will convince employees that this is a genuine part of the organization. This will lead to changes in behavior, changes in mindsets, and eventually to changes in organizational culture.

3. **Develop help systems.** When we help each other, we support each other as employees and as people. This improves relationships and also helps to change behaviors, which then leads to changes in behavior. Working in organizations that have supportive mechanism builds engagement and enablement, leading to more rewarding workplaces.

4. **Allow team members to be themselves.** Respectful organizations value each team member for who they are. Employees will feel comfortable being themselves and will be valued as a productive team member. Organize team activities that allow team members to interact

outside the office. This allows team members to get to know each other and to find out more about one another.[107]

5. **Develop bridge builders**. Find team members who have high interpersonal skills and who are respectful and nominate them as bridge builders. They can coach team members when problem arise and work with leaders to create a respectful inclusive environment.

6. **Embrace creative abrasion and use conflict as a learning mechanism**. Discuss conflict and abrasion within the framework of respect and inclusion and encourage openness. Create a solution focused framework for these discussions and work towards employees understanding that they can expect a respectful environment.

Building and maintaining respectful environments is what will end up empowering your employees; they will feel valued. It will lead to a culture of engagement and enablement that will benefit your organization in so many ways.

Integrating Purpose Into Your Organizational DNA

"Never doubt that a small group of thoughtful, concerned citizens can change world. Indeed, it is the only thing that ever has."

—*Margaret Mead*

Purpose is taken for granted. It is assumed that organizations make something, they have a product and that is their sole goal and mission. So long as organizations are making more, producing more, and improving the bottom line, then their purpose is clear. Leaders who lead this process are seen as leading with purpose. Teams that meet their KPIs are said to be working with purpose.

---

[107] https://www.entrepreneur.com/article/247932

This is not integrated purpose.

Our purpose is more than just what we have made or what our bottom looks like. Our purpose is also more than our KPIs. Purpose is always linked to the question: WHY? Purpose is not about results, but it is about why. Why are you pursuing that result? Purpose is about motivation. What motivates you to achieve that result?

Our purpose powers our passion but our purpose does not have to be linked to social or moral debates. Consider what Steve Jobs thought was the purpose of Apple. He set the purpose as producing the most innovative exciting technological products on the planet. This is quite a purpose. It is a definitely a grand purpose; a key objective that could be used to guide every action within the entire organization. If any team member of the Apple company wanted to know if they were working towards this goal, they could easily ask themselves a few questions about their work to determine this. It is easy to measure. We return to an idea discussed in the first section of this book – hard goals. Just as goals need to be hard, so does our purpose. Steve Jobs could have set the organizations purpose as making a nice laptop. They achieved this. Many times. Once it had been achieved, they may have needed a new purpose if they wanted to avoid losing motivation and engagement.

Purpose statements should be brief, and they should be broad. This sounds like an impossible task, but it sums up purpose very well. We need succinct descriptions of what we are trying to achieve but we also need them to be large enough to be adaptable. Our products, processes, services, and teams may change over time, but the focus of the organization must last. Statements of purpose should become macro guidelines for everything your teams do. It is a top-down process, with leaders setting the stage.

To integrate purpose into your organization's DNA ask yourself these questions about your purpose statement:

- Does your product or service contribute to your target society or community?
- Why is your work important?
- How is your work motivational and inspirational?
- What powerful words are used to describe your purpose?
- Is your purpose easy to remember? Can it be easily passed on?
- Is your purpose wide enough to be adapted, changed, and shaped by future opportunities?[108]

While writing this book, I have thought a lot about purpose. I have thought a lot about what my purpose has been in all of the roles I have had throughout my career. I have answered this question by writing this book.

- My purpose is to help organizations move beyond tolerance.
- My purpose is to help to create organizations that are based on respect.
- My purpose is to help develop working environments that are based on cultures of inclusion and RESPECT.

Writing this book is just part of that process. I wrote this through one of the most turbulent political periods of our country. It made me realize there is still a lot of work to do.

In some ways I am lucky. I am optimistic about our country's future; I know what we are capable of and I know that as a nation we are always striving to do better. The current political climate seems to have thrown us back into a climate of tolerance. I understand what this means. We have a long journey ahead of us moving towards respect and inclusion. We will get there. It is a long

108 https://sheilamargolis.com/core-culture-and-five-ps/the-five-ps-and-organizational-alignment/purpose/

journey that will have more setbacks and we have to learn from many more mistakes. I know this will happen because this is not what I do; this is who I am.

Part of this process will be led by organizations in our country. They will start these processes, driven by considerations of productivity, bottom lines, and ROIs. These are powerful motivations and are the gas that we will use on the journey.

We will start by making personal decisions to start this journey. We will look at our own behaviors, our own interactions, and we will use our courage to decide to start this journey.

We will develop teams that will join us on this journey. These teams will be coached to become performing teams. They will disrupt the status quo to become innovative and enabled.

We will be driven by leaders who are inclusive, respectful, and who lead with purpose. They will be looking through the windshield with a clear understanding of where they want to go. These leaders will make mistakes but their commitment to the journey will not fade. They will build other courageous leaders, they will change behaviors, and they will develop inclusive mindsets. They will generate organizational change that is inclusive and long-lasting.

This will create respectful and inclusive organizations that we will feel proud to work in. The journey will not stop there. We will continue to be courageous and ensure that the move beyond tolerance is a permanent one. I know this is possible because I have seen it many times before. My optimism is derived from these experiences of seeing organizations and communities successfully navigate a journey towards respect and inclusion. I know that a successful journey is also possible for your organization.

So what are you waiting for?

References

- Arthur, M. B., & Rousseau, D. (1996). A new career lexicon for the 21st century. The Academy of Management Executive, 10(4), 28-39.

- Beneke, C. (2006). Beyond toleration: The religious origins of American pluralism. New York: Oxford University Press.

- Branscombe, N. R., Spears, R., Ellemers, N., & Doosje, B. (2002). Intragroup and intergroup evaluation effects on group behavior. Personality & Social Psychology Bulletin, 28(6), 744–753.

- Brehm, S. S., & Brehm, J. W. (1981). Psychological reactance — A theory of freedom and control. New York: Academic Press.

- Clayton, Craig B Sr (2010). The Diversity Profit Equation dPE. The Diversity Factor Journal. Rutgers University 18 (3):

- Cortina, Lilia M.; Magley, Vicki J.; Williams, Jill Hunter; Langhout, Regina Day (2001). "Incivility in the workplace: Incidence and impact". Journal of Occupational Health Psychology. 6 (1): 64–80.

- Darwall, S. L. (1977). Two kinds of respect. Ethics, 88(1), 36–49.

- De Cremer, D. (2002). Respect and cooperation in social dilemmas: The importance of feeling included. Personality & Social Psychology Bulletin, 28(10), 1335–1341.

- De Cremer, D. (2003). Noneconomic motives predicting cooperation in public good dilemmas: The effect of received respect on contributions. Social Justice Research, 16(4), 367–377.

- De Cremer, D., & Mulder, L. B. (in press). A passion for respect: On understanding the role of human needs and morality.

- De Cremer, D., & Tyler, T. R. (2005a). Am I respected or not? Inclusion and reputation as issues in group membership. Social Justice Research, 18(2), 121–153.

- De Cremer, D., & Tyler, T. R. (2005b). A matter of intragroup status: The importance of respect for the viability of groups. In M. Thomas-Hunt (Ed.), Research on managing groups and teams (Vol. 7, pp. 1–21). Greenwich. CT: Elsevier Science Press.

- de Gaulle, C. (1968, 5/12). The thoughts of Charles de Gaulle. New York Times Magazine

- Derrida, J. (2001). Philosophie in Zeiten des Terrors. Berlin Philo Verlag.

- Dreikurs Ferguson, E., & Page, L. J. (2003). Work relationships, lifestyle, and mutual respect. Journal of Individual Psychology, 59(4), 501–506.

- Eagly, A. H., & Chaiken, S. (1993). The psychology of attitudes. Orlando, FL: Harcourt Brace Jovanovich College Publishers.

- Ellemers, N., Doosje, B., & Spears, R. (2004). Sources of respect: The effects of being liked by in groups and outgroups. European Journal of Social Psychology, 34(2), 155 172.

- Hill, T. E., Jr. (1998). Respect for persons. In E. Craig (Ed.), Routledge Encyclopedia of Philosophy (Vol. 2004). London: Routledge.

- Hollander, E. P. (1964). Leaders, groups, and influence. New York: Oxford University Press.

- Honneth, A. (1996). The struggle for recognition: The moral grammar of social conflicts (Studies in contemporary German social thought) The MIT Press.

- Horton, J. (1998). Toleration. Routledge Encyclopedia of Philosophy Version 1.0.

- Hudson, S. D. (1986). Human character and morality: Reflections from the history of ideas. Boston: Routledge and Kegan Paul.

- Kahneman, D. (2011). Thinking, fast and slow. New York: Farrar, Straus and Giroux.

- Kant, I. (1988). Groundwork of the metaphysics of morals. Cambridge: Cambridge University Press.

- Kruglanski, A. W. (2001). That "Vision Thing": The state of theory in social and personality psychology at the edge of the new millennium. Journal of Personality and Social Psychology, 80(6), 871–875.

- Lalljee, M., Laham, S. M., & Tam, T. (in press). Unconditional respect for persons: A social psychological analysis.

- Lind, E. A., & Tyler, T. R. (1988). The social psychology of procedural justice. Critical issues in social justice. New York & London: Plenum Press.

- Locke, J. (1689). A letter concerning toleration ed. R. Kilbansky, trans. J. W. Gough, (1968). An accurate modern translation of Locke's letter.

Oxford: Clarendon Press.

- Margalit, A. (1998). The decent society (N. Goldblum, Trans.): Harvard University Press.

- Merton, R. K. (1968). Social Theory and Social Structure. New York: Free Press.

- Miller, D. T. (2001). Disrespect and the experience of injustice. Annual Review of Psychology, 52, 527–552.

- Murphy, M. (2010). Hard Goals: The Secret to Getting from Where You Are to Where You Want to Be. London: McGraw Hill Professional

- Murphy, M. (2017).

  https://www.leadershipiq.com/blogs/leadershipiq/video-goal-setting-requires-hard-goals

- Rowe MP (1990) Barriers to equality: The power of subtle discrimination to maintain unequal opportunity. Employee Responsibilities and Rights Journal 3(2): 153–163.

- Schmidtz, D. (2006). Elements of Justice: Part 4 Equal respect and equal shares. New York: Cambridge University Scholar

- Sennett, R. (2003). Respect in a world of inequality (1st ed.). New York: W.W. Norton.

- Simon, B. (in press). Respect, equality, and power: A social psychological perspective.

• Simon, B., & Stürmer, S. (2003). Respect for group members: Intragroup determinants of collective identification and group-serving behavior. Personality & Social Psychology Bulletin, 29(2), 183–193.

• Simon, B., & Stürmer, S. (2005). In search of the active ingredient of respect: A closer look at the role of acceptance. European Journal of Social Psychology, 35(6), 809–818.

• Sleebos, E., Ellemers, N., & de Gilder, D. (2006a). The carrot and the stick: Affective commitment and acceptance anxiety as motives for discretionary group efforts by respected and disrespected group members. Personality and Social Psychology Bulletin, 32(2), 244–255.

• Sleebos, E., Ellemers, N., & de Gilder, D. (2006b). The paradox of the disrespected: Disrespected group members' engagement in group-serving efforts. Journal of Experimental Social Psychology, 42(4), 413–427.

• Sleebos, E., Ellemers, N., & De Gilder, D. (in press). Explaining the motivational forces of (dis)respect: How self-focused and group-focused concerns can result in the display of group serving efforts.

• Spears, R., Ellemers, N., & Doosje, B. (2005). Let me count the ways in which I respect thee: Does competence compensate or compromise lack of liking from the group? European Journal of Social Psychology, 35(2), 263–279.

• Thompson, L., Kray, L. J., & Lind, E. (1998). Cohesion and respect: An examination of group decision making in social and escalation dilemmas. Journal of Experimental Social Psychology, 34(3), 289–311.

- Toosi, M. (2012). Projections of the labor force to 2050: a visual essay. Monthly Labor Review, October (10), pp. 3–16.

- Tulshyan, Ruchika. (2015).

  https://www.forbes.com/sites/ruchikatulshyan/2015/01/30/racially-diverse-companies-outperform-industry-norms-by-30/

- Tyler, T. R., Degoey, P., & Smith, H. (1996). Understanding why the justice of group procedures matters: A test of the psychological dynamics of the group-value model. Journal of Personality and Social Psychology, 70(5), 913–930.

- Tyler, T. R., & Lind, E. A. (1992). A relational model of authority in groups. In M. P. Zanna (Ed.), Advances in experimental social psychology, Vol. 25 (pp. 115–191).

- Zauderer, D. G. "Workplace Incivility and the Management of Human Capital: How to Build a Community Where People Feel Included, Welcomed, and Work Together With Mutual Respect to Enhance Individual and Organizational Productivity." The Public Manager, 3: 36-42, 2002.

"Workplace Incivility and the Management of Human Capital." Author: Don Zander, Senior Fellow, Brookings Institute & American University. Journal Title: The Public Manager.

Social Investment Forum: National nonprofit membership organization. http://www.socialinvest.org

"A New Career Lexicon for the 21st Century." Authors: M.B Arthur & D. M. Rousseau. Journal Title: The Academy of Management Executives

"Assessing & Attacking Workplace Incivility." Authors: Pearson, Andersson & Porath – Journal Title: Organizational Dynamics, Fall 2000.

AMA. "American Management Association Study Finds Diverse Leadership Teams Are More Productive." For more information, see http://www.amanet.org/research